Centerville Library
DISCARD
Washington-Centerville Public Library
Centerville, Ohio

D1253605

# THE COEN BROTHERS' AMERICA

# THE COEN BROTHERS' AMERICA

## M. Keith Booker

ROWMAN & LITTLEFIELD
Lanham • Boulder • New York • London

Published by Rowman & Littlefield
An imprint of The Rowman & Littlefield Publishing Group, Inc.
4501 Forbes Boulevard, Suite 200, Lanham, Maryland 20706
www.rowman.com

6 Tinworth Street, London SE11 5AL

Copyright © 2019 by The Rowman & Littlefield Publishing Group, Inc.

*All rights reserved.* No part of this book may be reproduced in any form or by any electronic or mechanical means, including information storage and retrieval systems, without written permission from the publisher, except by a reviewer who may quote passages in a review.

British Library Cataloguing in Publication Information Available

**Library of Congress Cataloging-in-Publication Data**

Names: Booker, M. Keith, author.
Title: The Coen Brothers' America / M. Keith Booker.
Description: Lanham : Rowman & Littlefield, 2019. | Includes bibliographical references and index.
Identifiers: LCCN 2018052705 (print) | LCCN 2018054682 (ebook) | ISBN 9781538120873 (Electronic) | ISBN 9781538120866 (cloth : alk. paper)
Subjects: LCSH: Coen, Joel—Criticism and interpretation. | Coen, Ethan—Criticism and interpretation. | United States—In motion pictures. | National characteristics, American, in motion pictures.
Classification: LCC PN1998.3.C6635 (ebook) | LCC PN1998.3.C6635 B66 2019 (print) | DDC 791.4302/330922—dc23
LC record available at https://lccn.loc.gov/2018052705

∞ ™ The paper used in this publication meets the minimum requirements of American National Standard for Information Sciences Permanence of Paper for Printed Library Materials, ANSI/NISO Z39.48-1992.

Printed in the United States of America

# CONTENTS

# INTRODUCTION

## Alternate Realities: The Inside-Out World of Joel and Ethan Coen

The America we see in the films of Joel and Ethan Coen is a sort of alternate-reality America that produces fresh (though slightly skewed) perspectives on real-world cultural history. Though they have worked on a few other projects, the Coens' principal oeuvre consists of the nineteen feature films that they have written, directed, and produced in tandem—from *Blood Simple* (1984) to *The Ballad of Buster Scruggs* (2018). Each of these films is set in a fictional version of a specific American time and place; in each case, however, the fictional version involved does not quite seem to coincide with the same time and place in the *real* America but is instead slightly offset from reality (and in ways that are distinct to the Coens). Building their films from bits and pieces extracted from American cultural history, the Coens have produced some of the most intricately crafted and intellectually sophisticated films of the past several decades, yet they have done so largely without sacrificing intelligibility or entertainment value. The Coens' films are complex enough, however, that it does help to approach them armed with a few special insights and interpretive tools, which this volume will endeavor to supply.

The Brothers Coen are two of the most original and distinctive American filmmakers of the past three and a half decades. Joel was born in 1954, Ethan three years later. The brothers grew up in St. Louis

Park, Minnesota, a suburb of Minneapolis. From the beginning, then, they saw American society from the seemingly mainstream position of a middle-class suburban family in the Midwest. The brothers had what was in many ways a classic American upbringing, living in material comfort, their minds nourished by the still-new medium of television, especially when they were driven indoors during the long Minnesota winters. On the other hand, as the children of Jewish intellectuals, they also grew up viewing America from a decidedly off-center position. This situation of being both insiders and outsiders relative to the American mainstream is, I think, also quite descriptive of their films and of the unique point of view from which their films observe American culture and American society.

## THE COEN BROTHERS AND ALTERNATE REALITY

Most of the films of the Coens are, at least to an extent, reworkings of classic Hollywood film genres. However, the Coens approach these genres from a distinctly contemporary point of view, even if they also approach the genres with affection and respect, with little in the way of real revisionary intent. Indeed, they have pursued their creative engagement with a variety of different well-established film genres largely because they themselves are such big fans of genres such as film noir, the Western, and screwball comedies. In addition, individual Coen Brothers films often engage with several different genres at once, producing new and unique combinations. It's always fun to try to guess which genre (or genres) they might take on next.

They have, however, avoided one major film genre almost entirely and have, in fact, ruled out ever working in that genre: science fiction. As Ethan once said in an interview, we should never expect to find them working in science fiction because "neither of us is drawn to that kind of fiction. I don't think we could get our minds around the whole spacesuit thing."[1] Thus, in the spirit of subverting genre expectations, in the following study of the films of the Coen Brothers, I employ a concept from science fiction to tie all of their work together.

That concept, as I suggested above, is the alternate-reality (or alternate-history) narrative, in which the story takes place in a world that is very much like our own but differs from it in subtle ways, most commonly because some historical event in the past turned out differently than it did in our reality—such as the Germans winning World War II, which is the premise of any number of such narratives. At least this concept doesn't generally require spacesuits. What it does require is a fairly detailed evocation of place and time, providing enough details gradually to make clear the fact that the reality of the story is not our own, a situation that also very nicely describes the films of the Coen Brothers. The Coens, as much as any filmmakers living or dead, set their films in specific and vividly realized places and times (often places that have figured prominently in American cultural history), from the Texas plains and honky-tonks of their first film, *Blood Simple* (1984), to the Hollywood Hills and soundstages of *Hail, Caesar!* (2016). The films also tend to take place in clearly delineated time periods, very often in specific years and at crucial points in American history, as when *Barton Fink* (1991) is set in late 1941, just before and after the U.S. entry into World War II, or when *A Serious Man* (2009) is placed, by a variety of contextual clues, in 1967, the year of the Summer of Love. And yet, the Coens also sprinkle their films with small (and sometimes large) anachronisms and inconsistencies that announce, not that they are sloppy filmmakers, but that they are very meticulous filmmakers who want us to realize that the places and times in which their films occur do not, in fact, quite correspond to places and times in the real world. Jeffrey Adams is clearly correct when he notes that the Coens seem to see themselves as American filmmakers who are "dedicated to making films in and about the United States of America."[2] But it is equally clear that their version of the United States resides in a different reality (or realities) than our own. Their films take place, in short, in alternate realities.

This is not to say that the Coens are secretly (or inadvertently) making science-fiction films or that their claim to have an aversion to the genre is an attempt at misdirection (or a case of misrecognition). Nor do the Coens create this alternate-reality effect for the same reasons that motivate science-fiction writers, who often create worlds that differ from our own in a mode of political satire that produces fresh perspectives on our own reality, often for the purpose of making subtle political points about the fact that our own world doesn't have to be the way it is. The Coens, in contrast, employ their alternate-reality technique primarily out of a self-consciously postmodern awareness that their films are fictions and that the worlds shown to us within fictional films can *never* be the same as the real world, no matter how scrupulously the filmmakers might attempt to match up their fictional worlds with the real one. Rather than make such an attempt, the Coens embrace the fictionality of their filmic worlds and use it as a crucial resource in constructing their films. Going well beyond the trivial observation that fictional worlds are never quite the same as the real one, the Coens carefully create fictional worlds that differ from the real one in specific ways that are, first and foremost, entertaining.

## THE FILMS OF THE COEN BROTHERS: THAT'S ENTERTAINMENT

In certain circles, of course, "entertainment" is a bad word. For some, it connotes the bland, insipid, superficial products of a popular culture designed to numb minds, blunt critical thinking, and convert its audiences into an army of programmed, smiling robots, lacking in self-awareness and blindly devoted to the consumption of more and more of the products of modern capitalism—including popular culture itself. The Frankfurt School Marxist theorists Max Horkheimer and Theodor Adorno began warning us about the dire effects of this sort of entertainment culture as long ago as the 1940s, with Hollywood films as a central target of their critique. Beginning in the 1950s, the rise of commercial television broadened the urgency of such critiques, as cultural critics on both the left and the right became concerned about the detrimental effects of the new "mass" medium. This new wave of concern perhaps culminated in Neil Postman's best-selling 1985 volume, *Amusing Ourselves to Death*, which still stands as an influential expression of concern that contemporary popular culture, designed merely to amuse and entertain, was not only incapable of conveying serious ideas but even acted to render its consumers incapable of processing such ideas—much in the mold (as Postman himself notes) of the mind-numbing popular culture envisioned in Aldous Huxley's 1932 dystopian classic, *Brave New World*.

*Brave New World*, of course, is a science-fiction satire set in an alternate reality that is precisely intended to warn readers of dangerous trends in their own contemporary world, long before the rise of television made that warning more urgent than ever. Postman's critique, meanwhile, focuses first and foremost on television, but the subsequent development of Internet and then cell-phone culture has in many ways made his observations seem even more cogent. On the other hand, a number of recent "quality" television series—including such stellar examples as *The Sopranos* (1999–2007), *Mad Men* (2007–2015), and *Breaking Bad* (2008–2013)—have ushered in what many critics have called a Golden Age of Television, calling into question Postman's belief that certain media (such as television) simply cannot bear the weight of quality content.[3] Still, despite occasional concerns in some circles about its potential negative effects on the morals of viewers (especially children), film has to some extent succeeded in maintaining a reputation as a medium that retains the potential ability to produce genuinely thoughtful and artistic works, even if the box office is dominated by a seemingly endless stream of mindless comedies, flashy action films, and interchangeable superhero extravaganzas.

The Coens are pioneers in the kind of innovative, independent filmmaking that has helped to promulgate the notion that film has a greater potential to produce quality products than does television. At the same time, the Coens (almost despite themselves) have also been pioneers in breaking down conventional distinctions among media. For example, the FX cable network series *Fargo* (which premiered in 2014 and is still in production as of this writing) was inspired by the 1996 Coen Brothers film of the same title and has managed, through the three seasons produced thus far, to maintain a Coenesque feel even without the active participation of the brothers in its production (though both are listed among the executive producers of the series). Perhaps more tellingly, *The Ballad of Buster Scruggs* (2018), the Coens' latest effort, was originally announced as a television series to air on Netflix but eventually released as an anthology film just in time to premiere in competition at the Venice International Film Festival. *Buster Scruggs*, then, becomes a prime example of the ways in which the boundaries among different media (especially film and television) are under siege in the age of Netflix.

All of the films of the Coens are highly entertaining and most of them are quite funny—even the grim *No Country for Old Men* (2007) has its amusing moments. And the brothers have consistently maintained that they have no serious agenda (political or otherwise) in their films. But the works of the Coen Brothers suggest that the dichotomy between "serious" culture and "entertainment" culture is a false one. Thus, entertainment or no entertainment—and even though the Coens do not appear to employ their alternate-reality technique in the specifically satirical mode of much science fiction—their technique of creating alternate versions of America and American cultural history does effectively suggest some new ways of looking at America and its history that have the potential to change our ways of thinking, whether the Coens intended this effect or not.

## THE COMPLEX AND CONTRADICTORY WORLD(S) OF THE COEN BROTHERS

The Coens' films break down all sorts of distinctions, in addition to the one between "serious" and "entertainment" programming. The films are highly original, with a distinctive quality that makes them almost immediately recognizable as a film by the brothers. Yet the Coens borrow material from previous films (and other sources) more extensively and more overtly than almost any other filmmakers in the history of the medium. The brothers write their own films (and generally write *only* their own films), yet their most important foray into writing for others—the 2015 Cold War espionage drama *Bridge of Spies*—was written for the ultimate mainstream director, Steven Spielberg, and won the brothers (along with collaborator Matt Chapman) an Oscar nomination for Best Original Screenplay. The Coens are intensely independent filmmakers whose own quirky films are well outside the mainstream, both artistically and commercially. Yet films they have written and directed have won a total of thirty-six Oscar nominations (though only six victories), and they have been able to attract some of Hollywood's biggest stars—George Clooney, Tom Hanks, Brad Pitt, Jeff Bridges, and Billy Bob Thornton immediately come to mind—to appear in their films. Other actors have *become* stars partly because of their roles in Coen Brothers films, including Josh Brolin, Oscar Isaac, and Frances McDormand (who also happens to have been married to Joel Coen since 1984). The brothers have even helped to propel virtually unknown teenage actors—Scarlett Johansson and Hailee Steinfeld—into important show-business careers. Yet the Coens' films are not generally star-making vehicles but feature ensemble casts made up largely of talented character actors who have appeared in multiple films for the brothers. When John Turturro, John Goodman, Steve Buscemi, Richard Jenkins, Michael Badalucco, Jon Polito, and others appear on-screen in a Coen Brothers film, it is almost like meeting an old friend. Clooney, who has appeared in four of the Coens' films, should be included in this group of character actors as well, despite the fact that he is a major star even apart from his work with the brothers. In fact, all of these highly recognizable actors have had success outside of Coen Brothers films. McDormand, for example, won a Best Actress Oscar for the Coens' *Fargo* but also won one for the non-Coen film *Three Billboards Outside Ebbing, Missouri* (2017). And some of her most memorable work with the Coens is in small but outrageous character roles (such as in *Raising Arizona* and *Hail, Caesar!*). Still, the appearances of all these actors with the Coens have a special flavor; with the Coens, they seem almost like a group of (very gifted) friends and neighbors who regularly perform together in their local community theater.

One of the most remarkable features of the Coens' films is that each film seems distinctly different from the others, yet all are nevertheless distinctively Coenesque. The Coens make brilliant use of the resources of the medium of film, from the effective use of the actors noted above, to the dazzling (but often eccentric) camera work of British cinematographer Roger Deakins (who has shot most of their films), to a use of music (aided by collaborators such as Carter Burwell and T Bone Burnett) that is perhaps more effective than in the films of any other contemporary filmmakers—despite the fact that the brothers have never made a film that could be rightly described as a "musical." On the other hand, the style of a Coen Brothers film can vary significantly from one film to another, partly because they work in a number of entirely different genres (or combinations of genres). But even films that participate in the same principal genre can vary substantially. *Blood Simple* (1984), *Fargo* (1996), *The Big Lebowski* (1999), *The Ladykillers* (2004), and *No Country for Old Men* (2007) are all primarily crime films, yet each one differs sharply from the others, ranging from the slapstick farce of *The Ladykillers* to the dark and brooding menace of *No Country for Old Men*.

What really ties the Coen Brothers' films together as a distinctive, immediately recognizable body of work is the fact that each of their films engages in a dialogue with some aspect (or aspects) of American culture, history, and society in a way that is uniquely their own. In many cases, the most important engagement is with a specific film genre, but engagements with specific places and times—from the skewed perspective of the alternate-history mode that I have outlined—are also crucial. Together, their films constitute a sort of reconstruction of American history from the late nineteenth century to the early twenty-first century. As their frequent collaborator Burnett puts it, "The Coens are not just inspired filmmakers, but brilliant archaeologists, as well. They dig their films out of the past."[4]

Burnett is right, but the "past" that the Coens sift through is a complex and multiple past that consists not just of material reality but of cultural representations of reality in a variety of forms. A period piece such as *Miller's Crossing* is not an attempt to create a representation of urban life at the end of the 1920s; it is an attempt to represent the cultural *memory* of that life as found in a variety of sources, especially including hard-boiled detective fiction and classic gangster films. Similarly, *O Brother, Where Art Thou?* tells us very little about the reality of life in the American South during the Great Depression, but it tells us a great deal about how the Depression-era South has been represented in a variety of other films—with an important additional dose of cultural memory derived from American roots music of the period. *The Man Who Wasn't There*, set in California in 1949, does not attempt to recall that actual setting but is instead a re-creation of the films noir of that period, while also reaching back in important ways to the kinds of hard-boiled fiction on which those films were frequently based. And so on.

## THE COENS AND THE REPRESENTATION OF "REALITY"

In their films, the Coens produce representations of representations rather than representations of reality, a strategy that places their films at a double remove from the real world, creating the sense I have noted that their films are set in alternate realities. This phenomenon is actually quite common in the contemporary media environment. To cite a well-known example, I might note the family of superhero films and television shows that are set in the "Marvel Cinematic Universe," placing those narratives within a particular reality that differs from our own in important ways—most obviously in that this reality is inhabited by a variety of superheroes and supervillains. And this universe results from the fact that the films and shows involved are not representations of our world but of the world of Marvel comic books, which have long attempted to maintain a certain narrative continuity (or at least consistency) among different comics.

The Coens have no reason to try to produce this sort of consistency, so it probably makes less sense to try to place all of their films in a single universe, though there are occasional crossovers from one film to another, as when a character early in *Raising Arizona* (played by M. Emmet Walsh, who had been a star of *Blood Simple* three years earlier) is shown wearing a jumpsuit that identifies him as an employee of Hudsucker Industries, thus anticipating *The Hudsucker Proxy*, which would be released seven years later. In a sense, then, this moment combines the worlds of three different films (appearing over the course of a decade) into a single shot. Similarly, the Coens' two films about the Hollywood film industry (*Barton Fink* and *Hail, Caesar!*), though released a quarter of a century apart, are overtly set in the same universe (and even involve the same fictional film studio). In general, though, there is little to suggest that various Coen Brothers films are literally set in the same universe. Instead, what they all have in common is that they are set in avowedly and self-consciously *fictional* universes that resemble, but are not identical to, our own and that derive from a variety of cultural sources, including literature, film, and music. This realization helps, I think, to explain the off-kilter feel of the Coens' films, as if the universes of their films are just slightly out of phase with our own—but also as if the usual rules governing the distinction between fiction and reality in our universe do not apply in the worlds of these films. The result is a delightful and diverse array of films that together constitute one of the most entertaining and distinctive bodies of work produced by any directors in the history of American film.

This book traces the development of that body of work. Each chapter looks at the Coens' engagement with a specific genre or motif, beginning with the film in which that genre or motif first took center stage and then looking at one or more later films that returned to the same general territory. For example, chapter 1 begins with the Coens' reinscription of film noir in *Blood Simple* and then looks at their return to film noir nearly two decades later in *The Man Who Wasn't There*.

Chapter 2 looks at the turn to anarchic, almost cartoonish comedy in the brothers' second film, *Raising Arizona*, and then at the return to that mode in *The Ladykillers* and *Burn After Reading*. Subsequent chapters then look at the Coens' engagement with hard-boiled detective fiction (in *Miller's Crossing* and *The Big Lebowski*), the Hollywood film industry (in *Barton Fink* and *Hail, Caesar!*), screwball comedy (in *The Hudsucker Proxy* and *Intolerable Cruelty*), black comedy (in *Fargo* and *A Serious Man*), the American music industry (in *O Brother, Where Art Thou?* and *Inside Llewyn Davis*), and the Western (*No Country for Old Men*, *True Grit*, and *The Ballad of Buster Scruggs*). Together, these chapters demonstrate the wide variety of modes and genres in which the Coens work and the wide variety of materials that they draw upon in constructing their films. In so doing, they illuminate the work of the Coens in such a way that viewers can return to the films themselves armed with the sort of information that will make the appreciation and enjoyment of the films all the easier.

# 1

# PAINT IT BLACK

Film Noir, *Blood Simple*, and *The Man Who Wasn't There*

In a story by the famed Argentinian writer Jorge Luis Borges, written in the form of a piece of literary criticism, a fictional modern French writer, Pierre Menard, is described as having independently authored a text that turns out to be identical, word for word, with the pioneering 1602 Spanish novel *Don Quixote*, by Miguel Cervantes. In this story/critical discussion—titled "Pierre Menard, Author of the Quixote" (1939)—it is concluded that, due to differences in historical context, Menard's *Quixote* is, in fact, an entirely different work than the one authored by Cervantes. Moreover, the piece concludes that Menard's novel is actually the superior of the two, having gained richness and resonance from the intervening four hundred years of history. Put differently, because of the change in historical context, Menard's narrative takes place in a different universe than does Cervantes's. The Coen Brothers re-create earlier cultural artifacts less exactly than Menard replicates Cervantes, but in a sense the effect is a similar one that involves breathing new life into old motifs by reintroducing them in new contexts. One of the clearest ways in which this revision occurs in the work of the Coens is in their frequent use of images and ideas from earlier genres, such as film noir, a genre whose motifs were already being widely replicated and revitalized through the phenomenon of neo-noir, even before the Coens came along to give neo-noir their own distinctive twist.

## *BLOOD SIMPLE*: TEXAS NOIR

When the Coen Brothers' first film, *Blood Simple*, was released in 1984, neo-noir films had already gained considerable momentum. After a few scattered false starts in the 1960s, this resurrection of film noir had begun in earnest when Roman Polanski's *Chinatown* (1974) so convincingly demonstrated that film noir, very much a creature of the 1940s and 1950s, still had considerable unexplored potential for the post-Code, New Hollywood generation of filmmakers. Several other important neo-noir films appeared in the 1970s (such as Arthur Penn's *Night Moves*, in 1975), but it wasn't until the early 1980s when neo-noir really began to gather steam. In 1981, Bob Rafelson's remake of 1946 noir classic *The Postman Always Rings Twice* didn't really go that far beyond the original, but it did give a boost to the neo-noir movement by featuring A-list Hollywood stars in Jack Nicholson and Jessica Lange. That same year, Lawrence Kasdan's *Body Heat* demonstrated the potential for graphic eroticism of a noir form now freed of the shackles of Production Code censorship; then, in 1982, Ridley Scott's *Blade Runner* demonstrated the ability of the basic noir formula to spill over into other genres—in this case sophisticated science fiction. After that it was off to the races, as any number of filmmakers tried their hands at taking noir into new territory, whether it be generic, thematic, or geographic.

Enter the Coen Brothers. While many neo-noir films were moving into the realm of big-budget Hollywood extravaganzas, *Blood Simple* was a decidedly low-budget affair, financed with contributions from individual private investors (mostly rich Jews from Minnesota) solicited via Joel's one-on-one pitch campaign that involved a simple homemade trailer that prominently featured a shot of light shining through bullet holes in a wall. An unknown who had previously worked mostly in porn, Barry Sonnenfeld, came on as the cinematographer, and an unknown actress, Frances McDormand, was cast as the female lead after the Coens' first choice, Holly Hunter (at the time, not that well known herself), turned them down. In short, the film had many of the gritty, outside-the-mainstream ingredients that had made so many noir films special in the first place. It also seemed like anything but a guaranteed success.

Sonnenfeld, of course, would go on to become a successful director in his own right, if not a particularly inventive one. For her own part,

McDormand would go on to become one of the greatest actors of her generation, a true treasure of American cinema. And the Coens would go on to become the Coens. They were, in fact, already the Coens back in 1984, and their first film, despite the low budget and the inexperience of almost everyone involved, shows a surprising number of the elements that would distinguish their entire career. One of these was their unique way of engaging with genre. *Blood Simple* was certainly an important contribution to the rising tide of neo-noir, and it is rightly considered by many to be among the greatest of all neo-noir films. But even in this film, the Coens already showed a daring willingness to step outside of the conventions of genre altogether. As Cathleen Falsani aptly puts it, the film "is in many ways an homage to Hammett and film noir but with decidedly modern twists. *Blood Simple* uses the film noir themes of alienation, uncertainty, subterfuge, and double-cross—but it cleverly subverts and inverts them."[1]

One unusual aspect of *Blood Simple* as a film noir is its Texas setting, so different from the urban settings of most noir films, which tend to be set in places like Los Angeles or New York.[2] The film begins with a sequence of shots of a desolate Texas landscape, oil rigs and refineries off in the distance to emphasize the setting. Indeed, the film was shot on location in Austin, Texas, where Joel had briefly attended graduate film school, setting a precedent for the location shooting that would become a consistent feature of the Coens' work—though the film never specifies that the action is taking place in Austin, only that it is taking place in Texas. Meanwhile, the film begins (as would many subsequent films by the Coens) with a voice-over narration. In this case, the narrator issues ominous warnings about all the things that can go wrong in life, followed by the somewhat surprising declaration that "in Russia, they got it mapped out so that everyone pulls for everyone else: that's the theory, anyway. But what I know about is Texas. And down here, you're on your own."

The film thus foregrounds its Texas setting from the very beginning, making it clear that this setting will be important. Meanwhile, this opening narration identifies Texas as a land of stark individualism—a characterization that has long been central to the cinematic depiction of the state. It is perhaps also typical of the state's representation in popular culture to see it as the opposite of the Soviet Union. What is not typical, however, is that this comparison appears here to work to the advantage of the Soviets, emphasizing not the strength and independence of the state's individuals but the utter inability of anyone in the state to rely on anyone else for support.

Of course, the narrator who delivers this message is a shabby, folksy Texas private eye by the name of Loren Visser (M. Emmet Walsh), a less than admirable character in the film. Visser is also an extreme cynic, so perhaps his negative assessment of Texas should be taken with a grain of salt. On the other hand, the neo-noir story of deception and betrayal that follows appears to back up Visser's every-man-for-himself vision of Texas culture. In any case, the Texas of *Blood Simple* is a lonely place, its wide-open spaces serving as a visual emblem of the emotional distances that separate the characters, its stretches of empty highway echoing the empty hearts (and minds) of almost everyone in the film.

In this sense, though the film might appear, at first glance, to be oriented toward pure entertainment, it can actually be read as a rather effective critique of Texas individualism that reveals the dark heart of the self-reliance that has conventionally been presented so positively in American culture. In this sense, the Coens, who cannot be described as political filmmakers in any conventional sense, nevertheless produce a film that can be read as *highly* political, especially given that the ideology of individualism is one of the key underpinnings of American capitalism—and of the American "way." Such criticisms of the fundamentals of American ideology are highly unusual for Hollywood film today, though they are not necessarily unusual in film noir. Indeed, this aspect of *Blood Simple* also reveals that Texas is, in fact, an ideal setting for film noir, precisely because its individualist culture lends itself to the loneliness and treachery that are central to the genre.

This is not to say, of course, that the Coens were intentionally constructing a brilliant Marxist critique of alienation under capitalism or a profound existentialist commentary on the loneliness of human existence in the modern world, using the Texas setting to help them make their points. The Coens have made it clear in multiple interviews that they are perfectly happy to have people see their films in such ways but that they themselves do not. More than anything, they make films of the kind they themselves like to watch, adding their own spin. In the case of *Blood Simple*, a big part of that spin is the Texas setting. In addition to their effective use of the Texas landscape, for example, the Coens get a great deal of mileage out of the Texas accents of many of the characters, a technique the Coens would use in many of their subsequent films, perhaps most effectively with their use of the Minnesota accents of most of the characters in *Fargo* (1996). In any case, one gauge of the effectiveness of the Texas setting of *Blood Simple* is that the film, when remade by the great Chinese director Zhang Yimou (as *A Woman, a Gun, and a Noodle Shop*) in 2009, simply did not translate well to its new Chinese setting, despite Zhang's immense talents.

What is perhaps most impressive about the use of the Texas setting in *Blood Simple* is that the Coens, two fancily educated Jewish boys from way up north, treat the setting in a way that is entirely free of condescension or hostility, despite the fact that none of the members of the love triangle at the heart of the film seems to be very bright. These characters include Abby (McDormand) and her husband, Julian Marty (Dan Hedaya), the proprietor of a local dive, "Julian's Dessau Dance Hall," which supplies a suitably seedy setting for much of the action of the film—reminiscent of the run-down bars and diners and roadhouses that populate so many noir films. The third member of the triangle is Ray (John Getz), a bartender who works for Marty.

One could argue that Ray's and Abby's Texas accents make them seem even dumber than they otherwise would. But the evil Visser, who seems to be the smartest of the major characters (even though he bungles the killing of Abby, leading to his own death), also has a Texas accent, while Marty (who is both dumb *and* evil) does *not* have a Texas accent but is simply played in the natural accent of Hedaya, a New York Jew. In any case, the film never suggests that its characters are dumb *because* they are from Texas—they're just dumb people who *happen* to live in Texas.

In terms of the Texas setting, it is worth mentioning that Meurice, Ray's fellow bartender at the "dance hall," is black but that his race has essentially nothing to do with his role in the film. Indeed, in this alternate-reality Texas, race does not seem to be an issue at all. For example, Meurice is given to dating white women, but no one in town seems to care. Meanwhile, there is a scene early in the film when Meurice follows a live country band in the bar by playing Motown music on the juke box, and one almost expects that the good old boys in the bar might react with violence. Instead, no one really reacts at all because this isn't that kind of film—or that kind of Texas. Instead, Meurice steps unmolested over the bar in his white high-top Converse Chuck Taylor All-Star sneakers, a brand of basketball shoe with no particular racial associations (the original Taylor was white)—as opposed to the trendy basketball shoes that were just becoming popular in America (the original Air Jordans were introduced in 1984, the year of the film) and that have a special association with black culture. Meurice's shoes, of course, feature a lone star on the side, providing another winking reminder of the Texas setting. In this alternate-reality version of the Lone Star State, race might not matter, but clever visual puns do. And Meurice definitely seems to have arrived in the film from another reality, a fact that might be signaled in his very name, which recalls the swank Hotel Le Meurice in Paris, a favorite staying place of surrealist painter Salvador Dali.[3]

It should also be noted that the slow-thinking, slow-talking characters of the film seem rather out of place in a genre noted for its snappy dialogue delivered at a rapid-fire pace, adding a further twist to the play with genre in the film. In addition, where films such as *Body Heat* had ramped up the simmering sexual energies of noir, bringing it to full boil, *Blood Simple* tones *down* these energies. Ray falls in love with Abby (or thinks he does), though in an oddly dispassionate way; for her part, she doesn't particularly seem to be all that into him (or anything else). Both seem strangely affectless, and the sexual chemistry between them is tepid at best. Indeed, they come off as two damaged individuals already so wounded by life that they hardly have the energy left to generate any real emotions. Abby generally seems overwhelmed by events, a condition that is brilliantly enacted by McDormand—though she herself has attributed her performance not to acting skill but to the fact that she literally *was* overwhelmed by the experience of making the film (and more than a little bit afraid that the Coens didn't really know what they were doing and would never finish the project). Intentional or not, her deer-staring-into-headlights performance places Abby in direct opposition to her structural function as the man-destroying femme fatale of the film, a role usually filled by scheming, manipulative, diabolically clever women. Meanwhile, the two other most important elements that the Coens brought to the film that seem foreign to film noir are generic ones. In particular, *Blood Simple* is far funnier than one would typically expect from a noir film, while the film also draws strongly (especially in its visual style) upon the horror genre and especially upon the slasher film, which was in its golden age at the time *Blood Simple* was made.

The most interesting character in *Blood Simple* is probably neither of the protagonists but Visser, the film's private-detective narrator. Private detectives are, of course, common in film noir (as are voice-over narrators), but Visser is unusual in that he is ultimately the villain of the piece—though in point of fact virtually everyone in this film seems to be roughly on the same moral (or immoral) level. The aging, overweight Visser is also an unusual private eye in a number of other ways, including most obviously the laid-back, folksy style that always seems on the verge of becoming a parody of itself, giving the entire character a humorous tinge that belies his murderous nature and that contrasts sharply with the cultural memory of private dicks such as Sam Spade or Philip Marlowe. Add in the touch that Visser drives around town doing his private-eye business in a Volkswagen Beetle, and Visser becomes the sort of colorful, over-the-top figure that would populate so many of the Coens' later films.

Visser also helps to create an overall sense that the entire film is an elaborate joke and that the dark material it presents is never to be taken too seriously. Of course, film noir itself sometimes pushes things so far that they spill over into humor—as in the scene in Edgar G. Ulmer's *Detour* (1945) in which luckless protagonist Al Roberts (Tom Neal) inadvertently strangles femme fatale Vera (Ann Savage) by yanking on the cord to a phone on which she is attempting to talk in the next room. But *Blood Simple* pushes *everything* too far and never lets up, from the peculiar opening narration of Visser to the numerous self-referential touches that never let us forget that this was a film self-consciously made in imitation of other films, a fact that is perhaps most cleverly brought home from the fact that Meurice keeps playing the Four Tops' 1965 classic "It's the Same Old Song" on the jukebox in the bar. Of course, that song also reminds us that this same old song now has a different meaning, which serves as an announcement that the Coens might be recycling material from earlier films but are still putting their own spin on that material. As Adams puts it, this song "signals the filmmakers' ironic self-awareness that they are telling an archetypal story, but also revising and updating it."[4]

Sonnenberg's camera work is also worth mentioning in this regard. Though mostly straightforward (the Coens couldn't afford a lot of fancy equipment), the cinematography does include a number of very artfully composed shots—such as that shot of brilliant light streaming through bullet holes in a wall, which seems to be the Coens' way of trying to up the ante on all those film noir shots of light streaming through Venetian blinds to form patterns of light and shadow.[5] It's a wonderful visual, but it's also an excessive one: the bullet holes are far too large and perfectly round to be realistic and the brightness of the light beaming through the holes is out of all proportion to the actual level of light on the other side of the wall. At the same time, the brilliance of the light streaming through the perfectly round holes into a relatively dark space emphasizes the fact that, while *Blood Simple* plays on patterns of darkness and light as does film noir, it flips the usual meaning of the two, making light an ominous sign of danger and darkness a place of relative safety. This pattern, in fact, runs throughout the film—as when Ray attempts to get Abby to leave off the light in her apartment so that Visser can't see in, only to have her flip the light on instead, enabling Visser to shoot Ray through the window. The film's symbolic use of darkness and light thus both recalls film noir and goes beyond it into new territory, echoing the way in which the muted color scheme of the film is clearly designed to achieve much of the atmospheric effect of the black-and-white cinematography so intimately associated with film noir, yet can include splashes of brilliant color, especially red.

There are also other moments of particularly intrusive camera work/editing that complicate the generic makeup of *Blood Simple*. In perhaps the most noticeable example of cinematic dexterity in the film (shot via an elaborate mechanical contrivance—based on a sex device advertised in *Hustler* magazine),[6] Abby starts to fall backward in the back room of the dance hall, apparently fainting, then lands on her bed in her apartment. It's a nifty bit of cinematographic ingenuity that has nothing to do with the plot of the film but serves largely as a reminder that this low-budget film by first-time filmmakers is not to be taken lightly. Recalling more than anything the elaborate moving-camera shots that are sprinkled through the films of Alfred Hitchcock, the shot seems to say that this is *art*, and in an intrusive way that genuine film noir, with its quest for grittiness, would be unlikely to employ.

In another (perhaps more important) sequence, Marty attacks Abby after finding her in Ray's bed. He drags her out of Ray's house, apparently intending to kill her. A shot from across the lawn shows them exiting the house; the camera then moves rapidly across the lawn as tense music builds toward a crescendo. We expect some sort of violent climax, and we get it, in a way, but it's really more of an anticlimax, as Abby bites Marty's finger, breaks free, and then kicks him in the groin, sending him to the ground in agony. Such tense moments can often be found in film noir, but the particular rapid camera movement in this shot feels much more like something from a 1980s slasher film, in which such intrusive camera movements are often used to signal an impending violent event.

Soon after this encounter, Marty hires Visser to kill Abby and Ray. Visser sends Marty out of town on a fishing trip, presumably so that he will have an alibi for the killings. Then Visser goes to Ray's house as Ray and Abby sleep in Ray's bed. We are less than halfway through the film, but it seems very possible that the couple might be killed. Camera movement is again used to enhance the tension as the camera moves slowly through the house toward the door where Visser is picking the lock to come inside. The composition of this shot is once again more reminiscent of slasher films than of film noir, but the resolution of the sequence is more artful than violent. By the time Visser leaves, we are left uncertain whether Ray and Abby have actually been killed, and it will only be later that we learn that Visser has simply photographed the sleeping couple so that he can doctor the photo to make Marty think they have been killed.

In a classic film noir betrayal, Visser meets up with Marty in the back room of the seedy bar so that he can extract his payment from Marty for the killings, then promptly shoots Marty in cold blood so that his scam will not be uncovered. But Visser shoots Marty with Abby's gun, which he stole from Ray's house. At this moment, it is still unclear whether Visser has also killed Abby and Ray, but the film itself takes a sudden Coenesque turn as Visser snarls at Marty (who has consistently shown contempt for Visser through the film), "Who looks stupid now?" It's a perfectly appropriate line for the scene, and it is likely that most of the film's original audience would take it that way. However, the line is actually borrowed from the 1955 British comedy crime film *The Lady-killers*, a film that the Coens themselves would remake in 2004. Recognizing this bit of allusive verbal dexterity tends to ironize the entire preceding scene between Visser and Marty, and the scene is then immediately complicated still further by an artfully composed shot of the

The sleeping Ray (John Getz) and Abby (Frances McDormand) as photographed by the private detective Visser (M. Emmet Walsh) in *Blood Simple*. Circle Films / Photofest © Circle Films

dead Marty, slumped back in his chair with blood oozing from his chest wound, the bloody fish he has brought back from his trip lying on the desk in front of him to complete the atmosphere of blood and death. It's a brilliant shot, composed like a painting, made even more effective as the camera moves to an overhead position, giving us a view of Marty and the fish from above, as the slowly moving blade of a ceiling fan sweeps between the camera and the carnage below, momentarily blotting the screen to black. Ceiling fans are in fact used throughout the film to create a noir-like atmospheric effect, playing almost the same role as that played by Venetian blinds in the original film noir cycle, but this sequence is almost *too* artistic, *too* brilliant. Even more than the later scene of Abby falling in the dance hall and landing in her bed, it's an intrusive moment of art that seems just slightly out of place in such a tawdry story, creating the off-kilter effect that would become a trademark of the Coens' filmmaking.

Of course, such effects are not entirely foreign to film noir; the combination of high technique with low subject matter that marks this scene is in fact highly reminiscent of the same combination used so deftly by Orson Welles's *Touch of Evil* (1958), one of the great noir films of all time. Of course, *Touch of Evil* is also often regarded as the film that finished off the original noir cycle, having taken the form about as far as it could go and already tottering on the brink of self-parody, occupying an eccentric and unstable position that the Coens have made very much their own home territory. In their case, however, they typically reach this position not merely by pushing the conventions of genre to their extreme but also by mixing in elements of multiple genres.

In addition to certain camera movements that evoke the feeling of slasher films, *Blood Simple* draws upon the horror genre more overtly as well. Immediately after the killing of Marty, Ray appears at the dance hall, almost as if risen from the dead. He then finds Marty's body and Abby's gun. He puts two and two together and concludes that Abby has shot Marty, so he decides to dispose of the body in order to protect Abby. First, though, he rather incompetently cleans up the blood from the floor, beginning a sequence of events that, more than any other, earns the film its title. As Falsani notes, the term "blood simple" is used in Dashiell Hammett's novel *Red Harvest* to suggest "a kind of mania that takes over when people are exposed to bloody violence."[7] It is certainly the case that Ray is not thinking clearly in this sequence, but then clear thinking was never his forte to begin with. In an unlikely turn of events that again comes dangerously close to black comedy (but also veers into horror film territory), Marty *does* rise from the dead, reviving before Ray can bury him and then attempting to escape by crawling away from Ray's car because he is too badly wounded to walk. For his part, Ray contemplates re-killing Marty, first by running him over with his car and then by braining him with a shovel, but he doesn't have the stomach for either. Eventually, he decides to bury Marty alive, along with Abby's gun—and nearly gets shot by Marty in the process. He retrieves the gun after staring into it dumbly as Marty pulls the trigger three times.[8] To make matters worse, he drives his car into a freshly plowed field to bury the body, leaving clearly visible tire tracks that virtually assure the quick discovery of the body. In the process, he also leaves an array of handprints and footprints, while soaking the backseat of his car with Marty's blood.

There is, in fact, a great deal of blood in this film, as perhaps the title already predicts. In another horror-film sequence, after Abby falls from the dance hall to her apartment, she apparently discovers Marty in her apartment, somehow having risen once more from the dead. They have a brief conversation, then he drops to his knees and vomits a torrent of blood. Then Abby awakes and we realize that the encounter with Marty was a nightmare. Such inserted dream sequences are, of course, common in classic American films, and the Coens employ them in a number of clever ways throughout their career. In any case, Marty's final gush of blood is clearly far more reminiscent of horror films than film noir, which is essentially bloodless, despite its emphasis on violence and murder.

In its final sequence, *Blood Simple* shifts into all-out slasher film mode, as a desperate Visser, suddenly turned far more sinister than he had previously seemed, shows up determined to kill both Ray and Abby. Ray is no problem, but Abby proves far more difficult. Indeed, it is Visser who is finally killed, leaving Abby as the film's Final Girl, after an incredibly tense sequence in which Visser tries everything he can to finish her, including (at one point) resorting to a knife that she had previously plunged through his hand, pinning it to a windowsill. Meanwhile, in one final bit of irony, the whole scene of Visser chasing Abby occurs while the two remain in different rooms: Abby, in fact, thinks that Marty is indeed alive and that he is her assailant almost until the very end. For his part, Visser takes so much punishment in this scene before he is finally shot and killed by Abby that the sequence hovers on the brink of comedy, almost in the mode of Road Runner and Wile E. Coyote. However, the sequence never quite goes over the edge into all-out comedy—though Visser himself literally dies laughing after he discovers Abby's misidentification of her attacker. Nevertheless, the sequence actually remains a quite effective one, filled with tension and suspense, visually built around the film's signature shot of that light streaming through those bullet holes. A better referent for the sequence than Road Runner cartoons, in fact, is James Cameron's *The Terminator*, released in the same year as *Blood Simple* and drawing in a similar way upon the slasher film, though belonging primarily to another genre. Like Visser, Arnold Schwarzenegger's Terminator takes an incredible amount of punishment before he finally succumbs, greatly increasing the tension of the final scenes as he comes back from seeming destruction again and again.

All in all, the horror film and film noir elements of *Blood Simple* are blended quite seamlessly and work very well together. It is, in fact, a meticulously constructed film, with scenes carefully composed to echo other scenes and lines of dialogue cleverly written to echo earlier lines of dialogue. The Coens, in making the film, seemed already to be budding masters of their craft, the virtual opposites of all the characters in the film, who can't seem to do anything right. *Blood Simple* was, in fact, so well made that it has been widely credited as starting a whole new era of well-crafted, low-budget, independent films, a category that had formerly been dominated by slipshod workmanship, its products often being entertaining primarily because they were so laughably bad. The film certainly took neo-noir in new directions, though the Coens themselves would perhaps be the best example of neo-noir filmmakers who followed its path.

## THE MAN WHO WASN'T THERE: RAISING CAIN

Virtually all Coen Brothers films contain some sort of elements that are reminiscent of film noir and its literary forebear, hard-boiled detective fiction, though in differing ways and to varying extents. For example, if *Blood Simple* is a primarily neo-noir film that also has comic aspects, their next film, *Raising Arizona* (1987), is a primarily comic film that has neo-noir elements. And if *Blood Simple* seems to owe a certain amount of its hard-boiled flavor to Dashiell Hammett, then *Miller's Crossing* (1990) owes even more to Hammett, while *The Big Lebowski* (1998) owes a great deal to Raymond Chandler. In 2001, meanwhile, the brothers would undertake their most concerted effort to make a seemingly genuine replica of a film noir in the form of *The Man Who Wasn't There*, a film that was shot (or at least developed) in black and white[9] and whose classic film noir plot is set in 1949, about the time when the noir cycle was at an absolute peak. At that time, such classic noir films as *The Postman Always Rings Twice* (1946), *The Big Sleep* (1946), *The Killers* (1946), *Body and Soul* (1947), *Crossfire* (1947), *The Lady from Shanghai* (1947), *Nightmare Alley* (1947), *Kiss of Death* (1947), *Out of the Past* (1947), *The Naked City* (1948), *Key Largo*

(1948), *Criss Cross* (1949), and *White Heat* (1949) had all been released in the past three years.

Nevertheless, despite the mutual interest in noir, *The Man Who Wasn't There* could hardly be described as a return to the mode of *Blood Simple*. As Nathan puts it, these two films "couldn't be more diametrically opposed in style or mood and yet still be recognizably part of the Coen canon."[10] Thus, while *The Man Who Wasn't There* can certainly be categorized as a neo-noir film, numerous elements of it continue to suggest the Coens' habitual refusal to be tied to generic purity or historical accuracy. As Peter Bradshaw (calling the film the Coens' "masterpiece") puts it, *The Man Who Wasn't There* is "a thriller in the style of James M. Cain, set in suburban California in 1949 and obviously influenced by the movies of the period, yet somehow transmitting the atmospheric crackle of a strange tale from *The Twilight Zone*."[11] Cain's 1943 novel *Double Indemnity* (first published in serial form in 1936) does seem to be the main literary referent of *The Man Who Wasn't There*, with a dash of Cain's earlier *The Postman Always Rings Twice* (1934) thrown in for good measure, but there are numerous other potential sources as well.[12]

Both of these Cain novels, of course, were adapted into classic noir films, and both of the latter provide important glosses on *The Man Who Wasn't There*, whose most obvious *cinematic* referent is Billy Wilder's adaptation of *Double Indemnity* (1944), regarded by many as the quintessential film noir. Still, as is so often the case with the Coens, their dialogue with *Double Indemnity* is more directly with the source material in Cain than with Wilder's film. Like both versions of *Double Indemnity* (and like *Blood Simple*, for that matter), *The Man Who Wasn't There* features a deadly love triangle, this time including barber Ed Crane (Billy Bob Thornton) and his hard-drinking accountant wife, Doris (McDormand again), who is having an affair with her boss, Big Dave Brewster (James Gandolfini), who will eventually be killed by Ed. Brewster is the manager of the Santa Rosa, California, department store where Doris keeps the books. That store happens to be called "Nirdlinger's Department Store" and is owned by Brewster's wife, the former Ann Nirdlinger (Katherine Borowitz). Most of this situation does not appear to be particularly closely related to Wilder's *Double Indemnity*, though that film does feature a love-triangle plot of sorts, as femme fatale Phyllis Dietrichson (Barbara Stanwyck) seduces insurance salesman Walter Neff (Fred MacMurray) into helping her kill her husband so that she can collect the payoff from the life insurance policy that Neff himself sold her. Cain's novel is built around this same basic plot structure, except that there Phyllis's last name is *Nirdlinger*.[13]

This hint at a connection between Cain's novel and *The Man Who Wasn't There* is only one of numerous hints that Cain's fiction is the primary source for the film, though it is certainly the case that the Coens' film is also meticulously constructed to resemble an authentic film noir in many ways. Again, however, even if the Coens' film was *exactly* like an authentic film noir, it still wouldn't *be* an authentic film noir: it simply doesn't mean the same thing to make a film noir in 2001 as it did to make a film noir in 1949, much in the same way that Menard's Quixote could not possibly mean the same thing as Cervantes's original. If nothing else, it is impossible to see *The Man Who Wasn't There* as anything other than an imitation, or pastiche, of a film noir, rather than as a film noir proper. However, as with the case of Menard, this seeming lack of originality actually enriches the film because it introduces a whole new form of intertextual dialogue that would not be available to a film made amid the original noir cycle.

In *The Man Who Wasn't There*, Crane has absolutely no dedication to his work as a barber, which he regards as a form of Sisyphean tedium—he keeps cutting the hair, and it keeps growing back, in an endless cycle, just as the barber pole that serves as a central visual image in the film keeps turning, sending its stripes spiraling upward, yet never moving beyond the pole. Then again, the morose and laconic Crane seemingly has little enthusiasm for anything. He even goes so far as to say (in his remarkably unenthusiastic voice-over that opens the film) that he does not even really consider himself a barber. He's just someone who stumbled into working in the barbershop because it is owned by Doris's loquacious brother, Frank Raffo (Michael Badalucco). Crane seems to have stumbled into his marriage as well. In fact, he seems to be stumbling aimlessly through life, passively waiting for things to happen to him. His (non)reaction to his realization that Doris is having an affair with Brewster is typical: "It's a free country."

The late 1940s were a key time in American history, as well as in film noir history, and the Coens, in their typical fashion, lace their film with allusions to both mainstream and marginal historical references. For example, there are multiple references in *The Man Who Wasn't There*

**Billy Bob Thornton as Ed Crane in *The Man Who Wasn't There*. USA Films / Photofest © USA Films**

to UFOs, even though UFOs really have nothing whatsoever to do with the plot of the film. Still, it was in June of 1947 that pilot Kenneth Arnold made the first high-profile claim to have seen UFOs, which he reportedly observed while flying near Mt. Rainier in Washington State. Two weeks later, a downed UFO was supposedly discovered in the desert near Roswell, New Mexico, in what remains the most prominent UFO rumor in American history. Probably the second most prominent UFO rumor involves photos that were supposedly taken of a UFO by farmer Paul Trent near McMinnville, Oregon, in 1950. Oregon, in fact, has long been a central locus for UFO sightings, which becomes relevant in the film when a paranoid-seeming Ann Brewster visits Crane in the middle of the night, while his wife awaits trial for Ann's husband's murder. Ann assures Ed that she knows Doris is innocent and reveals her theory that Big Dave had been killed as part of a conspiracy to cover up the fact that he had been abducted by aliens and taken aboard their spacecraft the year before, when the Brewsters were on a camping trip near Eugene, Oregon.

Such sightings and rumors might well have been spurred by the atmosphere of tension and paranoia that reigned in American society in the late 1940s, the time when the Cold War kicked into high gear. Indeed, the tensions involving World War II and then subsequently the Cold War nuclear arms race (figured most directly and spectacularly in Robert Aldrich's 1955 noir film *Kiss Me Deadly*) formed an important part of the atmospheric backdrop of film noir in general. The Cold War figures directly in *The Man Who Wasn't There* as well. For example, in one early scene, Raffo reads a newspaper in the barbershop and notes with exasperation that "the Russians exploded an A-bomb, and there's not a damn thing we can do about it." Given that the Soviets did, in fact, test their first A-bomb in 1949, this evocation of Cold War fears is highly appropriate. It was, after all, only a couple of years earlier, in 1947, that Bernard Baruch coined the very term "Cold War," and it was also in that year that the Truman administration took its first major steps toward the active conduct of this war, initiating the program of prevention of Soviet expansion known as the Truman Doctrine, beginning with massive military and economic aid to Greece and Turkey. The summer of 1947 also saw Truman sign the National Security Act, which established much of the administrative apparatus for conducting the Cold War, including the founding of the Central Intelligence Agency (CIA).

Ultimately, however, the paranoid and pessimistic outlook of the original film noir cycle (especially in the postwar years) owes less to fear that communists might destroy America's capitalist way of life than to fear that there was something rotten at the heart of American capitalism to begin with. This same suspicion centrally informs *The Man Who Wasn't There* as well. In fact, the entire plot of the film is driven by business considerations and is kicked into gear when entrepreneur Creighton Tolliver (Jon Polito) shows up in the barbershop and informs Crane that he is in town from Sacramento looking for investors in his plan to found a business empire based on the revolutionary new technology of dry cleaning. Not surprisingly, dry cleaning was not an entirely new technology in 1949 but had in fact been in use in its modern form since the 1930s, with precursors dating well back into the nineteenth century.[14] Indeed, one of the key moments that marks *The Man Who Wasn't There* as set in 1949 comes as Crane sits in the barbershop late in the film reading the September 19, 1949, issue of *Life* magazine, which can clearly be identified from the authentic cover, featuring actress Arlene Dahl on the front and a young Lucille Ball (in an advertisement for Chesterfield cigarettes) on the back. However, Crane reads an article titled "Dry Cleaning: The Wave of the Future," by one Ezra Moorestone. He then flips to the next article, titled "Mysteries of Roswell, New Mexico." Both articles resonate surprisingly well with the thematic content of the film. Then again, the articles are plants: neither actually appeared in that issue of *Life*. We even get an extended view of some of the text of the second article. It is, of course, nonsense that sounds like it might have been generated by some sort of algorithm designed to produce bureaucratic gobbledygook: "The outlined situation is currently under debate. Issues were selected and are being prioritized on the basis of common agreement. The widest possible latitude is being allowed, to more carefully assess all salient points." As a general rule, the more authentic elements in a Coen Brothers film appear to be, the more likely they are to be fake; the more outlandish elements in a Coen Brothers film appear to be, the more likely they are to be authentic.

But Tolliver's plan is very much in tune with the *spirit* of American capitalism in 1949, as American business kicked into an expansionist mode that seemed to put quick riches within the reach of everyone. Even the normally passive Crane catches money fever after he hears Tolliver's pitch, triggering a tragic chain of events that leads to the deaths of almost all of the major characters in the film. Crane anonymously blackmails Brewster with the threat of revealing his affair with Doris in order to get the $10,000 he needs to invest in Tolliver's dry-cleaning scheme. Brewster pays up, but the loss of the cash puts such a dent into his own business plans (he hopes to open an "annex" to Nirdlinger's Department Store) that he flies into a rage and ends up beating Tolliver to death, initially thinking Tolliver to be the blackmailer. In the process, however, he learns from Tolliver that Crane is the actual blackmailer. When he violently confronts Crane, Crane kills Brewster in self-defense. Doris is charged with Brewster's murder and commits suicide while in jail. Things then go full circle, as Crane is convicted of Tolliver's murder and sentenced to death.

In addition to the fact that all the main action is triggered by a business deal, *The Man Who Wasn't There* is chock full of allusions to the burgeoning consumerist culture of postwar America. "These are boom times in retailing," as Big Dave describes it. Crane's opening voice-over also informs us that he and Doris live "in a little bungalow," complete with "an electric ice box, a gas hearth, and a garbage grinder built into the sink. You might say I had it made." Of course, whatever *you* might say, it is clear that Crane doesn't think he has it made, despite this catalog of consumerist dream devices with which his household is equipped, suggesting that the suburban dream might not be all it is cracked up to be. In terms of consumerist imagery, it is of course significant that so much of the action of *The Man Who Wasn't There* revolves around a department store, perhaps the ultimate consumerist institution. Immediately after describing the amenities available in his home, Crane introduces us to Doris by noting that she keeps the books at Nirdlinger's Department Store. He also notes, as if this is one of the most important things to know about her, that Doris gets a 10 percent discount on whatever she wants at Nirdlinger's. Her wants, we are told, include "nylon stockings, make-up, and perfume," a list that suggests her concern with her sexual attractiveness—though not, we will soon realize, to Crane, their relationship having been asexual for "many years."

Other aspects of the American way are also called into question in the film. For example, like the good Americans they are, the Cranes go to church weekly. However, they usually only go on Tuesday nights, when there are no religious services but merely a bingo game. "Doris," Crane tells us in his ongoing voice-over, "wasn't big on divine worship." In this way, the film undercuts the myth of American piety. It also undercuts the myth of the wholesome American town—and the film's Santa Rosa certainly seems, on the surface, to meet this description—as a perfect place to raise virtuous, hardworking children. But Santa Rosa, we should remember, also serves as the setting for Alfred Hitchcock's noirish 1943 thriller *Shadow of a Doubt*, which employs the seemingly idyllic setting of the town precisely in order to deliver a reminder that violence and evil can easily intrude into such settings—and even into the domestic family sphere within such settings. [15]

The final half hour of *The Man Who Wasn't There* becomes increasingly strange and surreal as the basic film noir matrix begins to break down, though it might perhaps be more to the point to say that the noir matrix (which already contains a certain amount of strangeness and surrealism) is pushed to its logical conclusion. There is, for example, lots of courtroom drama in film noir, though there is nothing quite like the scene in which flamboyant, high-priced Sacramento defense attorney Freddy Riedenschneider (Tony Shalhoub), recruited by Crane to defend Doris in her murder trial, discourses to them on his defense strategy, which involves creating a reasonable doubt in the minds of the jurors concerning Doris's guilt.[16] This strategy, of course, is a very conventional one. What is not conventional is the way Riedenschneider frames the creation of this doubt as a version of the Heisenberg uncertainty principle, even though he cannot remember Werner Heisenberg's name, recalling only that the principle was formulated by some German guy named "Fritz, or Werner, or whatever." Indeed, Riedenschneider's explanation of the uncertainty principle makes it clear that he doesn't really understand it at all, making it more a question of phenomenology than of physics. What is also unusual about this scene is the extreme expressionist lighting, in which Riedenschneider paces about a large jail visitation cell, as if performing in a spotlight. For example, the scene begins as he stands with brilliant light on his mouth, while the rest of his face is obscured in shadow, emphasizing the lawyer's role as the mouthpiece for his clients. Granted, expressionist lighting is common to film noir as well, but this scene is clearly more Franz Kafka than Billy Wilder.[17] Indeed, the lighting here serves almost as a parody of noir lighting, with the prison bars creating an exaggerated version of the Venetian blind effect so common to film noir.

Doris commits suicide before we learn whether Riedenschneider's Heisenbergian defense would have been successful, something that disappoints Riedenschneider immensely. Doris's death also sends Raffo into a depression that forces Crane to assume responsibility for keeping the barbershop going—which he does, with his customary stoicism. His wife's death seems to have affected him very little: he was emotionally dead already. And yet, now that she is dead, he suddenly feels the urge to talk to her, especially after he learns from the local medical examiner that Doris had been pregnant (with Brewster's child). This discovery sends Crane to seek the services of a weird medium to try to contact Doris, even though he clearly expects the woman to be a charlatan. This expectation is accurate, and Crane quickly abandons the séance. He decides, reasonably enough, that, if he is to move forward, he needs to leave the dead and the past behind.

However, Crane's turn to the future and to the living is no more sensible than his visit to the medium. Earlier, during a Christmas party for employees of Nirdlinger's (and their families), Crane had overheard local teenager Rachel "Birdy" Abundas (played by a then-unknown Scarlett Johansson) playing the slow second movement of Beethoven's Piano Sonata Number 8 ("Pathétique"). Birdy is the daughter of alcoholic local lawyer Walter Abundas (Coen regular Richard Jenkins), with whom Crane is vaguely acquainted, primarily as a customer in the barbershop. Perhaps because the feel of the music matches his own pathetic predicament, Crane is mesmerized by the sonata, though he is so ignorant of such things that he asks Birdy if it is her own composition. "Oh, no," she says with absolute seriousness. "No, that was written by Ludwig van Beethoven." She then goes on the explain that Beethoven "wrote some beautiful piano sonatas."

Those sonatas—including passages from Sonatas 14 ("Moonlight"), 15 ("Pastorale"), 23 ("Appassionata"), 25, and 30—form the core of the soundtrack of *The Man Who Wasn't There*, creating considerable postmodern irony from the mismatch between the intense passion of the music, a key expression of Romantic emotionalism, and the dispassion of Crane. The prominence of this music in the film should come as no surprise, both because music is so important in the Coens' films in general and because classical music in particular was crucial to the soundtracks of the 1940s films that the Coens draw upon so extensively in so many of their films, including this one. Caryl Flinn has documented the use of classical music in classic Hollywood cinema, noting that this music often carries with it strong utopian and emotional resonances that reinforce the thematic content of the films. However, in the case of *The Man Who Wasn't There*, Beethoven's sonatas are important precisely because their sweep and grandeur and emotional power do *not* match the overall thrust of the film or condition of its protagonist.

From this point forward, Crane becomes more and more enamored of Birdy's talents as a pianist, visiting the Abundas home almost nightly to hear Birdy play, while Doris awaits trial and Mr. Abundas sits numbly by, apparently unconcerned that a middle-aged man seems so fascinated by his attractive teenage daughter. Crane, of course, denies (even to himself) that there is anything sexual in his attraction, instead finding in his perception of the beauty of her playing an escape from the emptiness and tedium of his life as a barber. Still, he pathetically imagines himself spending his life with her, becoming her manager and mentor and helping her to turn her musical ability into a major career. The problem, though, is that Birdy is not nearly as gifted as Crane believes—a fact of which Crane is informed after he takes her to audition for a fancy music teacher in San Francisco.[18] For her part, Birdy is not especially interested in a musical career—and possibly not in *any* career—though she thinks she might want to be a veterinarian. Birdy, in short, is just an ordinary 1940s girl, however much Crane might have aestheticized her, confusing her personal qualities with the qualities of the music she plays. Then again, as Flinn notes, musical utopias in film noir are quite commonly associated with women, such films tending "to associate femininity with lost, musical moments."[19]

In one of the strange moments that punctuate the second half of *The Man Who Wasn't There*, Crane is driving Birdy back to Santa Rosa from her failed audition for the teacher in San Francisco. She thanks him for his help but informs him of her lack of ambition to be a concert pianist. Then she reveals, in one of the film's most ironic moments, that she has misperceived his true nature as much as he has misjudged hers. "You know what you are?" she asks him. "You're an enthusiast." Crane, of course, couldn't be further from an enthusiast in general, however much he might have idealized Birdy. Their mutual lack of understanding then reaches its peak when Birdy attempts to fellate Crane as he drives, leading to a surreal scene in which Crane drives the car off the side of a mountain and we see it flying through the air in slow motion, while Crane's voice-over informs us that an undertaker once told him that human hair continues to grow even after death. Crane clearly expects to die as the car sails through the treetops. When the car hits the ground, a hubcap shakes loose and rolls improbably far along the ground in a classic Coen motif, while Crane continues to meditate on the status of one's hair after death. We then see a shot of Crane's crumpled body in the wreck of the car, leading us to believe that he might be dead, or at least dying. To top off the scene, the rolling hubcap then morphs into a flying saucer and zips off into the distance, disappearing into darkness.

The film then suddenly cuts to Crane, sitting on the porch of his bungalow, smoking a cigarette (as usual). His life seems to have returned to normal, and the approach of a salesman who attempts to interest him in having his driveway paved with "tar macadam" emphasizes the ordinariness of the scene even more. Then Doris pulls into the driveway, hops out of the car, and sends the unfortunate salesman packing. She heads into the house and grabs a drink, then joins Crane on the couch, where they sit at opposite ends, as alienated from each other as ever. Then there is another cut back to the darkness, out of which the flying saucer reemerges, this time morphing into a round examination mirror strapped to the forehead of a doctor who has been treating Crane's injuries from the car wreck.

It thus becomes clear that Crane's encounter with the resurrected Doris had simply been a dream while he was lying unconscious, sending us for the time being back into a relatively realistic world. Then, in a moment of delicious irony, the two police detectives who had earlier arrived at the barbershop to inform Crane of Doris's arrest (and who seem to have emerged from *Dragnet* via Kafka's *The Trial*) arrive at the hospital. In a comic scene in which the two policemen and the doctor form a sort of comedy team, they inform Crane that he himself is now under arrest—for the murder of Tolliver, whom we now realize had been beaten to death by Brewster.

The film then quickly skims through Crane's murder trial, in which Crane has to sign over his house in order to pay Riedenschneider to defend him. In this new trial, the lawyer shifts from physics to philosophy, attempting to portray Crane as an embodiment of the existential predicament of "modern man," something the Coens themselves in fact do throughout the film.[20] Crane is, Riedenschneider argues, very much in the same boat as the jury members themselves, hoping that they will feel sympathy for him. The jury seems sympathetic, but then Raffo interrupts the proceeding to attack Crane, whom he now blames for Doris's death. A mistrial is declared. Unable to afford Riedenschneider in his retrial, Crane is sentenced to death, which he accepts with his customary stoicism.

As Crane awaits execution by writing his story in his prison cell (for publication in a men's magazine), we experience one last moment of cinematic strangeness as Crane walks numbly out of his prison cell and into the yard outside, there to encounter a flying saucer. He is then shaken awake to be taken to the electric chair (even though executions in California at the time would have been carried out via the gas chamber), once again revealing a strange scene in the film to be a dream. The screen cuts to black as Crane is electrocuted—though the execution

sequence itself is so surreal that one almost expects it also to be revealed as a dream.

Crane's ultimate end evokes a number of noir films in which innocent men are wrongly accused, perhaps most notably Hitchcock's *The
Wrong Man* (1956). However, the most direct predecessor is *The Postman Always Rings Twice*, in which both the 1934 novel and the 1946
film version end with protagonist Frank Chambers (played in the film
by John Garfield) awaiting execution after a conviction for the murder
of his lover Cora (Lana Turner in the film), even though she was actually killed in an accidental car crash that Chambers survived. The parallel
with Crane's crash with Birdy is obvious—though Birdy suffers only a
broken collarbone and is otherwise fine. More importantly, Chambers
accepts his wrongful conviction as poetic justice, given that he had
earlier conspired with Cora to kill her husband, while Crane seems
calmly to accept his conviction in the death of Tolliver as rightful retribution for "all the pain I caused other people," perhaps including the
killing of Brewster. Finally, as *Postman* reaches its end, Chambers is
writing his story for potential publication, just as Crane writes his at the
end of *The Man Who Wasn't There*.

All in all, *The Man Who Wasn't There* shows the Coens at the peak
of their powers, demonstrating a mastery of the genre of film noir so
complete that they can make what seems to be an authentic noir film
even while including so many elements that would be out of place in
the films of the original noir cycle. Indeed, even the elements of the
film that might seem out of place in a noir film—the flying saucers, the
Heisenberg-quoting defense attorney, Crane's scheme to become Birdy's manager—seem to have been carefully chosen to be twenty-first-
century versions of the excessive elements that sometimes appeared in
the noir films of the 1940s and 1950s, such as the drug-induced halluci-
nations of Edward Dmytryk's *Murder, My Sweet* (1944) or the battle to
the death in a mannequin factory at the end of Stanley Kubrick's *Killer's
Kiss* (1955). It is clear that, in the seventeen years between *Blood Simple* and *The Man Who Wasn't There*, the brothers honed their craft
considerably (while also gaining the ability to attract better financing
and distribution). As a result, the later film is altogether more accomplished than the first, while nevertheless maintaining much of the gritty
look and feel of film noir and never appearing *too* polished. *The Man
Who Wasn't There*, despite its over-the-top moments, is an altogether

more serious film than *Blood Simple* had been. Then again, by this time, the Coens had already established that they were able to work in a variety of registers, including an ability to explore serious aspects of the modern existential predicament. They had also, beginning with their second film, *Raising Arizona* (1987), established the complementary ability to do all-out comedy without seeming entirely silly.

# 2

# WHAT'S UP, DOC?

Anarchic Comedy in *Raising Arizona*, *The Ladykillers*, and *Burn After Reading*

Karl Marx once proposed that historical phenomena tend to occur twice, first as tragedy, then as farce. If *Blood Simple* is ultimately tragic, with most of the characters winding up gruesomely dead, the Coens' second film, *Raising Arizona* (1987), definitely moves into the realm of farce. In fact, the ability to do both tragedy and farce (sometimes within the same film) would go on to become a hallmark of the Coens' filmmaking. The particularly farcical, cartoonish comedy of *Raising Arizona* shows up here and there throughout the Coens' body of work, and it is the dominant mode in at least three otherwise very different films: *Raising Arizona* itself, *The Ladykillers* (2004), and *Burn After Reading* (2008). Each of these films takes a potentially serious genre (the domestic drama, the heist film, and the espionage film, respectively) and turns it on its head, injecting a gleefully anarchic note of silliness that can nevertheless also include a certain amount of violence and bloodshed. The films are also typical of the work of the Coens in the way they foreground their settings in specific geographic locations and specific cultural milieus, while at the same time producing what are essentially alternate-reality versions of those settings that never correspond exactly to anything in the real, physical world.

## *RAISING ARIZONA*: REAGAN-ERA FAMILY VALUES

In some ways, *Raising Arizona* foregrounds its setting more than almost any other Coen Brothers film. Not only is the name of the setting in the title of the film, but no less than seven characters in the film are themselves named "Arizona," while a chain of furniture stores called "Unpainted Arizona" is a prominent motif. The irony is that the setting of *Raising Arizona* is actually less important to the overall functioning of the film than in virtually any other Coen Brothers film.[1] In addition, the relationship between the real Arizona and the fictional "Arizona" of the film is even less direct than is typically the case with the Coens' films. Indeed, the Arizona of the film seems so much like a parallel-universe version of Arizona that critic Roger Ebert (apparently not at that time yet accustomed to the Coens' unique play with place) trashed the film on its initial release for its unsteady relationship with its world, arguing that one cannot tell whether it "exists in the real world of trailer parks and 7-Elevens and Pampers, or in a fantasy world of characters from another dimension. . . . It moves so uneasily from one level of reality to another that finally we're just baffled."[2]

Noting Ebert's criticism, Jeffrey Adams suggests that it is typical of critics who "judged the movie by conventional standards of cinematic realism, with the expectation that unless presented explicitly as fantasy, a movie should depict a unified and credible reality. Movies can be either realistic or fantastic, but apparently not both simultaneously."[3] But of course it is precisely this combination of the realistic and the fantastic that helps to give the films of the Coens their unique feel, especially in terms of the places in which they are set. Indeed, while the silliness of *Raising Arizona* might make it seem to be a rather minor Coen Brothers film, it is quite typical of their work in a number of ways.

Like *Blood Simple*, *Raising Arizona* begins with a voice-over narration, this time delivered by male lead Herbert I. "Hi" McDunnough (a wild-haired Nicolas Cage), a small-time habitual criminal who explains, in this opening sequence, how his multiple run-ins with the law brought him into contact with a young woman police officer named "Ed" (short for Edwina, played by Holly Hunter), who has been responsible for shooting the mugshots associated with his various arrests. Love blooms as Hi returns to jail again and again, in the process delivering a bit of political commentary through his voice-over: "I tried to stand up and fly straight, but it wasn't easy with that sumbitch Reagan in the White House." Hi, of course, is hardly an authoritative political commentator, so his distaste for Reagan hardly stands as devastating critique. In fact, given the overall tenor of the film, such comments read more like a *parody* of political commentary than like commentary itself, a tendency that would appear again and again in subsequent films by the Coens.

After this opening prologue, the real plot of the film kicks in as Hi decides that the chance to have a life with Ed is sufficient reason to turn away from his life of crime. The two get married after his latest release from prison, then move into a trailer in suburban Tempe. Hi, trying mightily to settle into the daily grind of law-abiding life, gets a job in a machine shop (apparently run by Hudsucker Industries), though he finds the work rather tedious. In what could again be taken as a commentator on the drudgery of workaday life under modern capitalism, Hi declares (in his ongoing voice-over) that "most ways, the job was a lot like prison." Again, though, this commentary is really more like mock commentary, and—in any case—Hi is happy when at home with Ed: "These were the happy days, the 'salad' days, as they say."

Just who "they" are is unclear, but much of Hi's voice-over seems like he is quoting from *somewhere*, even if that somewhere often seems to be a catalog of clichés. Indeed, this voice-over is itself worthy of extended commentary and serves as a key part of establishing the setting in an Arizona that isn't quite real. In a sense, Cage simply takes the voice-over delivered in *Blood Simple* by Walsh (who also has a minor role in *Raising Arizona*) and cranks it up a notch, into the realm of comic exaggeration. For one thing, Walsh's opening narration runs less than a minute, while Cage's runs for all of eleven minutes, providing commentary on a significant number of scenes. Cage, meanwhile, delivers his narration in a vaguely Southern accent, just as Hunter plays Ed with her own distinctive Southern accent, which itself had been the main reason the Coens had originally wanted Hunter to star in *Blood Simple*. Most of the other characters have accents as well, but each character seems to have an accent of his or her own, making it difficult to locate their speech as "Arizonan." For some critics, the Coens took these odd speech habits a bit too far. For example, Hi employs such strange speech patterns and such an unusual vocabulary (especially given his background) that Ebert found his manner of speech (and for that matter the speech patterns of all the characters) to be distracting and annoying. Hi's speech, Ebert concludes, is a bit too artificial and constructed. He sounds, says the critic, "as if he just graduated from the Rooster Cogburn school of elocution," referring to John Wayne's grumpy U.S. marshal in the 1969 Western classic *True Grit*, a characterization that would prove retroactively ironic when the Coens remade that film in 2010 (or at least re-adapted the 1968 Charles Portis novel on which the 1969 film was based).

*Raising Arizona* itself, while an original story, takes inspiration from a variety of literary sources as well. Josh Levine, for example, lists such literary luminaries as John Steinbeck and William Faulkner as possible inspirations, writers known for their representation of common people and of the South, respectively, and this film certainly has a Southern feel and certainly deals with common folk.[4] In an interview, Joel himself identified Faulkner and Flannery O'Connor as influences on the film,[5] and it is notable that both of these writers are associated exclusively with the South, not the Southwest, just as much of the texture of *Raising Arizona* seems more like the film might have just as easily been titled *Raising Mississippi*. The film uses other cultural resources as well. Hi's narration, for example, is filled with proverbs and biblical quotations. Particularly worthy of mention in terms of the film's delineation of place is the title music, a comically folksy, yodeling cowboy song that strongly helps to establish both the comic tone and the Southwestern setting of the film. And the song sounds goofy for a reason: it is actually a classic by legendary folksinger Pete Seeger titled "Goofing-Off Suite," from his 1955 album of the same title. Seeger, of course, was also something of a voice of the common folk, but the Manhattan-born son of two classical musicians was hardly an authentic cowboy. Thus, while the sound of the song might be perfect for this particular film, it is made even more so because it is an artificial construct made mostly in fun, much like the film itself.

Ebert was not alone among early critics who reacted negatively to *Raising Arizona*, but the film has also had its supporters, and its critical reputation has generally grown over the years, perhaps because critics have come to better understand what the Coens are about. In 1987, though, *Raising Arizona* must have been a hard film to categorize, partly because it didn't seem much like the Coens' previous film and partly because it didn't seem much like anything else being produced in Hollywood. Whatever social and political commentary *Raising Arizona* might contain, for example, it certainly has little in common with the biting satire of capitalist soullessness to be found in Oliver Stone's *Wall Street*, the signature cinematic denunciation of late-Reagan America. On the other hand, much of the American popular culture of 1987 had a lighthearted, escapist quality, designed to provide a respite from Reagan-era America rather than a comment upon it. Several of the films of the year even featured adventures with infants. Yet, while one might be tempted to place *Raising Arizona* with other 1987 "baby" comedies, the texture of the Coens' film has little in common with the cuteness and sweetness of films such as *Three Men and a Baby* or *Baby Boom* or the slightly later *Look Who's Talking* (1989). After all, Bergan notes, *Raising Arizona* deals with the treatment of babies as "consumer goods, good publicity, and as objects for kidnapping, not a subject one generally makes jokes about."[6]

One reason *Raising Arizona* is so hard to categorize is that it includes elements from a variety of different genres. For example, the plot certainly does involve cute babies, but it also involves kidnapping, robbery, a prison break, and a murderous bounty hunter. Bergan notes that Joel Coen described the film in an interview as having all of the "essential elements of popular cinema: 'Babies, Harleys, and explosives.'"[7] One should not read too much into such off-the-cuff remarks, of course, but this suggestion does point to the highly self-conscious and self-referential way in which this film—like all of the Coens' films—comments not only on itself and its own construction but also on the state of the film industry as a whole, with its increasing tendency to toss in diverse elements simply because those elements seemed to be popular in other films.

The real plot of *Raising Arizona* begins when Hi and Ed reach a crisis in their marriage after discovering that she is unable to conceive a child. Hearing the news, Hi at first can't believe it, given that Ed looks to him "as fertile as the Tennessee Valley." But, he tells us in his own inimical style, "the doctor explained that her insides were a rocky place, where my seed could find no purchase." As luck would have it, however, they get this news just as Florence Arizona (Lynne Dumin Kitei), the wife of local furniture magnate Nathan Arizona (Trey Wilson), has given birth to quintuplets after undergoing fertility treatments. Hi is not the clearest thinker in the world, but he immediately puts two and two together and concludes that it makes sense for Ed and himself to snatch one of the Arizona quints for themselves. As he explains it in his voice-over narration, "We thought it was unfair that some should have so many, while others should have so few." If it were not clear enough already, this line makes it obvious that this heist narrative of the redistribution of baby wealth can be read as a sort of off-beat political allegory about the unequal distribution of wealth in Reagan-era America.

This film, however, is far too farcical to be taken very seriously as any sort of political commentary. As usual with the Coens, this is a film more about other films than about its real-world context. The heist itself is an extended bit of slapstick in which Hi climbs through the window of the Arizona nursery, then gets overwhelmed by the horde of babies that is suddenly swarming everywhere, constantly on the verge of disaster, as Hi attempts to take one. It's like something from a Chaplin movie or a Popeye cartoon. And of course it comes as no surprise that, after one false start, Hi and Ed finally do successfully make off with a baby (Nathan Jr. apparently) and that all the other babies are unhurt.

Soon after the McDunnoughs have snatched Nathan Jr. (or Hi Jr. or Ed Jr.; the name keeps shifting), the film suddenly switches from being a highly unconventional heist film to being a highly unconventional prison break film as we observe one Gale Snoats (John Goodman) pushing his way through from beneath the mud during a driving rainstorm. It is a scene with clearly mythical (though comical) resonances, and Gale's appearance is clearly figured as a sort of birth scene as he emerges, screaming and yelling, from the loins of mother earth, recalling the role of the primordial goddess Gaia, mother of all life on earth and the personification of the earth itself, in Greek mythology. He then pulls his brother Evelle (William Forsythe) from the same hole, though this one is a breech birth, Evelle emerging feet first.

After this mythical birth scene, Gale and Evelle go on the run in a way that might be reminiscent of any number of crime films, except for the fact that everything they do is cartoonishly overdone and ridiculous. Hi is an old prison acquaintance, so they eventually take refuge, uninvited, with the McDunnoughs, much to Ed's displeasure. Soon afterward, the film takes a turn into still another form of crime film when Hi dreams of a hellish biker (described by Hi as "the lone biker of the apocalypse"),[8] who then appears in the "real" world of the film in the person of bounty hunter Leonard Smalls (former professional kickboxer and then professional heavyweight boxer Randall "Tex" Cobb). Smalls is an imposing figure of doom, a seeming escapee from the *Road Warrior* films who takes great pleasure in destroying small, defenseless animals. Smalls has come to Tempe to seek a reward from Nathan Sr. for recovering Nathan Jr., thus becoming a crucial part of the plot, even though he really doesn't seem to belong in this particular story.

The film takes a detour into domestic comedy as Hi and Ed experience marital troubles due to their odd situation. "It ain't Ozzie and Harriet," Hi acknowledges. More domestic comedy ensues when Hi and Ed host his boss Glen (Sam McMurray) and Glen's wife, Dot (Frances McDormand), for a cookout—along with Glen and Dot's five bratty children, who nearly wreck the McDunnough trailer. McDormand's hyperactive, over-the-top performance (virtually the exact opposite of her stunned performance in *Blood Simple*) as the overbearing Dot (who insists that the baby be given a diph-tet vaccine immediately) is a comic tour de force. But when Glen smarmily suggests to Hi that the two couples execute a wife-swap, Hi reacts angrily and punches out his boss, leading not only to Hi's firing but to Glen's attempt to force Hi to hand the baby over to him and Dot because Dot wants a baby to cuddle and they can't have any more because something has "gone wrong" with his semen.

A series of comic robbery scenes, comic chase scenes, and comic fight scenes ensues, making clear just how cartoonish this "crime" film really is, its antecedents clearly to be found in actual cartoons and in slapstick comedy more than in the dark world of film noir or more serious films about kidnappings and robberies. Many of these scenes appear to place the stolen baby in extreme danger, but by this time it is abundantly clear that this is not the type of film in which the baby might suffer any real damage, even when he is momentarily acquired by the demonic Smalls. Unlike in the 1993 film *The Sandlot*, Smalls isn't killing anybody in this film, and it is no surprise that it is Smalls himself who is finally blown to oblivion, hoist on his own petard, or at least blown to smithereens by his own grenade—but no one is bemoaning the demise of Smalls, partly because he is so evil and partly because he seems more a nightmare vision than an actual person.

Ultimately, Hi and Ed return Nathan Jr. to Nathan Sr., while the film ends with one last dream-vision on the part of Hi, in which he envisions a distant future in which he and Ed have not only children but

Frances McDormand as Dot and Holly Hunter as Ed in *Raising Arizona*. 20th Century Fox / Photofest © 20th Century Fox

grandchildren. The vision appears to exist in a perfect dream world, "if not Arizona, then a land not too far away, where all parents are strong and wise and capable, and all children are happy and beloved. I don't know. Maybe it was Utah." This, the last word spoken in the film, before the credits role and "Goofing-Off Suite" again plays, once more blurs the boundary between fiction and reality by suggesting that the never-never land envisioned by Hi might actually be a real place (and one that most Americans do not particularly associate with utopian social conditions).

## *THE LADYKILLERS:* GOIN' SOUTH

The Coens did not return to the mode of all-out anarchic comedy that is central to *Raising Arizona* until 2004, with the release of their version of *The Ladykillers*, a film that was unprecedented for the Coens because it was a remake of an earlier film, the 1955 British comedy classic directed by Alexander Mackendrick. *The Ladykillers* was also unusual in that the Coens had originally scripted it for their old pal Barry Sonnenfeld and then agreed to direct only after Sonnenfeld bowed out. One reason why the Coens agreed to direct *The Ladykillers*, despite the fact that they had not written it with an eye toward directing it, was no doubt the fact that the film, being produced via the deep pockets of Disney's Touchstone Pictures, had already lined up Tom Hanks to play the lead role. The Coens, no matter how far outside the Hollywood mainstream they might be in some ways, clearly love working with big movie stars. Moreover, big stars seem to love working with the Coens—who don't always show them in a flattering light but typically give them things to do that they don't normally get to do as big movie stars.

As it turns out, Hanks might, however, be the weakest part of the Coens' version of *The Ladykillers*. Of course, he had big shoes to fill, given that his role as Professor Goldthwaite Higginson Dorr, the leader of a criminal gang involved in a riverboat casino heist, was a near-direct reprisal of a similar role that had been played in the 1955 original by British screen legend Sir John Gielgud. And Hanks acquits himself well, though his performance (so over the top that it feels almost like a parody of Gielgud's performance) does get a little tedious at times. However, almost all of the other characters are more entertaining than the corresponding British characters (though most of them do not exactly match up one for one with characters in the British film). In addition, as an ensemble, the colorful band of misfit felons of the Coens' version of the film is far more comically grotesque than their predecessors. This is especially the case with Garth Pancake, the movie special effects technician who serves as the group's demolitions expert—and who nearly steals the film from Hanks. Played to the hilt by Coen regular J. K. Simmons, Pancake's overly talky explanation of his techniques and his constant, confident reassurances that every difficult task that arises is the "easiest thing in the world" provide some of the film's most amusing dialogue. On the other hand, the film might perhaps have been able to get along without the running joke concerning Pancake's troubles with IBS. The attempt to add black humor by having Pancake blow off his own finger, which is then made off with by a cat, is similarly unsuccessful. But then this whole film is something of a hit-or-miss affair, seemingly constructed according to the old bit of wisdom about throwing mud (or something similar) against a wall and hoping some of it will stick.

The heist element that is so prominent in the Coens' film is an added feature that goes well beyond the British original, which places almost no emphasis on the central heist, an event that takes place quickly and neatly. Instead, the original focuses on the attempts of the gang to get away with the cash they have stolen, and in particular on their bumbling attempts to do away with an old lady, Mrs. Wilberforce (Katie Johnson), who has found them out (thus the title of the film). The bulk of the film essentially plays out as a sort of darkly comic riff on the Agatha Christie classic *And Then There Were None* (1939, adapted several times to film as *Ten Little Indians*), in which the gang itself is killed off, one by one, then dumped onto a freight train that passes beneath an overpass near Mrs. Wilberforce's home. This element is still present in the Coens' version, with Mrs. Wilberforce replaced by Marva Munson (delightfully

**Professor Goldthwaite Higginson Dorr (Tom Hanks) and his crew in *The Ladykillers*. Touchstone Pictures / Photofest © Touchstone Pictures**

played by Irma P. Hall), a churchly widow with whom the professor boards so that he and his gang, posing as a group of musicians who specialize in Renaissance-era music, can tunnel from her basement into the nearby vault where a riverboat casino keeps its cash.

That this heist element in fact becomes the most important part of the film suggests the way in which the Coens' "remake" goes well beyond the British original to engage in a comic dialogue with the whole tradition of the heist film, one of the classic forms of crime-based cinema. Indeed, the Coens are able to hang onto the basic structure of Mackendrick's original, while loading in an almost entire extra film that has more to do with classic noir heist films of the same period as Mackendrick's film—John Huston's *Asphalt Jungle* (1950), Jules Dassin's *Rififi* (1955), Stanley Kubrick's *The Killing* (1956)—than with the original *Ladykillers*. Indeed, the tunneling-into-a-vault technique featured in the Coens' film is one that has been featured in fiction at least as far back as Arthur Conan Doyle's 1891 Sherlock Holmes story "The Red-Headed League." The technique has also been featured in numerous films—not to mention real robberies, perhaps most famously in the 1971 Baker Street Robbery in London (which itself became the inspiration for the 2008 British heist film *The Bank Job*). Even the subsequent unraveling of the gang in the Coens' *Ladykillers*, while closely paralleling the main plot of the British original, also resembles (except for the comic tone) the typical denouement of the heist film.[9]

That Pancake has developed his demolitions expertise as a special effects technician for the movies adds still another dimension (or another ball of mud) to the Coens' film in that it can be taken as a satirical jab at the excessive role being assumed by special effects in the films of the early twenty-first century. This satire even includes a good-natured poke at Coen pal Sam Raimi's then-recent *Spider-Man* (2002), which had featured Simmons in a key role. Pancake (a former civil rights activist, or so he says) lectures Gawain (Marlon Wayans), the gang's lone black member, by noting, "With equal rights comes equal responsibility," thus offering a fairly transparent riff on *Spider-Man*'s most famous line, "With great power comes great responsibility."

Such elements, along with the multicultural aspects of the film's engagement with black Southern culture, make the Coens' version of *The Ladykillers* much richer and more complex than the British original. Much of this richness comes from the setting of the film amid the black culture of the American South. If the setting of *Raising Arizona* is somewhat ambiguous despite the title and the clearly identified location of the action in and around Tempe, blurring the boundary between Southern and Southwestern, the setting of the much later *The Ladykillers* is quite clearly identified as Mississippi, and all the markers of the film (including Tom Hanks's outrageous Southern accent) bear out that location. In addition, not only is the action in this remake transplanted from London to Mississippi, but it is set specifically amid the *black* culture of Mississippi. This multiculturalism adds a new dimension to the Coens' version (though some of the racial humor comes uncomfortably close to *racist* humor). Similarly, Roger Deakins's off-kilter cinematography is also far more interesting than anything in the visuals of the original British version of *The Ladykillers*. Several shots of lone buildings in the Mississippi town, standing in isolation as if each is the only building for miles, are especially striking (and especially Coenesque), though the visual highlight of the film just might be the several shots of the film's criminal gang throwing the bodies of its own members one after another from a bridge onto a garbage barge (replacing a train in the British original) that seems to pass beneath suspiciously often. Among other things, these shots call attention to the important presence of the Mississippi River, which adds to the regional flavor of the film. In addition, the fact that the barges are carrying garbage to an artificial island of refuse in the middle of the majestic river potentially produces some environmentalist commentary, reminding us that the Mississippi of the film is far from a pastoral paradise. This is not Huck Finn's Mississippi.

As usual with the political aspects of their films, the Coens do not particularly invite such interpretations or call attention to the environmentalist implications of the film. Similarly, they put little or no energy into exploring the complex and problematic racial politics of Mississippi, despite placing so much of the film within a black cultural context. There is no indication, for example, that the black characters of the film are discriminated against. Indeed, the main representative of official power in the film is the local sheriff (played by comedian George Wallace), who is himself black (and has a white deputy who shows no signs of racism). Perhaps the most important aspect of *The Ladykillers* with regard to race is the soundtrack, which is made up mostly of black gospel music. This music, organized by T Bone Burnett in a replication of the role he had played with the bluegrass music of *O Brother, Where Art Thou?*, is crucial to the cultural context and overall feel of *The Ladykillers*, even though Ronald Bergan has seen the use of this music as possibly being a "blatant grab for an ancillary market," following the great commercial success of the soundtrack of *O Brother*.[10] That the film employs this music in such a prominent way can be taken as a tribute to its aesthetic richness and its cultural importance, but again the Coens seem relatively uninterested in the political role of such music in the civil rights movement and other aspects of African American history.

This lack of interest in politics might seem like a missed opportunity to add an important new dimension to the film. However, it is also the case that, if anything, the Coens' version of *The Ladykillers* might already be *too* rich, containing too many diverse elements that never quite mesh into a coherent whole. A certain amount of anarchy reigns in even the best Coen films, of course, but here there is no central thread to hold it all even loosely together. In this sense, the much more compact and modest British version works much better, and it is no wonder that so many critics who are normally enthusiastic about the work of the Coens have found this film lacking. Bergan's conclusion that the British original "celebrates the victory of gentility over criminality," while the Coens' version has virtually nothing to say is fairly typical.[11]

## *BURN AFTER READING*: THE DUMBING OF AMERICA

Summarized in their briefest forms, one would have to say that *Raising Arizona* is a film about the kidnapping of an infant, while *The Ladykillers* is about a casino heist that turns deadly. These summaries, though, would completely fail to capture the real texture of these films, which are mostly anarchic comedies the silliness of which borders on the cartoonish. In *Burn After Reading* (2008), the Coens similarly take a potentially very serious genre (this time the espionage narrative) and deploy it to comic effect. However, even more than *Raising Arizona* or *The Ladykillers*, *Burn After Reading* needs to be read in conjunction with its generic predecessors in order to be fully appreciated. For example, Bergan has noted the way in which the cinematography of the film resembles the "rather flat, functional photography of the seventies spy thriller," a fact that adds significantly to an appreciation of the artistry of what mostly seems to be such a lightweight film.[12] Meanwhile, Bergan lists a number of films that can be considered important predecessors to *Burn After Reading*, ranging from darkly paranoid thrillers of the seventies, such as Alan J. Pakula's *The Parallax View* (1974) and Sydney Pollack's *Three Days of the Condor* (1975), to later spoofs of spy thrillers, such as *Top Secret!* (1984) and *Spies Like Us* (1985). Ultimately, though, Bergan finds that Billy Wilder's Cold War spy comedy *One, Two, Three* (1961) "might have been the best model."[13]

Such intensive engagements with cinematic predecessors are typical of the Coens, but, otherwise, *Burn After Reading* was something of a departure for the Coens, particularly as the genre of the espionage drama does not really seem up their alley—or at least it didn't until they cowrote the Oscar-nominated screenplay for Steven Spielberg's Cold War drama *Bridge of Spies* (2015). Perhaps more importantly, the subject matter of *Burn After Reading* is highly political, even if that matter is not treated very seriously. While the film contains the typical mixture of elements and tones and genres that audiences had come to expect from the Coens, it functions most obviously as a satire of Washington bureaucracy (especially in the intelligence community) and as a commentary on the increasing lack of privacy in a contemporary American society in which the American government employs high-tech resources to keep its own citizens under surveillance. At another level, though, *Burn After Reading* suggests that the cynical and amoral operations of the U.S. government are symptoms of a larger cultural malaise that plagues American society as a whole.

Such concerns are important ones, but they also seem a bit out of character for the Coens, who have so assiduously avoided overt political engagement throughout their careers. Indeed, *Burn After Reading* does feel a bit different than most Coen Brothers films, but then we should also remember that even Preston Sturges, who in many ways seems to be the Coens' role model in avoiding political engagement in filmmaking, began his writing and directing career with a political satire, *The Great McGinty* (1940). Still, *Burn After Reading* contains what appears to be some genuine satirical commentary, as opposed to most Coen Brothers films, which appear to scoff at the potential of satire to produce anything like serious commentary on important issues.

Among other things, *Burn After Reading* employs one of the most impressive ensemble casts ever put in a film. It is a film without a true protagonist (because there are so many characters of approximately equal importance), but it is also a film with many stars (because so many members of the cast are important Hollywood names). If nothing else, *Burn After Reading* stands as a powerful reminder of the stature of the troupe of regulars that the Coens have built up over the years. George Clooney returns as still another in the series of self-involved, morally challenged idiots he has now played so many times for the Coens—this time as sex-crazed deputy U.S. Marshal Harry Pfarrer, who is so busy cheating on his wife that he is completely oblivious to the fact that she is also cheating on him (and planning a divorce). Pfarrer's most important dalliance in the film is with Dr. Katie Cox (played by another Coen veteran, Tilda Swinton, a major global star who has played only supporting roles for the Coens). Dr. Cox is a pediatrician who appears to hate children, which is perfectly in tune with the emotional tenor of this entire film. The affair between Katie and Harry is almost entirely lacking in passion: the two "lovers" don't even appear to like each other. They are, instead, just going through the motions, seeking moments of respite from the emptiness of their lives (and their minds). Pfarrer also becomes involved with Linda Litzke (Frances McDormand), an employee of Hardbodies Fitness Center who is convinced that she needs a series of cosmetic surgeries in order to be able to live a fulfilling life. Hardbodies is managed by Ted (Richard Jenkins), an ineffectual former Greek Orthodox priest who has an undeclared crush on Linda. All of these veterans of multiple Coen films, meanwhile, are joined by Brad Pitt, as Linda's friend Chad Feldheimer, an airhead trainer at Hardbodies, and John Malkovich, as Osbourne Cox, an alcoholic CIA analyst.

Clooney, McDormand, Swinton, and Jenkins represent one of the most impressive collections of Coen regulars in all of the brothers' films, while Pitt and Malkovich constitute a formidable addition of major stars from outside the fold. Indeed, the film boasts such an impressive collection of top stars (all acting like idiots) that Ian Nathan has suggested that, in addition to its other satire, the film might be read as a "satire on venal celebrity culture."[14] However, amid this impressive top-billed ensemble cast, another Coen regular, J. K. Simmons (in a minor role that only gives him a few minutes of screen time), comes up with another scene-stealing performance as Gardner Chubb, a completely

**Brad Pitt as airheaded personal trainer Chad Feldheimer in *Burn After Reading.***
**Focus Features / Photofest © Focus Features**

amoral high-level CIA executive.[15] *Burn After Reading* is a sort of comedy of errors in which ordinary people (such as the employees of Hardbodies Gym) inadvertently become entangled with members of the U.S. intelligence community. No real issues of national security are at stake, and no real spying is involved. Instead, the CIA in the film seems less concerned with spying or national security and more concerned simply with covering its own ass and trying to avoid any potentially embarrassing publicity.

*Burn After Reading* begins with a dramatic shot of the earth from high above the clouds. The shot scans the surface and gradually zooms in on the top of a building. A cut to the inside of the building reveals it to be CIA Headquarters in Langley, Virginia. Apparently, in this world of high-tech spy satellites, even the CIA is subject to surveillance from outer space (whether by itself, by rival forces within the U.S. government, or by rival governments is not made clear). Cox walks down a spacious hallway and enters an office where he will be informed that his "drinking problem" has led him to be reassigned to a less sensitive position than his current job as an intelligence analyst on the "Balkans desk." Cox reacts angrily and resigns, hoping to get revenge by writing a tell-all memoir about his time in the agency, setting in motion the events that will constitute the remainder of the plot of the film.

The newly unemployed Cox feels that his memoir might be "pretty explosive." As he apologetically explains to his father, a retired career State Department officer, government service has changed since the older man's days. Possibly due to the end of the Cold War, "now it seems like it's all bureaucracy and no mission." But things aren't going much better for the beleaguered Cox at home, where Katie, already fed up with her husband's excessive drinking (and already involved in her affair with Pfarrer), does not take the news of his resignation well. The news, in fact, sends her into a series of secret meetings with a divorce lawyer, who advises her to begin gathering all of the information she can about the family finances preparatory to divorce proceedings—and before Cox can try to hide assets, as a man professionally trained in deceit might be prone to do. Dr. Cox sets about gathering as much data as she can, storing the information on a CD to deliver to her attorney. When the CD subsequently gets lost by the lawyer's assistant at Hardbodies, Chad and Linda misinterpret the data on it as something related to national security and attempt to extort money from Cox for the return of the disk, especially as Linda so badly needs money for the surgeries that she is convinced will change her life.

Cox assumes that Chad and Linda have somehow gotten their hands on a copy of his preliminary work on his memoir. He's puzzled because the work doesn't really seem all that valuable at this point, but he quickly realizes that Chad is an idiot, punches him in the nose, and sends him packing. Linda *really* wants those surgeries, though, so she angrily responds by dragging Chad (and the disk) to the Russian embassy, assuming the Russians might be the best market for the data. Cold War habits die hard. The Russians are, in fact, intrigued enough to examine the disk, which encourages Linda to try to gather even more information from Cox, sending Chad on a mission to the Cox home during which he will be shot and killed by Pfarrer (who carries a gun as part of his job as a U.S. marshal but has apparently never fired it until he encounters Chad hiding in Cox's closet). Linda isn't sure what happened to Chad, only knowing that he has disappeared. Yet she still continues to try to gather more information, even after the Russians have declared a lack of interest, thinking that perhaps she can market the data to the Chinese. So she sends Ted to the Cox home hoping to gather more data, whereupon he too will be killed, this time by Cox.

This portrayal of the depth of Linda's obsession with self-improvement through surgery, combined with Chad's empty-headed devotion to diet, exercise, and hydration, forms an important part of the satire of *Burn After Reading*, much of which can be read as a not entirely good-natured skewering of the shallow, superficial concerns of a large segment of the American population in the early twenty-first century.[16] The fitness craze is a crucial target of this satire. In addition to Chad and Linda, Pfarrer (who couldn't be more shallow and superficial) is also obsessed with fitness (he tends to try to "get a run in" after each of his illicit sexual encounters), and even Cox is shown exercising in the film. Still, the Hardbodies Gym itself stands as the film's central emblem of a cultural fascination with fitness that is clearly meant to suggest an emptiness and meaninglessness at the heart of contemporary American life. From this point of view, it is not insignificant that Ted is a former priest, suggesting that fitness is now being used as a sort of substitute religion, attempting to fill a spiritual hole at the heart of the American psyche. Or, as Cox tells Ted when he discovers him in his basement trying to pull more information off his computer so that Linda can try to sell it to the highest bidder, Ted and the people at Hardbodies "represent the idiocy of today."

Unfortunately, the fitness craze doesn't seem to be very effective as a substitute for religion, and nothing at all seems to be filling the *intellectual* holes in the psyches of the various characters in this film. The Coens' films feature lots of characters of questionable intelligence, but the characters of *Burn After Reading* might just take the cake. Chad is the champion in this regard for sure, but none of the characters behaves in particularly intelligent ways, a fact that is particularly telling given that so many of them occupy professional positions that one would expect to require at least a certain modicum of intelligence.

This aspect of the film involves a pun of sorts, given that many of the stupid characters in the film literally work in intelligence—though we don't actually see them doing a lot of that work. We're not really sure exactly *what* Pfarrer does in his job, for example, as he doesn't appear to work at all but instead spends all of his time in the film pursuing his "hobbies." The motif of surveillance in the film is reinforced by the fact that, wherever Pfarrer goes (and almost everywhere he goes is somewhere he shouldn't be), he notices that someone seems to be following him. Through much of the film, we might wonder if he is simply paranoid because he is constantly cheating on his wife, though one might also suspect that he is mixed up in something more sinister that we know nothing about. In one sequence, for example, he makes a trip to a home improvement store to buy materials that look like they might go into the construction of a mysterious device that the overall setting of the film tends to suggest might have some sort of espionage-related purpose, especially as someone does indeed seem to be following him as he brings the materials home from the store. Given Pfarrer's preoccupations throughout the film, however, it comes as no big surprise when we ultimately learn that he is using the materials to construct a sex machine in his basement workshop—though perhaps we should at least give him credit for the fact that the device is designed to deliver pleasure to *women* rather than directly to Pfarrer himself.

Meanwhile, if this device turns out to have a far different application than we might have first expected, the mysterious man who has been following Pfarrer turns out simply to be an investigator hired by Pfarrer's wife to collect evidence of his philandering, a fact we discover when Pfarrer finally manages to tackle the man. This bit of divorce drama, of course, clearly echoes the action of *Intolerable Cruelty*, in which the shoe had been on the other foot as Clooney's divorce lawyer employed an investigator to gather the same sorts of information that is now being gathered concerning Pfarrer. Pfarrer asks the man if he works for the CIA or NSC (which would sound paranoid, except that by this time we already know that he *is*, in fact, also under surveillance by the CIA). Learning the truth about his wife's divorce plans, Pfarrer staggers away, blubbering like a baby. "Grow up, man," the investigator (still on the ground) cynically advises him. "It happens to everybody."

This cynical notion that everyone will ultimately be betrayed by those they love is central to the portrayal of the moral and intellectual bankruptcy of modern American life in *Burn After Reading*. It is also central to the atmosphere of distrust that makes everyone assume that everyone else is plotting against them. Paranoia reigns supreme. After Chad's disappearance, Linda asks Pfarrer's help in locating him: of course, neither she nor Pfarrer knows that Pfarrer has killed Chad. Pfarrer assures her that, with his connections, finding Chad will be a "piece of cake." After all, he explains, while finding missing persons might once have been an art, with today's technology, it is trivial: "Now, with cell phones, I mean pretty soon, everybody's gonna know where you are at any given moment." As their conversation continues, however, Pfarrer suddenly realizes that Chad was the man he killed in Cox's house. He draws back from Linda in terror, assuming that she is part of some sort of conspiracy against him. As he did with the divorce investigator, he immediately asks her who she works for, this time including the military in addition to the CIA and NSC as possibilities. Though she professes her innocence of any such connections, he leaps from the park bench where they have been talking and looks around him in confusion and paranoia, noting all the people with cell phones, cameras, and other devices that might perhaps be used in spying on him. He panics and runs away. Bewildered, Linda goes to her car to drive home, but on the way she is also overcome with an attack of paranoia as she believes she detects another car (possibly multiple cars) following her, then realizes that a helicopter is hovering directly over her vehicle. We will eventually learn that she is, in fact, about to be taken into custody by the CIA, even though the CIA would not be allowed, theoretically, to take an American citizen into custody on American soil. After all, this CIA doesn't mind breaking the rules, as long as they don't get caught.

This suggestion provides an important gloss on one of the important targets of the satire of *Burn After Reading*—the notion that Washington, D.C., is now a world populated by self-serving bureaucracies that have no real purpose other than their own perpetuation. The bureaucracy that we see the most of is the CIA, the organization that was perhaps affected more than any other by the end of the Cold War. And the CIA's position, per the film, is encapsulated most clearly in the attitude of Simmons's Chubb, who reacts to each piece of developing news with a self-serving cynicism so shameless and complete as to be comical. Chubb is first introduced when his subordinate brings him news (via "our man in the Russian embassy") that the Russians have gotten their hands on some sort of files involving Cox. At first, Chubb is mostly puzzled that the Russians would be involved at all, but then the news gets more complicated when he is informed that the Russians seem to have gotten their information from Linda, described as "an associate" of Pfarrer, who is in turn described as a "Treasury guy who has been screwing Mrs. Cox." "They all seem to be sleeping with each other," he adds, making it clear that the intelligence gathering of the U.S. government seems to go well beyond matters of national security to include the private lives of individual citizens. Chubb doesn't really want to know the details but is then informed that matters have become complicated by the fact that Pfarrer has just shot somebody in Cox's house, a fact he knows because the house was under CIA surveillance. Simmons's character is still not all that concerned (the shooting is "no biggie," he says), given that Cox's clearance level is not all that high, but he does instruct his subordinate to keep an eye on things and to dispose of Chad's (unidentified) body, making sure that "those idiots" at the FBI don't find out about the whole situation because they would just make it even more complicated.

When next we see Chubb, he is being informed—in a scene that serves as a sort of coda to the film—that Pfarrer is being detained at Dulles airport after attempting to board a flight to Venezuela, a country with which the United States has no extradition. Chubb's solution? "For fuck's sake, put him on the next flight for Venezuela," thus effectively removing Pfarrer from the equation, whatever that equation might be. Meanwhile, the subordinate informs Chubb that Cox has killed Ted but that the body has been taken care of. Unfortunately, though, there is a "snag": the CIA agent assigned to keep watch on Cox's house observed Cox hacking Ted to death on the sidewalk outside the house and subsequently shot Cox. "Good," says Chubb, without batting an eye. "Great. Is he dead?" To Chubb's disappointment, Cox is still alive, but he is not expected to recover and seems to have no brain function. That leaves only Linda as a loose end, at least for now, and she is in CIA custody, offering to remain silent about all that has happened if the government will agree to pay for her plastic surgeries. Still completely uncertain as to what *has* happened, Simmons's character nevertheless quickly accedes to her demand. The film then draws to a close with a reverse of the opening shot as we zoom back out into space in a final reminder that those spy satellites are still out there, still collecting data, even though the bulk of the film has suggested to us that the intelligence community might not have much of an idea what to do with those data once they are collected.

Though the Coens have (characteristically) denied that they had any intention of producing a serious satire of the intelligence community— or of the culture of Washington, D.C., in general—it is certainly possible to read such satire into *Burn After Reading*. Meanwhile, Jeet Heer, in an article published in the *New Republic* in the summer of 2017, has pointed out that the climate produced by the Trump presidency has given the film a second life as a satire of the Trump years. For Heer, the film

> stands as singularly prophetic of the Trump era. The Coen Brothers' black comedy echoes this unique period in history not only because of the Trump campaign's collusion with Russian operatives, but the wider culture of deceit that made Donald Trump's rise possible. More than just a satire on espionage, the movie is a scathing critique of modern America as a superficial, post-political society where cheating of all sorts comes all too easily. [17]

For Heer, *Burn After Reading* might just be the most nihilistic of the Coens' films, its characters having few defining qualities other than a shared stupidity and deceitfulness. For him, these characteristics make the film highly relevant to the Trump years (especially with the Russians thrown into the mix), though he ultimately concludes that the combination of stupidity and malevolence that he sees as defining the Trump administration goes well beyond anything in the film, which is, in comparison, almost optimistic in its vision that the powers that be might finally be able to retain at least *some* sort of order. In any case, that *Burn After Reading* could still function effectively as topical political satire more than a decade after its original release suggests the extent to which the film, however seemingly silly, touches on some very real truths about the state of American politics—and American life—in the early decades of the twenty-first century.

## 3

# JOEL AND ETHAN DO HAMMETT AND CHANDLER

*Miller's Crossing, The Big Lebowski,* and the
Hard-Boiled Tradition

*Raising Arizona* was so different from *Blood Simple* that critics and audiences of the two films must have wondered just what kind of filmmakers the Coens really were. That confusion could then have only been heightened by the release of *Miller's Crossing* in 1990. Despite having the same musical director and cinematographer as *Raising Arizona* and *Blood Simple*, the Coens' third film looks, feels, and sounds unlike either of the first two. The geographical setting is also considerably different, moving from the Southwestern locales of the first two films to a vaguely Northeastern one, though for once the actual location of the film's action is unspecified. Similarly, while the first two films are set in times roughly contemporaneous with those in which they were made, *Miller's Crossing* is very much a period piece (and a lavish one at that), set vaguely around the end of the 1920s, though again the film's exact placement in time is not entirely clear. Retrospectively, though, *Miller's Crossing* fits very nicely within the Coens' entire oeuvre, a fact that only began to come clearly into focus some years later with the release of *The Big Lebowski* (1998), a film that also seems like something of an odd duck among the Coens' other films but that begins to make sense once it is read properly within the context of the impact of hard-boiled detective fiction on the Coens' work as a whole. *Miller's*

*Crossing* is strongly connected to the fiction of Dashiell Hammett, while *The Big Lebowski* has an important connection to the work of Raymond Chandler, thus bringing the Coens into contact with the two most important writers of hard-boiled detective fiction. The addition of James M. Cain to this list of inspirations with *The Man Who Wasn't There* then completed a sort of hard-boiled trifecta.[1]

## MILLER'S CROSSING: HATS OFF TO HAMMETT

Gustave Flaubert's *Madame Bovary* (1857) is one of the monumental works of nineteenth-century French literature and one of the works that comments with particular acidity and bile on the growing power of capitalist consumerism that marked Flaubert's contemporary France, particularly during the reign of Louis Napoleon Bonaparte, singled out by Marx in *The Eighteenth Brumaire* as a paragon of bourgeois stupidity and mediocrity. Flaubert skewers the emergent consumerist culture of his society, including the use of consumerist objects to help us understand his characters, thereby suggesting their immersion in the world of consumerism. One of the novel's most remembered scenes, for example, occurs at the very beginning, as Charles Bovary is introduced as a schoolboy in a sort of flashback scene. The narrator, one of Charles's schoolmates, describes for us the new hat that was worn by Charles, a new student at the school:

> It was one of those head-gears of composite order, in which we can find traces of the bearskin, shako, billycock hat, sealskin cap, and cotton night-cap; one of those poor things, in fine, whose dumb ugliness has depths of expression, like an imbecile's face. Oval, stiffened with whalebone, it began with three round knobs; then came in succession lozenges of velvet and rabbit-skin separated by a red band; after that a sort of bag that ended in a cardboard polygon covered with complicated braiding, from which hung, at the end of a long thin cord, small twisted gold threads in the manner of a tassel. The cap was new; its peak shone.[2]

This hat, clearly intended to impress Charles's new classmates, does just the opposite, identifying him to them as a rube with no sense of style and as a philistine who believes that garish excess is a form of elegance.

On the other hand, Charles is still young, and his obvious lack of sophistication in this scene wins for him a certain amount of sympathy from readers, if not from his classmates or teacher.

Hats, in fact, feature prominently as signifiers of class and character in modern literature—and even more so in a visual medium such as film, where the hats can actually be seen. By and large, this emphasis on hats in fiction reflects the role of hats in reality. Arthur Asa Berger, for example, singles out hats as being among the consumer objects whose particular branding and style have the strongest meanings attached to them, while also noting that Freud's discussion of hats as phallic symbols suggests more symbolic significance: "If Freud is correct, the hat has, at a subconscious level, a much deeper and more profound significance for our psyches than we imagine and is connected with anxieties about castration."[3]

Few films, of course, put more emphasis on hats than does *Miller's Crossing*, in which hats are perhaps *the* most important visual motif, even if the significance of this motif is open to debate. I will, in fact, return to that debate at the end of this section. But first I will start with a consideration of the importance of the fiction of Hammett in that film, an importance that has been universally acknowledged by critics. William H. Mooney, for example, sees *Miller's Crossing* as a "reading" of Hammett's 1931 novel *The Glass Key*, as well as of the 1935 and 1942 film adaptations of that novel. For Mooney, however, *Miller's Crossing* is far more than a simple remake, and a proper understanding of the film requires that audiences understand both its sources and its particular use of nostalgia as a cinematic tool. He argues that the film is successful because it

> addresses the potential difficulties directly: nostalgia is always tempered with irony, the past viewed through the lens of the present even while the present offers a pastiche of the earlier works. The Coen brothers, withholding attribution of the film's sources, insist on identifying them through a deliberate excess of narrative, visual, and verbal citation.[4]

At the same time, Mooney acknowledges that other critics have faulted *Miller's Crossing* for being *too* directly evocative of its sources, as when Gary Giddins argued in the *Village Voice* that the film is "so clever about its sources . . . that it has little life of its own," or when John

Harkness wrote in *Sight and Sound* that it was a wonder the Coens hadn't been sued for plagiarism by the Hammett estate.[5] As Mooney points out, however, such a charge would have been unfair because the Coens, despite leaving their debt to Hammett unstated in the literal sense, go out of their way to call attention to Hammett's fundamental influence.[6]

Jeffrey Adams also regards *Miller's Crossing* essentially as an adaptation of *The Glass Key*, providing, in fact, significantly more discussion of the parallels between the two works than does Mooney. Indeed, *Miller's Crossing* might very well be the most stylish—or perhaps *stylized*— of all the Coens' films. Its characters and its plot seem drawn almost directly from Hammett, filtered through gangster films and film noir. And Mooney is certainly right that the basic plot of *Miller's Crossing* owes more to *The Glass Key* than to any other Hammett work, but I would argue that the overall texture of the film owes almost as much to *Red Harvest*, the 1929 novel that supplied the title for *Blood Simple*. In fact, I would say that *Miller's Crossing* as a whole derives more from a generalized Hammett*esque* vision rather than from any specific work by Hammett. It is almost as if this particular alternate reality were derived from a *Star Trek* episode in which the complete works of Hammett were inadvertently left behind on a developing planet, which mistook the works for a sacred text and then evolved an entire civilization based on the worldview of Hammett's fiction.

The central character of *Miller's Crossing* is Tom Reagan (Gabriel Byrne), the right-hand man of mob boss Leo O'Bannon (Albert Finney) in a city that seems to have some things in common with Prohibition-era Boston and New York but doesn't quite seem to be either. Actually filmed primarily in New Orleans, the city it resembles most, in fact, might be Personville (or Poisonville), the setting of *Red Harvest*, while the relationship between O'Bannon and Reagan has much in common with that between Paul Madvig and Ned Beaumont in *The Glass Key*. The aging O'Bannon has been a dominant power in the city for years (and he is still a formidable force), but he has one major soft spot—his feelings for cold-hearted "twist" Verna Bernbaum (Marcia Gay Harden). Among other things, these feelings cause O'Bannon to protect Verna's brother, bookie Bernie Bernbaum (John Turturro), from Italian gangster Johnny Caspar (Jon Polito), leading to an inter-ethnic gang war that drives the main plot of the film. And yet this plot is almost beside the point in a film that is clearly so much more concerned with how it looks and the mood it projects than with telling a story.

This concern with style was highlighted by Roger Ebert in his initial (lukewarm) review of the film, in which he complained that the set design of *Miller's Crossing* was simply too *designed*. Concentrating in particular on O'Bannon's office, Ebert notes that it is a "wonderful" room, but perhaps just a bit *too* wonderful:

> I do not really think that Leo would have such an office. I believe it is the kind of office that would be created by a good interior designer with contacts in England, and supplied to a rich lawyer. I am not sure a rackets boss in a big American city in 1929 would occupy such a space, even though it does set him off as a sinister presence among the shadows.[7]

Ebert has similar complaints about other aspects of the film as well, noting that it seems altogether "like a movie that is constantly aware of itself, instead of a movie that gets on with business." For Ebert, the set design, the wardrobe, the makeup and haircuts, and (perhaps especial-

Tom Reagan (Gabriel Byrne) and Verna Bernbaum (Marcia Gay Harden) in *Miller's Crossing*. 20th Century Fox / Photofest © 20th Century Fox

ly) the dialogue are all extremely well crafted—so well crafted that they make us aware of the craft and distract us from the story.

Ebert, of course, was a great fan of cinematic realism—his highest praise was always for films whose characters and plots were "believable." Believability in this sense means the creation of a cinematic world that seems to operate very much according to the same principles as the real world, and this kind of believability is never high on the Coens' list of priorities. It is understandable that this fact would be confusing in a film such as *Miller's Crossing*, which seems to go so far out of its way to pay attention to even the tiniest detail in its quest to create an authentic-looking world, but the emphasis here is on "looking"—and this authenticity is of a sort that relies on internal self-consistency and not on any kind of consistency with the expectations we have gained from our experience of the real world. Put differently, *Miller's Crossing* is not intended to provide audiences with an authentic vision of how real Prohibition-era gangsters might have looked and acted. It is intended to provide a highly self-conscious vision of how *fictional* Prohibition-era gangsters (filtered through the fiction of Hammett but with new elements of postmodern play mixed in) should look and act.

*Miller's Crossing*, despite the lavish attention to period detail, calls attention to its status as a work of fiction in a number of ways, including the insertion of several scenes and motifs that simply have no place in a realistic movie about gangsters at the end of the 1920s. Two of these occur within a few minutes of each other around a third of the way through the film—just in case some viewers were, this far in, still trying to view *Miller's Crossing* as a conventional gangster film. In the first (and more spectacular) of these two set pieces, two henchmen working for Caspar invade the home of O'Bannon with murderous intent, Thompson submachine guns in hand. O'Bannon dives under his bed as they invade his bedroom, machine guns blaring. Somehow, the bed manages to shield O'Bannon from their bullets. He shoots and kills one of the gunmen (in a particularly colorful fashion), which sends the second gunman scurrying out of the room, giving O'Bannon an opportunity to escape out the window with the first gunman's Thompson. When the second gunman reenters the bedroom looking for O'Bannon, the latter ventilates him with a barrage of bullets from the Thompson that sends him into an exaggerated and protracted dance of shuddering death that lasts all of twenty seconds, while the gunman's own Thompson goes off wildly, spraying bullets around the room, demolishing a chandelier, a painting, and even the gunman's toes. The car that brought the two gunmen then speeds away, another gunman inside the car spraying Thompson bullets back at O'Bannon, who calmly walks into the street behind the car, seemingly impervious to the shower of lead around him, and returns fire, until the car crashes and explodes. To make matters even more theatrical and even surreal, this entire sequence is accompanied by the strains of the sentimental Irish ballad "Danny Boy" playing on the gramophone in O'Bannon's bedroom, in a version recorded specifically for the film by the eminent Irish tenor Frank Patterson, just so the song could be perfectly synched with the bloody action.

This scene is a virtuoso piece of filmmaking. It's also ridiculous and entirely unrealistic, a fact that is quickly punctuated by the fact that it is followed only a few minutes later by another unrealistic scene in which Reagan confesses to O'Bannon that he has been sleeping with Verna. O'Bannon beats him mercilessly, sending him tumbling down not one, but two flights of stairs, finally winding up on the ground level of the Shenandoah Club, the elaborate speakeasy where O'Bannon's minions serve illegal hooch to an affluent-looking clientele, generally dressed in formal attire. If all of this weren't enough of a clue that this is not an ordinary gangster film, Reagan inadvertently winds up crashing into a matronly but well-dressed customer at the club, who screams in shock and pummels the hapless Reagan with her purse. Reagan, in fact, is constantly being pounded on in this film. As Bergan points out, Hammett's Beaumont gets beaten up quite a lot in *The Glass Key* as well, and it is certainly the case that being able to take a beating can be taken as an indicator of Reagan's tough-guy status.[8] Still, the amount of punishment he absorbs goes well beyond reason. Like many Coen characters, in fact, he seems to have the ability of a cartoon character to take punishment, so he survives all of this intact.

In addition to such specific scenes, it is also the case that the entire plot of *Miller's Crossing* doesn't particularly make sense. O'Bannon and his Irish mob have been running the town behind the scenes for years, with the mayor and the police in his pocket. And yet, after the Thompson attack on his house (an attack, mind you, in which O'Bannon single-handedly demolishes four of Caspar's top henchmen), O'Bannon is suddenly perceived as so weak that the city's official powers that be (almost all of whom appear to be Irish) quickly shift their allegiance to Caspar's Italian mob. Before we know it, O'Bannon has lost his public works contracts with the city, and the police are raiding the Shenandoah Club. Soon afterward, virtually the entire police force (accompanied and seemingly led by an Italian gangster, played by the Coens' old buddy Sam Raimi) shows up to firebomb the Sons of Erin Social Club, an establishment owned by O'Bannon that is a favorite hangout for the Irish mob. The mobsters inside return fire, giving Raimi an opportunity to do the Thompson death dance himself when he is hit by a hail of bullets, but then the cops obliterate the club with a preposterously excessive show of firepower.

Meanwhile, Caspar smoothly slides into O'Bannon's old position as the city's top political boss. The vulgar Caspar does, however, lack O'Bannon's class and style, a point that is driven home when we get a view of Caspar's office, which looks downright cramped and seedy compared with O'Bannon's roomy, well-decorated office. Never fear, though, Caspar simply boots the befuddled mayor out of *his* office and sets up shop there, though even the mayor's office is no match for O'Bannon's posh digs. Meanwhile, our trip to the mayor's office provides another reminder of just how *constructed* this whole film is when we see the mayor's secretary being played by Frances McDormand in a brief but amusing cameo that is one of the highlights of the film, even though it contributes essentially nothing to the narrative.

One of the great stylistic pleasures of *Miller's Crossing* comes from the dialogue, which is just as constructed as the sets, just as artificial as the plot. Reagan's tough-talking dialogue is particularly effective—and sounds very much like it might have come from a Hammett novel. His repeated declaration of ideas like "nobody knows anybody" not only reinforces his characterization as a cynic ("What heart?" he asks, as Bernie asks him to look in his heart just before he puts a bullet between Bernie's eyes) but also adds to the film's elaboration of the notion (first put forth at the beginning of *Blood Simple*) of the fundamental individualist isolation of one person from another in modern America. Importantly, though, these characters are not simply unknown to each other: they are all constantly plotting against and working to undermine each other, not only physically but verbally: each exchange of dialogue (even between friends or lovers) tends to turn into a battle for verbal supremacy.

Indeed, the whole verbal world of this film sounds like something from a hard-boiled novel—a genre to which an implied critique of the alienating effects of individualism is quite central as a whole. For example, multiple times in the film, one character asks another what is going on by inquiring, "What's the rumpus?" This expression was, in fact, in use in America in the 1920s and 1930s, including once in *Red Harvest*. However, some of the gangster slang of *Miller's Crossing* seems to have been entirely invented, as when various characters are told to "dangle" when someone wants to get rid of them. Other slang expressions are authentic but sound made up because they are no longer widely used, as when a character being disrespected is said to be given the "high hat."

This last expression sounds particularly artificial in this film, simply because hats in general are such an important visual motif running through the entire film. Indeed, hats are *so* important as to constitute a metafictional signal in their own right. American men often wore hats in 1929, and the main characters in 1930s gangster films and then later in film noir typically wore hats as well. As Bergan puts it, "Hats are an essential part of the aesthetic of the gangster movie from the 1930s to the 1950s."[9] Further, as Adams notes, hats are a particularly important motif in *The Glass Key*.[10] It is therefore perfectly understandable that so many of the men in *Miller's Crossing* wear hats. What is not quite as easy to understand is the way the film continually calls attention to the hat motif, with the camera consistently focusing in on hats as if to say, "Look, a hat!" During his beating at the hands of O'Bannon in the Shenandoah Club, for example, Reagan manages to keep his hat with him the whole time, including his tumbles down flights of stairs. At the end of the scene, O'Bannon hands him his hat, literalizing a common metaphorical expression for firing someone or unceremoniously sending someone away.

This aspect of the film is so intrusive that it seems to demand interpretation. Why all the focus on hats anyway? This demand for interpretation is reinforced by the fact that the hat imagery of the film revolves around one of the dream sequences of which the Coens make so much use in their films. Though it is not clear at the time, the opening title sequence (after a seven-minute prologue in which we are introduced to O'Bannon, Reagan, and Caspar and some of the tensions among them) consists, in fact, of this dream, which Reagan relates to Verna halfway through the film in one of the rare moments in which he comes close to opening up to anyone. In the dream, Reagan is walking in the woods outside town near Miller's Crossing, when his beloved hat is suddenly blown off his head and carried away along the ground by the breeze. At least since the time of Freud (and maybe even since the Old Testament), nothing in Western culture invites interpretation more than a dream, and many moments sprinkled throughout the film provide clues that this dream might be of crucial significance. Not only does the dream take place in the wooded area that gives the film its title, but this area is also the setting of some crucial moments in the film, as when Reagan fakes the execution-style slaying of Verna's brother there and when Reagan is himself nearly executed in the same spot. Moreover, the very fact that the dream is about a hat seems to lend it extra significance, given the obvious way that hats are foregrounded throughout the film.

Immediately after the opening credits, Reagan is awakened from his dream, only to find that his hat is, in fact, missing, having been lost in a poker game the night before. It might well be, then, that the dream simply re-stages the loss of the hat in the card game, this time, for once, a cigar being pretty much just a cigar. But, for Freud, hats could also sometimes be a phallic symbol, and when we learn that it is, in fact, Verna who has taken away his prize hat, we are tempted to see the dream as symbolizing Reagan's fear that his feelings for Verna will take away his heavily guarded masculine independence. Verna herself gets in on the interpretive act after Reagan tells her the dream and seems to want to see the hat as a symbol of *her*, its loss in the dream signifying Reagan's fear that she will be lost to him. Apparently excited by this possible meaning of the dream, Verna (who clearly wants Reagan to love her though she feigns lack of concern) interrupts and guesses that Reagan chased down his hat and picked it up, only to discover that it had been transformed into "something wonderful." However, much in the way that the Coens themselves often shoot down fancy symbolic or allegorical interpretations of their films, Reagan immediately deflates any expectation that this dream might reveal a crack in his affectless persona. It stayed a hat, he tells her, and in any case he didn't chase it down: "There's nothing more foolish than a man chasin' his hat," he grumbles, thus dismissing symbolic interpretations of the dream with a

statement that itself could have a number of different symbolic interpretations.

The Coens, not surprisingly, would appear to side with Reagan on
this one. In an interview, Joel Coen insisted that the hat has no particular symbolic significance: "It's an image that came to us, that we liked,
and it just implanted itself. It's a kind of practical guiding thread, but
there's no need to look for deep meanings."[11] Adams notes this dismis-
sal of symbolic significance for the hat motif in *Miller's Crossing* but
concludes that, while the hat imagery in *The Glass Key* seems legitimately to lack such meaning, the hats in the Coens' film do project
significance, whether the Coens like it or not. Adams sees the hats in
the film primarily as signifiers of social status and (especially) masculinity, with the loss of one's hat being a sign of weakness or vulnerability.
He concludes that the hat imagery does not really support Freudian
symbolic readings, despite its significance in terms of Adams's gender-
based reading of the film, a reading that, for Adams, could potentially
lead to a much better appreciation of the homoerotic subtext that runs
through *The Glass Key*.[12]

Adams is right but not *entirely* right, in the sense that his reading
does not encompass anything like a complete understanding of the
possible significance of the complex of hat imagery that runs through
*Miller's Crossing*, a complex that can have multiple interpretations. For
example, if we refer back to my discussion of *Madame Bovary* above,
we can see that the hat imagery of *Miller's Crossing* can potentially be
read as a critique of capitalism—and particularly as a critique of the
rampant commodification of everything brought about by capitalism in
its consumerist phase. After all, *Madame Bovary* is a novel that is chock
full of manufactured objects, many of which are pursued by Flaubert's
haplessly oblivious characters with a desire so intense as to be indistinguishable from the erotic. Hats are particularly prominent in the novel
in this sense—"emblematic," says Edward J. Ahearn, "of a world over-
flowing with manufactured things." Citing the prominent French critic
Claude Duchet's well-known suggestion that the famously eclectic hat
worn by young Charles Bovary at school in the novel's opening scene is
"the quintessential manufactured object," Ahearn concludes that the
hat imagery of *Madame Bovary* dramatizes the way in which the consumerist desire created by commodities in the novel exerts a warping
effect on interpersonal relations, with so much emotional energy spent

on desire for objects that none is left for proper relationships with other people."[13]

One might, I would suggest, read very much the same significance into the hats of *Miller's Crossing*, which makes those hats an ongoing reminder of the materialist desire that is never overtly expressed in the novel. In *The Sopranos*, Tony Soprano, following in the footsteps of *The Godfather's* Michael Corleone, continually reminds his viewers that he is "runnin' a business here," that his criminal enterprise is all about making money. *Miller's Crossing* provides no such overt reminders. Indeed, the gangsters of the film—especially those at the top, such as O'Bannon and Caspar—are certainly in the business of making money, but the cash they accumulate seems almost like an afterthought, more an indirect by-product of their desire to achieve power and respect (even love) than the direct object of desire in its own right. But the hats that run through the film serve as continual reminders of the kinds of consumer goods that can be bought with cash and that are required accoutrements of the well-equipped gangster.

This reading should not be surprising. Film noir, hard-boiled fiction, and the gangster film all quite commonly function as allegorical critiques of capitalism, suggesting that the dark side of the American consumerist dream as greed and corruption tends to overwhelm any sense of freedom and opportunity; the gangster film in particular quite typically suggests that corporate capitalism is really just another form of organized crime, this time operating in full view and with the full approval and support of American society. Hard-boiled detective fiction is often similarly cynical in its depiction of the consequences of capitalism. Yet, for most critics, *Miller's Crossing*—despite its close ties to all of these genres—seems relatively uninterested in deploying the resources of these genres to conduct a critique of capitalism. On the other hand, it is certainly the case that the individualist loneliness and lack of mutual trust shown by virtually all of the characters of *Miller's Crossing* could be seen as a result of precisely the sort of alienation that Marxist critics since Marx himself have seen as a central negative psychic consequence of life under the capitalist system, with its ethos of competition and its emphasis on specialization and division of labor.

Granted, the film does not overtly invite such readings, the isolation of the characters seeming more like an existential condition than a social or political one. Thus, I am not arguing that the hat imagery of

*Miller's Crossing* should be read as an allegory about commodification and consumerism, even though it clearly *can* be read this way. And I am certainly not arguing that the hats of *Miller's Crossing* somehow constitute an oblique reference to the hats of *Madame Bovary*. What I am suggesting, though, is that *Miller's Crossing*—and the films of the Coen Brothers in general—are filled with such a multiplicity of meaning and reference that no one interpretation of a Coen film (or of a specific motif within a Coen film) can generally be expected to be *the* correct interpretation. The Coens consistently construct films that reward viewers for knowledge and ingenuity, but they do not construct "puzzle" films in which audiences must decode clues in order to come up with the "right" solution to the various mysteries that the films convey.

## THE BIG LEBOWSKI: "THERE ARE A LOT OF FACETS TO THIS."

It is not difficult to think of *Miller's Crossing* and *The Big Lebowski* as somehow going together because the first is so clearly influenced by the hard-boiled fiction of Hammett, while the latter is so clearly influenced by the hard-boiled fiction of Raymond Chandler (which itself was heavily influenced by the fiction of Hammett). In almost every other way, though, these two films could not be more different. Stylistically and generically, *Miller's Crossing* is probably the most consistent of the Coens' films, sticking to the same period look and gangster milieu throughout. *The Big Lebowski*, on the other hand, probably combines more styles and genres (and pop cultural references) than any other Coen film, employing a variety of looks, none of which are even close to that of *Miller's Crossing*. Finally, it would be hard to imagine two film protagonists who are more dissimilar than the tightly wound Tom Reagan and the laid-back Jeff "The Dude" Lebowski (Jeff Bridges).

Christopher Raczkowski further notes that the two films seem based on fundamentally different aesthetic principles but argues that the difference between the films in this sense is similar to the difference between the aesthetic principles of Hammett and Chandler.[14] For Raczkowski, the central visual image of the tumbling hat in *Miller's Crossing* functions via a metonymy in which the hat "refers to" Reagan through its continual proximity to him but does not stand as a symbol *of* him. The tumbling tumbleweed in the opening sequence of *The Big Lebowski*, on the other hand, has no direct association *with* the Dude but stands as a symbol of the way he aimlessly drifts through life. Formulated by Raczkowski in terms of the noir literary aesthetics of Hammett and Chandler, "the striking difference between the noir vision of *Miller's Crossing* and *The Big Lebowski* is the difference between a metonymic aesthetic of impenetrable surface and a metaphoric aesthetic of depth and identity."[15]

The Chandler resonances in *The Big Lebowski* are clear, though (other than serving vaguely as a detective figure throughout the film) the Dude would seem to have little in common with Chandler's Marlowe. Indeed, the one moment in *The Big Lebowski* in which the Dude overtly attempts to play sleuth turns out to be a parodic one. After watching a pornographer make notes on a notepad during a phone conversation, then tear off the top sheet and take it away, the Dude employs the age-old trick of shading the next sheet of the notepad with a pencil to reveal the imprint of the writing from the previous sheet. What is revealed, however, is simply a doodle of a man with a giant erect penis. This moment then resonates with the other moment in the film in which the Dude is identified as a private detective. Here, he encounters another private detective (played by Coen vet Jon Polito) who enthusiastically expresses his pleasure at meeting a fellow "dick." For his own part, though, the Dude seems completely baffled by this greeting from a supposed professional colleague, clearly suggesting that he does not regard himself as a detective by trade.

Indeed, even Raczkowski grants that, while *Miller's Crossing* seems to adhere to Hammett's aesthetic quite closely (and is set in Hammett's time frame), *The Big Lebowski*'s relationship with Chandler is quite loose given that the film is set in the early 1990s and is informed by such an eclectic array of other influences as well. Multiplicity is perhaps the single most important defining characteristic of *The Big Lebowski*, a film whose mix of materials is drawn not just from hard-boiled detective fiction and film noir but also the Western, the buddy film, the stoner film, rock music, technopop, avant-garde art, interpretive dance, pornography, bowling, and German nihilism, among others.

*The Big Lebowski* functions largely as an eclectic collection of cultural references, its almost nonsensical plot serving merely as a framework designed to hold up its complex array of characters and allusions.

Given the cult status of *The Big Lebowski*, this plot is well known: as befits his directionless lifestyle, the Dude careens wildly from one cultural context to another seeking retribution for the damages he has suffered in an unlikely case of mistaken identity as two not-too-bright goons accost him in his seedy apartment in an attempt to collect a debt owed by one Bunny Lebowski (Tara Reid), the young trophy wife of an aging and disabled millionaire who also happens to be named Jeffrey Lebowski (David Huddleston). As a warning apparently meant to intimidate the Dude into coming up with the money, one of the goons pees on the Dude's favorite rug, an accessory that really ties his shabby living room together—and that, as a sort of MacGuffin in the mode of Hitchcock, loosely ties together the film by providing the initial impetus for the plot.

It is worth noting that the other goon (who is busy dunking the Dude's head into his not-too-sanitary-looking toilet) is played by Mark Pellegrino, who would play a similar dunderheaded thug a few years later in David Lynch's *Mulholland Drive* (2001), another film that takes place in a sort of alternate-reality Los Angeles (or perhaps in two different alternate-reality versions of Los Angeles). This bit of cross-casting was probably not an intentional nod to the Coens on the part of Lynch, but the fact that a similar character played by the same actor fits so nicely within the worlds of these two films suggests their mutual participation in a number of noir traditions having to do with the representation of Los Angeles in fiction and film. It also suggests the breadth of the Coens' reach in terms of the different kinds of films and filmmakers with which their work shares common tropes and common interests.

When he realizes the case of mistaken identity that has led to the sad fate of his rug, the Dude—egged on by his crusty sidekick Walter Sobchak (John Goodman)—goes to the other Lebowski seeking recompense for the damage to his rug. The rich Lebowski rebuffs him, but the Dude for once shows initiative and takes an expensive Persian rug from the Lebowski mansion as compensation anyway. Soon afterward, Bunny is apparently kidnapped, leading Mr. Lebowski seemingly to turn to the Dude to try to get her back—though we will eventually learn that he actually assumes that the Dude will bungle the task. The so-called kidnappers, meanwhile, are a group of German nihilists who have merely faked Bunny's kidnapping (echoing the semi-fake kidnap plot the brothers used in *Fargo* two years earlier) to try to extract the ransom. More trouble then brews when Mr. Lebowski convinces the nihilists that the Dude has stolen the ransom money (though in fact the elder Lebowski has stolen it for himself). This maneuver puts the Dude in direct conflict with the nihilists, but then the Dude (despite his laid-back demeanor) seems to have an astonishing ability to get into conflicts in this film, largely because of the truculence and bad advice of Walter. These conflicts, in turn, are part of a series of complicated plots and counterplots, all involving strange encounters with characters so eccentric that they seem to be playing parodies of eccentrics. The episodic structure of the film (which resembles the episodic construction of most Chandler novels and especially of *The Big Sleep*) allows the Dude to move through a series of extreme and diverse cultural contexts, navigating most of them with the "help" of Walter, whose assistance invariably makes things worse. "There are a lot of facets to this. A lot of interested parties," as the Dude says at one point.

The film begins with a voice-over narration delivered by "The Stranger" (Sam Elliott), whose deep, folksy, cowboyish voice seems perfectly suited to the Western landscape that we see on the screen and

**The Dude (Jeff Bridges) and Walter Sobchak (John Goodman) in *The Big Lebowski*. Gramercy Pictures / Photofest © Gramercy Pictures**

to the opening music, the Western classic "Tumbling Tumbleweeds," recorded by the Sons of the Pioneers in 1934. And the tumbleweeds in the song (and on the screen) do indeed serve as a metaphorical introduction to the directionless Dude. Otherwise, though, this entire opening sequence seems completely out of place in this film about a stoner in urban Los Angeles in the early 1990s. The Stranger himself seems to have wandered from another film that is completely foreign to this one. As he himself says, introducing the film's main character, "There was a lot about the Dude that didn't make a whole lotta sense to me—and a lot about where he lived, likewise."

As the Stranger continues with his opening voice-over, he explains that the story takes place during the American conflict with Iraq, which began with the Iraqi occupation of Kuwait on August 2, 1990, and ended as the U.S.-led coalition forces drove the Iraqis out of Kuwait at the end of February 1991. This historical setting is worth mentioning, the Stranger adds, because it helps us to understand the Dude as "the man for his time and place. He fits right in there. And that's the Dude. In Los Angeles." Unfortunately, the Stranger never explains what this has to do with the conflict in Iraq, which seems to have little or no relation to how the Dude functions as a representative Angelino—other than the fact that he would presumably have virtually no idea what is really going on in Iraq. Indeed, the Stranger at this point loses track of his train of thought about the Dude and decides that "I done introduced him enough," ending his opening voice-over in a haze of confusion—which is, of course, the Dude's own natural condition.

The Stranger's confusion might be attributed to the fact that he is so out of his element in the Dude's world—which makes the two scenes in which he suddenly appears at the Dude's favorite bowling alley and starts conversing with the Dude seem all the more absurd, while making the Stranger's character label seem all the more appropriate. Indeed, the fact that these two characters are identified either primarily or exclusively by descriptive labels rather than actual names indicates the way in which they both function as essentially allegorical figures, representatives of particular cultural positions rather than fully developed individual characters. The Stranger comes from the world of the Western, perhaps the most traditionally American of all genres—and one that the Coens would explore in much more detail in future films such as *No Country for Old Men* (2007) and *True Grit* (2010). In the case of *The Big Lebowski*, though, the evocation of the Western through the figure of the Stranger seems primarily designed as an indication of the foreignness of the world of the Western to the cultural world of the Dude, in which the values of heroism, rugged individualism, and violent solution of conflicts that are so central to the Western would seem to have little place.

But then the world of the Dude is itself a blurry one whose own values are ill defined. While the role he plays in *The Big Lebowski* does indeed seem to have been derived from the fiction of Chandler, the Dude himself seems to have emerged from the stoner/slacker culture embodied in a series of films ranging from Cheech and Chong's *Up in Smoke* (1978) to Richard Linklater's *Slacker* (1990) and *Dazed and Confused* (1993). However, while the stoner/slacker characters in such films tend to be young people who have simply not yet found a path in life, the Dude is a middle-aged man (Bridges was in his late forties during filming, and the Dude seems to be about the same) whose path is quite well established, even though it leads nowhere—a situation with which he seems quite content. Once apparently an active member of the 1960s counterculture,[16] the Dude now seems almost entirely apolitical and has been happily going nowhere for quite some time, his development apparently having been arrested sometime around the late 1960s or early 1970s, the heyday of his favorite band, Creedence Clearwater Revival (active 1967–1972).

Meanwhile, the Dude's closest associate is Walter, a Vietnam vet who never tires of reminding everyone he meets of his former military service, an experience that seems to have left him so tightly wound that he flies into violent furies at the slightest provocation. In terms of personality, then, Walter and the Dude are about as odd a match as a couple can be, while it should also be noted that Walter somehow manages to own and operate his own small business (a security company). Walter thus has a number of skills that would seem to be useful in a story of this kind, but his anger issues, combined with his generally distorted vision of the way the world works, mean that his "assistance" invariably makes the Dude's life more difficult, especially as the Dude, always seeking the path of least resistance, tends to take Walter's advice even when it seems wrong to him (and for him).

Walter and the Dude would seem to have only two things in common. The first of these is a shared interest in bowling, which in this sense functions as a sort of utopian enclave where bowlers from diverse cultural, religious, and ideological backgrounds can for a time come together to participate in the sport they love. Cultural critics who have studied sport in general have, in fact, often seen it in this way, and the bowling alley—with its fundamentally working-class intonations— would seem to have a particularly strong utopian potential as a communal gathering place, something along the lines of the bar in the classic television series *Cheers* (1982–1993). Peter Körte gives this idea a more philosophical spin, suggesting that the bowling alley in the film is to the bowlers "what the Doric temple was to the ancient philosophers. This is the navel of the world, a place where a quote from Lenin is no more unusual than a chat about the next tournament."[17] The problem is that the bowling alley in *The Big Lebowski* functions more as a locus of conflict than of community, and the always-on-edge Walter seems constantly primed for violent confrontations with other bowlers. In one early scene, for example, he pulls a gun on a rival bowler during a scoring dispute. Walter is even constantly hostile and abusive toward Donny Kerabatsos (Steve Buscemi), the third member of the league bowling team that also includes Walter and the Dude. In one of the film's many running jokes, Donny can hardly get a word in edgewise because every time he opens his mouth, Walter screams at him to "shut the fuck up, Donny!" Walter's silencing of Donny is so abusive, in fact, that it is only funny when read in combination with Buscemi's performance only two years earlier in the Coens' *Fargo* as small-time hood Carl Showalter, who practically never stops talking through the entire film, until he is finally axed to death and fed into a wood chipper by his partner Gaear Grimsrud (Peter Stormare).

The other thing that Walter and the Dude have in common is that Walter, too, seems to have stopped his intellectual and emotional development some time during the last years of the war in Vietnam—which also turn out to be almost exactly the same time period as the active years of Creedence Clearwater Revival (CCR). This sense of a lack of advancement beyond the late 1960s and early 1970s in fact informs the entire texture of the film. It is not insignificant, for example, that the film's opening titles play over scenes from the bowling alley, with Bob Dylan's "The Man in Me" (1970) providing musical accompaniment. The Dylan song (which is also used later in the film to accompany one of the Dude's dream visions) is an indication of the extent to which the eclectic soundtrack of the film relies on relatively well-known popular hits in a variety of genres but mostly originating in the 1960s and 1970s—though the versions used in the film of the Rolling Stones' "Dead Flowers" (1971) and the Eagles' "Hotel California" (1977) are actually covers (by Townes Van Zandt and the Gipsy Kings, respectively) from the 1990s, providing a sort of musical reminder of the way in which the historical context of the film seems to be a sort of mashup of the late 1960s/early 1970s and the 1990s. As Körte puts it, in this film we are "in a peculiar time warp where the 1970s are struggling under the weight of the 1990s, and where the pop culture icons of the recent past are shot through with allusions to the literary noir of the 1940s."[18]

Again, one reason why the cultural context of the film seems to conflate the 1990s with the 1970s is that both Walter and the Dude, while physically living in the early 1990s, seem mentally to be living in the early 1970s. But, once the condition of these two characters is extended to the film as a whole, one is tempted to read this collapsing of historical periods in a broader sense as an allegorical suggestion that American society as a whole progressed very little between the 1970s and the 1990s. By this reading, Walter's arrested development could be taken as an emblem of the failure of American society adequately to cope with the phenomenon of Vietnam and thus to move beyond it. Similarly, the Dude's failure to advance beyond the early 1970s could be taken to suggest the failure of the counterculture of the 1960s and early 1970s to transform American society in the way it had originally hoped.[19]

The mixture of cultural time frames in *The Big Lebowski* is presented most clearly in the soundtrack, which features period songs selected by T Bone Burnett, while the original music was composed by Carter Burwell, so that the soundtrack combines the talents of the Coens' two most important musical collaborators. The combination of such a wide variety of musical styles nicely parallels the eclecticism of the film as a whole, though the music is matched with the film's scenes in sometimes surprising ways—as when the relatively wholesome "Just Dropped In (To See What Condition My Condition Was In)," the 1968 pop hit by Kenny Rogers and the First Edition,[20] plays during a drug-induced dream in which the Dude imagines himself as the star of a pornographic movie.[21]

Music is also used in the film as a form of characterization. Thus, allegorical characters such as the Dude and the Stranger evoke not only specific film genres but also specific musical styles. "Tumbling Tumbleweeds" and the musical genre it represents thus serve as a sort of musical emblem of the Stranger, while the Dude's musical alter ego is the songs of Creedence Clearwater Revival, of which he carries around a liberal selection on cassette tapes in his beat-up car. Other characters also have such musical leitmotifs, as when pornographer Jackie Treehorn (Ben Gazzara) is represented by Henry Mancini's "Lujon" (1961), the sensuous song that plays in his pad as he hosts the Dude, drugging him and triggering a vision in which the Dude envisions himself as the star of one of Treehorn's productions (set, of course, in a bowling alley). This dreamwork is not very pornographic, though. It is marked mainly by an elaborate Busby Berkeley–style production number that anticipates the similar numbers in *Hail, Caesar!* It also features the German nihilists (who had earlier threatened to cut off the Dude's "Johnson") wielding giant scissors. Meanwhile, the German nihilists themselves are associated in *The Big Lebowski* with the 1970s technopop music of Kraftwerk, which became an international sensation with their 1974 album *Autobahn*—which also happens to be the name of the technopop group to which Uli Kunkel, the leader of the nihilists, had belonged "in the late 1970s."[22]

Kunkel (aka Karl Hungus, a part-time porn star in Treehorn's stable) is played by Stormare, who returns for his second outrageous role in a Coen film. Other than Polito's brief cameo, the smallest role filled by a true Coen regular in *The Big Lebowski* is that played by John Turturro, as the hilarious Jesus Quintana, who elevates bowling to the level of pansexual religious ecstasy but who is also a convicted pederast who is easily able to match Walter at making violent threats (though Quintana's are more obscene). Turturro's brief-but-audacious performance as Quintana is one of the highlights of the film, while his leitmotif (the Gipsy Kings' Spanish-language cover of "Hotel California") provides one of the film's funniest self-reflexive jokes by indirectly associating the "pervert" Quintana with the Eagles—though this joke fully pays off only later in the film, when the Dude famously declares, "I hate the fuckin' Eagles, man."

Given his love for CCR, this animosity toward their more commercially successful rivals is understandable. The Eagles, Adams notes, rep-

**Jesus Quintana (John Turturro) loves bowling in *The Big Lebowski*. Gramercy Pictures / Photofest © Gramercy Pictures**

resent a "belated and commercially diluted imitation of the roots rock revival led by CCR."[23] Thus, the Dude's distaste for the music of the Eagles comes about as close as anything in the film as a political statement on his part. He clearly sees CCR as an authentic expression of the worldview of the counterculture of which he was once a part, while viewing the Eagles as participants in the commodification of that counterculture, converting it into just another case of capitalist marketing. In this sense, the Dude seems rather perspicacious. One might compare here Thomas Frank's argument that the counterculture of the 1960s was quickly appropriated by American consumer capitalism (which then used the energy and imagery of the counterculture for its own purposes) or Dick Hebdige's well-known argument that youth "subcultures," if successful, tend to be appropriated by the mainstream culture and put to commercial use. For Hebdige, "youth cultural styles may begin by offering symbolic challenges, but they must inevitably end by establishing new sets of conventions; by creating new commodities, new industries, or rejuvenating old ones."[24]

Walter is one of the few characters who lacks a specific theme song from the soundtrack, perhaps because he lacks a coherent character and is so full of contradictions. He is, for example, a stickler for the rules of bowling but flagrantly breaks the rules of league play when he pulls a gun on a member of an opposing team. At times a supporter of political correctness, Walter chides the Dude for calling the thug who peed on his rug a "Chinaman" and points out that the preferred term is "Asian American." Yet Walter's racist animosity toward Arabs seems to know no bounds, and soon afterward we find him referring to Saddam Hussein as "that camel-fucker in Iraq." Still later, Walter waxes poetic about what worthy adversaries the Viet Cong had been in Vietnam, but then concludes that America's current enemies, the Iraqis, are just a "bunch of fig-eaters wearing towels on their heads and trying to find reverse on a Soviet tank. This is not a worthy fucking adversary."

Perhaps some of Walter's animosity toward Arabs is related to his devotion to Judaism, to which he converted (from being a Polish Catholic) when he married his now ex-wife. He staunchly observes the Jewish Sabbath (though his description of himself as "shomer fucking Shabbos" seems of questionable piety) and quotes from Theodor Herzl (the father of the modern Zionist movement). Yet, despite his claims of devotion to Judaism, Walter (a lover of systems and rules, and thus again the antithesis of the Dude) expresses a certain admiration for Nazis. When he learns that the Germans who have been threatening the Dude are not Nazis but nihilists, he finds that to be far worse. "Say what you will about the tenets of National Socialism," he opines. "At least it's an ethos." Finally, the fact that he apparently regards Moses and Sandy Koufax as the two greatest figures in the Jewish tradition seems questionable at best.

Though he doesn't have a song, Walter does have a specific work of pop culture with which he is associated—the 1960s television series *Branded* (1965–1966), created by the Coens' near namesake Larry Cohen, perhaps best known as the writer and director of a series of classic horror films in the 1970s. When Walter and the Dude go to the home of a fifteen-year-old they think may have stolen the missing ransom money, we learn that the boy is the son of one Arthur Digby Sellers, once a prominent television writer but now reduced to life in an iron lung because "he has health problems." According to Walter, the elder Sellers wrote 156 episodes of *Branded*, a claim that seems unlikely given that the series actually had only forty-eight episodes. In any case, Walter is reduced to tears as he relates to Sellers that "*Branded*, especially the early episodes, was truly a source of inspiration."

*Branded* was a Western series about Jason McCord (Chuck Connors), a man unjustly expelled from the U.S. Cavalry on false charges of cowardice under fire. He then spends the entirety of the series trying to prove his manhood in the face of this history. As the theme song of the series (which Walter and the Dude both seem to know by heart) puts it, "Wherever you go for the rest of your life, you must prove you're a man." This song and this series thus both resonate with one of the central concerns of *The Big Lebowski*: embattled masculinity, a theme that is particularly reinforced by the many images of threatened castration that run through the film, from the threats of the German nihilists to cut off the Dude's "Johnson" to the near attack on that same organ by the nihilists' ferret (which the Dude thinks is a marmot). The would-be severing of Bunny's little toe can also be taken as a castration image of sorts. This concern with (a possibly endangered) masculinity is foregrounded very early on, as "The Man in Me" plays over the opening credits. Almost all of the film's male characters are ineffectual, though Walter certainly works hard to try to establish his masculine power. Yet, he remains henpecked by his ex-wife, and the fact that he dog-sits for her while she goes off to Hawaii with her boyfriend is a strong indicator of just how precarious his masculinity is in this film. His penchant for violence and his seeming pride in his military service are taken to such a level that they seem like some sort of compensation, and the fact that he comes to tears when thinking of McCord's shaming in the military makes one wonder just what Walter really experienced in 'Nam.

The Dude fares little better in terms of his masculinity. It is, after all, his penis that is the object of most of the threatened genital violence in the film. Moreover, in one of his dream sequences, we see him flying through the air—according to Freud a dream image that frequently signifies an erection. But then, suddenly weighed down by a bowling ball, he plummets to the earth, obviously signifying the loss of that erection. Granted, the Dude is the only male character who successfully participates in an act of sexual intercourse in the film, but that intercourse occurs at the instigation of the rich Lebowski's daughter, Maude Lebowski (Julianne Moore), who only wants the Dude's sperm so she can conceive a child and then cast its father aside so he doesn't impinge on her life. Through most of the film, though, the Dude seems almost asexual, so much so that, when he complains, in the light of the nihilists' threats, that he needs his "fucking Johnson," Donny replies (without irony) by asking, "What do you need that for, Dude?"

The Dude is also highly incompetent at conventionally masculine tasks, such as driving nails with a hammer. Meanwhile, Treehorn (whose name certainly sounds phallic enough and who seems to be a stand-in for Hugh Hefner) comes off as more of a pretender than a stud, his claims to being an artist with high standards belied by the one example we see of his work, the clichéd porn film *Logjammin'*, which stars Kunkel and Bunny (as Bunny LaJoya).[25] Even Mr. Lebowski, the film's patriarch figure, is hardly a carrier of masculine power. Unable to control his young wife (who turns out really to be just a runaway Minnesota cheerleader), he is disabled and confined to a wheelchair.[26] He is able to function at all only with the aid of his effeminate assistant, Brandt (played by Philip Seymour Hoffman).[27] He isn't even really rich. All of the family money (which came from his wife's side of the family) is tied up in a trust controlled by Maude, who gives her father a meager allowance and allows him to live on the family estate in order to keep up the appearance of being wealthy.

In one scene, Mr. Lebowski openly poses the question of masculinity—and in a way that might suggest that he finds his under threat. "What makes a man, Mr. Lebowski? Is it being prepared to do the right thing? Whatever the price? Isn't that what makes a man?" We will eventually come to realize that Lebowski is here trying to rationalize his own attempt to steal Bunny's ransom money (which he embezzled from the trust), but the Dude responds with characteristic literalness: "That, and a pair of testicles." This seemingly straightforward biological addendum, however, comes under question when we realize that, except for the stereotypically masculine Stranger (who is so out of place in this film), Maude might very well be the most effectively masculine character in the entire film—though the most effectual *male* character might be Quintana, a convicted pederast of questionable sexual orientation. Strong though she may be, though, Maude is herself a rather pretentious figure, apparently inspired by the experimental Fluxus art movement that involved a variety of media—including painting, video art, music, and various forms of performance art—and that was at its peak (of course) in the 1960s and 1970s.[28]

Maude views herself as a feminist, and she notes to the Dude that her art "has been commended as strongly vaginal." It is not at all clear, though, just what feminist values her art represents or just what feminist agenda it promotes. In fact, Maude's art would appear to do for women exactly what Barton Fink's art does for the working class—nothing whatsoever. Artists and their art, from the phallic porn of Treehorn, to the vaginal paintings of Maude, to the ludicrous interpretive dance of the Dude's neighbor/landlord Marty (Jack Kehler), to the video art of Maude's giggling friend Knox Harrington (David Thewlis), do not come off well in this film. Here, all forms of art seem to be pointless and pretentious, especially in comparison with bowling, which comes off as the true art form of the film.

Artists, *The Big Lebowski* seems to want to tell us, tend to take their art far too seriously, whatever their level of talent—though we see little evidence of true artistic talent among the characters in the film. What we do see, though, is a clear attempt on the part of the Coens not to fall into this trap by taking their own art too seriously. Among other things, this means that their critique of *other* art is not to be taken seriously, either. Granted, Matthew K. Douglass and Jerry L. Walls have outlined the ways in which the Dude's devotion to laziness can be seen as an entire philosophy of life. And this philosophy is apparently an attractive one, given the legions of the Dude's devoted followers who have made *The Big Lebowski* into a genuine cult phenomenon. Meanwhile, the Dude's hatred of the commodified art of the Eagles (which matches the contempt for commercialized art that was central to the Fluxus movement) combines with his love of laziness to suggest that his personal philosophy is essentially the antithesis of the Protestant work ethic that drives capitalism. Conversely, Mr. Lebowski functions almost as a cartoon capitalist, his ineffectuality serving to undermine the notion of capitalist efficiency, his lack of ethics or empathy reminding us of the cutthroat nature of the capitalist system. However, by offering its critique of capitalism in a mode of absolute silliness, while offering no alternatives to the ethos of capitalism other than the laziness of the Dude or the pretentiousness of artists such as Maude, *The Big Lebowski* ensures that no one will mistake it for a serious statement about politics or art or anything else. Here, as elsewhere in their films, the Coens abide.

# 4

# HOW THE SAUSAGE GETS MADE

Inside the Hollywood Film Industry in
*Barton Fink* and *Hail, Caesar!*

**B**y the time of their fourth film, *Barton Fink* (1991), the Coens had established themselves as important independent filmmakers, a status that was reinforced when their new film won the Palme d'Or at the Cannes Film Festival, the highest prize given annually at that festival and one of the most prestigious awards in the entire film industry. By this time, the Coens had also made abundantly clear how thoroughly their films draw on earlier films and film genres in both their style and content. But *Barton Fink* draws upon film history even more extensively than had the earlier films of the Coens, especially as it is actually set *within* the Hollywood film industry. This seems a natural choice for the Coens, though, surprisingly, they would not return to the film industry itself as a setting for their films until *Hail, Caesar!* a quarter of a century later. *Hail, Caesar!* is a very different sort of film than is *Barton Fink*, but the films have in common the fact that they are not only set within the film industry but at very specific historical moments within that industry. In addition, both films strongly reinforce the sense that the Coens' films are set in an alternate reality: the Hollywood portrayed in the two films is clearly not quite the same Hollywood as the one in our own history.

That films set in Hollywood should have a special sense of unreality is not surprising: Los Angeles (and especially Hollywood) has long figured in the American imagination as a sort of unreal city, largely due to the crucial role played by the film industry in the history of the city. After all, Hollywood has long been envisioned (both positively and negatively) as a "dream factory," producing images that are distanced from American reality. In the sense that they take place in a world mediated by the movies, all of the Coens' films are set in Hollywood, but the films that are literally set within the Hollywood film industry might be expected to be doubly distanced from reality, as if occurring in an alternate version of an alternate reality. Interestingly, though, the Coens' other Los Angeles film, *The Big Lebowski*, also has a particularly unreal quality, despite not being directly about Hollywood. In fact, even *No Country for Old Men*, which is set in the West but not in California, acknowledges this mythic quality (while at the same time undermining it), suggesting that the special texture of the Coens' Western settings is related, not just to the role of Hollywood in American culture, but also to the mythic role of the West itself in American history.

## *BARTON FINK*: PORTRAIT OF AN ARTIST

Still, it is Hollywood in particular that sets the terms for films such as *Barton Fink*, so perhaps it is not surprising that, of all the Coens' films, this is probably the one that has caused the most critical commentary on its blurring of the boundary between fiction and reality. In particular, it appears possible that much of the action doesn't even take place in the world of the film at all, but only in the mind of the title character (played by John Turturro), a successful leftist playwright who has been recruited from the New York stage to come to Hollywood to "write for the pictures." And many of the scenes that clearly do happen within the "real" world of the film are set inside a single room in the claustrophobic and seedy Hotel Earle, a dilapidated establishment that might be located almost anywhere, including hell. After all, not only does the hotel eventually erupt in hellish, apocalyptic flames, but, when Fink first arrives to check in, we see the front desk clerk Chet (Steve Buscemi) weirdly emerge through a trap door in the floor, as if rising from a lower circle of hell.

We are repeatedly reminded, meanwhile, that Barton is a New York Jew (based to a large extent on the playwright-turned-screenwriter Clifford Odets) and clearly out of place in Hollywood, which further de-realizes the setting. From this point of view, it is significant that the film actually includes *two* important screenwriter characters and that the other one is also specifically associated with a geographic location other than California. That other writer would be one W. P. Mayhew, a drawling, hard-drinking, ultra-Southern, once-great novelist (a literary hero of Fink), now writing for Hollywood but with his creative powers seriously in decline. His work, in fact, is now secretly being largely written by his secretary and mistress Audrey Taylor (Judy Davis). That Mayhew is played by John Mahoney, a William Faulkner lookalike, is of course no accident, just as it is no accident that the Mayhew-Taylor relationship in many ways recalls Faulkner's well-known affair, while he worked as a Hollywood screenwriter, with Meta Carpenter, the beauti-ful script supervisor who also worked for famed director Howard Hawks. Of all regionalized stereotypical figures of the American writer, the lefty New York Jew and the alcoholic Southerner are probably the two most prominent, so the fact that these two figures are both featured in the film calls attention to the question of geography, while also fore-grounding the fact that most of the denizens of Hollywood (and Los Angeles in general) come from elsewhere, further contributing to the sense of the insubstantiality of the city. It is not so much a place as a transit point through which various people pass on their way to some-where else.

In this same vein, when Fink checks into the hotel, he is asked by Chet whether he is a "trans" or a "res" but is baffled by the question. When Chet explains that these terms are short for "transient" or "resi-dent," Fink is still unsure how to answer and simply says that he will be staying "indefinitely." Chet then marks him down as a "res," suggesting that, here, even the residents are not really permanent inhabitants but merely temporary visitors whose residency has no predefined expiration date. If William Leach's characterization of America in the late twenti-eth century as a "vast landscape of the temporary" was already becom-ing apt by 1941, this description clearly applied even more to California than to the rest of the country.[1]

Perhaps the most classically Californian setting in *Barton Fink* is the beach that is pictured in the advertisement-like painting that hangs in Fink's hotel room. But the fact that this setting occurs mostly in a painting, not in the actual world of the film, once again suggests the fundamental fictionality of California. The fact that Fink travels, at the end of the film, to an actual beach and finds the scene from the painting exactly replicated there does not, of course, serve to make the painting "real." Instead, it does just the opposite by suggesting how like a cheap painting the reality of Los Angeles can be. In addition, this ending is overtly contrived, thus serving as a commentary (though an ambiguous one) on the contrived endings of so many Hollywood films, a feature that syncs up perfectly with the artificiality of Los Angeles as a whole.

Thus, even the most specific foray into the "real" world of Los Angeles in *Barton Fink* can also be taken as just another engagement with the world of film and as a comment (though not necessarily a negative one) on the artificiality of that world. Indeed, the entire motif of the blurring of the boundary between fiction and reality (a key characteristic of postmodernist art in general) can be taken as a reminder of the way in which even the films of Hollywood's Golden Age tended to play fast and loose with such boundaries. After all, at the most literal level of categorization, *Barton Fink* is first and foremost a satire of the Hollywood film industry, even if that satire is so lighthearted (and, in some ways, clichéd) as to read almost like a parody of such satires.

**The final scene of *Barton Fink* replicates the painting on the wall of Fink's hotel room. 20th Century Fox / Photofest © 20th Century Fox**

The Hollywood satire of *Barton Fink* is further complicated by the fact that the Hollywood of the film is so patently not the same Hollywood as the one that exists in our material reality. The film is littered with allusions, direct or indirect, to films or people in the film industry, but these allusions are often just a bit askew, making it clear that we are once again within one of the Coens' alternate realities. In the world of the film, for example, Fink is assigned to write the script for a "wrestling picture," which is to star Wallace Beery, but for which he is otherwise given few other parameters. It is clear, however, that such wrestling films are a major Hollywood phenomenon in this world, which was simply never the case in the history of "our" Hollywood. Indeed, various characters in *Barton Fink* talk about the wrestling subgenre in a way that makes it clear that, in the Hollywood of the film, wrestling films play much the same role that boxing films have played in our reality. Thus, while it is difficult to name a truly important wrestling film at all (Darren Aronofsky's *The Wrestler*, from 2008, probably comes closest), boxing films from Rouben Mamoulian's *The Golden Boy* (1939), to Martin Scorsese's *Raging Bull* (1980), to Clint Eastwood's *Million Dollar Baby* (2004) have long been an important subgenre in American film—though they had not really become prominent by 1941.

Indeed, they would gain this prominence only in the era of film noir. Given the importance of film noir to the Coens, it is probably significant that boxing films such as *Body and Soul* (1947), *Champion* (1949), *The Set-Up* (1949), and *The Harder They Fall* (1956) formed a particularly important subgenre within film noir. It may be even more important, however, that *The Golden Boy*, an important forerunner of the cycle of noir boxing films, was based on a play by Odets, making Odets—the chief model for Barton Fink himself—one of the founding fathers of the boxing film subgenre, even though the real Odets, despite a relatively productive career as a screenwriter, would never script a film in the boxing genre.

The presence of Beery in *Barton Fink* is perhaps significant with regard to this swapping of the boxing film for the wrestling film, given that the real Beery is unique in Hollywood history for having starred, within a one-year period, in both a boxing film (*The Champ*, 1931) *and* a wrestling film (*Flesh*, 1932). Of course, the dates are a bit off, given that these films were developed a decade before Barton is writing his own Beery vehicle, but off-kilter dating is also typical of *Barton Fink*. In point of fact, Beery turned fifty-six in 1941 and would have surely been too old to star in a film as either a wrestler *or* a boxer. In fact, while he is described as a reliable star within *Barton Fink*, Beery's once highly successful career as a film actor (he won a Best Actor Oscar for *The Champ* and was for a time in the early 1930s the highest-paid actor in Hollywood) was significantly in decline by 1941. This skewed timing might have made Beery an appealing choice for the Coen Brothers, producing exactly the kind of alternate-reality effect they so favor. Beery, though, was an interesting choice as a motif in *Barton Fink* in a number of ways, even though he never actually appears on-screen within the film. For one thing, Beery's personal story makes him sound more like a Coen Brothers character than like a real actor. Thus, he was born on April Fools' Day in 1885, a fact that surely must have appealed to the zany sense of humor that informs so many of the Coens' choices—as might the fact that Beery began his career in show business as an elephant trainer in the circus.

If Beery's real-life story seems stranger than fiction, it is also the case that all of the film-industry figures Fink encounters in Hollywood are exaggerated and simplified stereotypes, including Jack Lipnick (Michael Lerner), the head of Capitol Pictures, the studio for which Fink is brought to Hollywood to write. Lipnick himself is a Hollywood grotesque; as Ronald Bergan notes, he is a sort of amalgam of real-world larger-than-life studio moguls such as Harry Cohn, Louis B. Mayer, and Jack Warner.[2] Feigning a dedication to art, the flamboyant Lipnick initially assures Fink that Capitol Pictures regards the writer as the "king" of the film industry. But then, when Fink finally completes and submits to Lipnick the screenplay for his wrestling film, titled *The Burlyman*, Lipnick reacts with scorn and derision. He admits that he knows very little about the actual process of making movies but claims to know a great deal about people. And people, he insists, will not be much interested in Barton's artsy-fartsy script that treats actual wrestling as a mere metaphor for the ways in which we all wrestle with our personal demons. People go to wrestling films to see wrestling, he insists, not existential angst. Meanwhile, he makes it clear that, far from being the king of Capitol Pictures, Fink and anything he creates are mere commodities owned by the studio, whose real priorities are perhaps signaled by the proximity of its name to "capital." As Lipnick's much-abused toady, Lou Breeze (Jon Polito), puts it, "Right now, the contents of your head are the property of Capitol Pictures."

The obviously Jewish Lipnick also seems strangely anti-Semitic, freely throwing about the word "kike"—and not in a good way. Some have seen the Coens as doing virtually the same in *Barton Fink*. Indeed, the negative depiction of both Lipnick and Fink—along with that of vulgar, hyperactive producer Ben Geisler (Tony Shalhoub)—triggered considerable criticism of the film. For example, J. Hoberman, in the *Village Voice* (August 27, 1991), found it irresponsible to set a film in 1941, at the "acme of worldwide anti-Semitism," a time when "America's two most potent Jewish stereotypes were the vulgar Hollywood mogul and the idealistic New York communist,"[3] and then to populate it with characters such as Lipnick and Fink. Of course, having fun with stereotypes is one of the things the Coens do best—and one could argue that their exaggerated use of stereotypes actually *undermines* those stereotypes rather than promulgating them. Moreover, one could argue that the stereotype of the hard-charging capitalistic Jewish studio mogul stands in direct conflict to the stereotype of the effetely intellectual Jewish lefty, suggesting that neither figure can be taken as representative of Jews as a whole and thus simultaneously undermining both as ethnic stereotypes.

In the case of Lipnick, James Mottram has quoted Joel Coen to the effect that the Capitol Pictures head is *not* a stereotype but a realistic figure: "You have these guys who were from Russia, Jews from the old country, and they used to build synagogues for their parents on the backlots. . . . On the other hand, they wouldn't admit anything about their own Jewishness and went around calling people kikes."[4] Fink, of course, is not just a stereotypical Jew but a stereotypical leftist writer, who serves as a send-up of the arrogance and pretentiousness of the Hollywood screenwriter who would presume to speak for the working class, despite having never done a day's work in his life. Early in the film, after Fink takes up residence in the hotel, where he plans to do his writing in suitably modest surroundings, he meets one Charlie Meadows (John Goodman), an affable and loquacious door-to-door insurance salesman who would appear to be precisely one of the ordinary folk of whom Fink is seeking to write. Explaining his work, Fink tells Charlie, "I write about people like you. The average working stiff." Seemingly impressed, Charlie proceeds to try to tell Fink about his experiences.

Caught up in his own life, Fink ignores this seeming opportunity to gain firsthand knowledge about the lives he is presumably seeking to represent. He seems interested in such lives only in theory, not in practice. On the other hand, our sympathy for Meadows is ultimately mediated by the fact that he apparently also lives a second life as serial killer Karl "Madman" Mundt.

Later, feeling triumphant after completing his screenplay for *The Burlyman*, Fink goes to a dance hall where some soldiers and sailors are trying to have a last night of fun with the local girls before shipping out. When a sailor asks to cut in while Fink is dancing with one of the girls, Fink haughtily refuses, explaining that he is a special person who deserves special privileges, such as dancing with the girl. "I'm a writer, you monsters! I create! I create for a living! I'm a creator! I am a creator!" He points to his head. "This is my uniform! This is how I serve the common man!" The sailor punches him out, triggering a brawl between the sailors and the soldiers. The critique of Fink (and of the real-world leftist writers, such as Odets) seems clear.

**Barton Fink (John Turturro) and Charlie Meadows (John Goodman) in *Barton Fink.***
**20th Century Fox / Photofest © 20th Century Fox**

Numerous critics (including I myself, several years ago) have felt that this criticism, especially coming from a film so filled with reminders of the rise of fascism (however ambiguous those images might be), is wrongheaded and irresponsible because it tends to make the disengagement from reality of leftist writers like Fink a key reason why fascism was able to become such a force in the modern world. In point of fact, leftist writers were one of the few groups of people who did attempt to warn the American public against the rise of fascism; however, with little support from corporate or political leaders, they were unable to get the public to listen. I thus had some harsh words to say about the Coens and *Barton Fink* a decade or so ago:

> That the Coens would choose to level a charge of irresponsibility against the only group in America that actively sought to oppose the rise of fascism is itself highly irresponsible and shows a complete ignorance of (or perhaps lack of interest in) historical reality.[5]

Over the years, I have come to view *Barton Fink* a bit more kindly. It still bothers me that the film seems to have no interest in making any real statement about the sensitive political issues to which it nevertheless overtly calls our attention. However, this lack of commitment also means that the film now seems to me less clear (and less weeping) in its condemnation of leftist writers than I once felt it was. For example, the complex (and often contradictory) political intonations of *Barton Fink* might also include the naming of Mundt, Karl E. Mundt having been a Republican congressman from South Dakota who, as a member of the House Un-American Activities Committee (HUAC) from 1943 to 1948, was active in investigations of possible communist activity in Hollywood. As usual, the years are off, but Fink is precisely the sort of writer who would have been investigated and possibly blacklisted as part of the HUAC hearings, though Odets himself avoided blacklisting by cooperating with HUAC in 1952, subsequently experiencing a resurgence in his screenwriting career (though also drawing considerable contempt from many of his former associates on the left).[6] If one reads Charlie/Mundt as a figure of HUAC and Fink as a figure of Odets, then it is also certainly possible to read *Barton Fink* not as a condemnation of leftist screenwriters as a whole but instead as a show of solidarity with the true leftists who were betrayed by finks such as Odets.

Charlie/Mundt is thus a complex figure who introduces a great deal of generic complexity into the film. For one thing, if his status as an insurance salesman suggests a possible connection to film noir, the fact that he is potentially a gruesome serial killer (and also potentially a supernatural figure of either evil or vengeance) introduces important elements of the horror genre. Indeed, despite the many comic moments in the film, there is an air of (possibly supernatural) menace that lingers throughout the film. The late apocalyptic scene in which Charlie/Mundt seemingly arises from the fires of hell to destroy the hotel (just as the United States plunges into World War II) merely adds an exclamation point to the series of images (ranging from the peeling, oozing wallpaper to the pivotal moment Barton wakes up with a nude, bloody, and brutally murdered Audrey in his bed) that gradually contribute to a growing sense that something is seriously wrong in the world of the film.

Exactly *what* is wrong, however, never becomes entirely clear. *Barton Fink* is a film filled with uncertainties and unsolved mysteries. Who, exactly, killed Audrey? Was it Mundt? Fink himself? What is in the box that Charlie/Mundt leaves with Fink and that Fink totes about with him until the end of the film? All signs point to the fact that it is Audrey's head, but we never really learn. Perhaps the biggest mystery in *Barton Fink* involves the question of just what sort of film this really is. This question is partly a generic one, as this film (like almost all of the Coens' films) participates in a complex combination of different genres. Meanwhile, to the extent that the film is first and foremost a satire of Hollywood, just what are the implications of this satire? The Coens themselves have denied that this film was intended as some sort of revenge for the wrongs that have been done to them by the powers that be in Hollywood. Their experience with those powers, they insist, has been pretty good. And, to the extent that *Barton Fink* engages in dialogue with specific Golden Age predecessors, this dialogue seems far less than bitterly critical. Moreover, among the specific films with which *Barton Fink* engages in dialogue, at least by implication, is a long line of films that *have* satirized Hollywood (though with widely varying degrees of rancor), and *Barton Fink* itself seemed to trigger a resurgence in this genre, via the subsequent appearance of such films as Robert Altman's *The Player* (1992), Tim Burton's *Ed Wood* (1994), and George Huang's *Swimming with Sharks* (1994).

*Sunset Boulevard* is probably *Barton Fink*'s most important predecessor among Hollywood satires, partly because it is a film very much in
the noir mode, providing a reminder that there are several Hollywood
satires in film noir, including such films as Nicholas Ray's rather vicious
Humphrey Bogart vehicle *In a Lonely Place* (also 1950) and Robert
Aldrich's *The Big Knife* (1955). Meanwhile, in an illustration of the
complex and sometimes wacky world of intertextual connections in the
work of the Coen Brothers, it is not entirely irrelevant that the most
memorable aspect of *Sunset Boulevard* is the deliciously over-the-top
performance by Gloria Swanson as former silentfilm star Norma De-
smond. Swanson herself was a silent film star, so perhaps she was well
prepared for the role. But she was also the ex-wife of Wallace Beery, in
one of the strange sorts of connections that frequently seem to pop up
in the world of the Coen Brothers.

*Barton Fink* contains so many obvious echoes of earlier films and
genres that viewers are clearly invited to seek such connections. For
example, the film indicates that Mayhew is currently working on a film
titled *Slave Ship*, which was indeed the title of a film based on a story by
Faulkner—though the film was released in 1937, not 1941. To make
matters even more interesting, the 1937 *Slave Ship* featured Wallace
Beery in a key role (though it was one of the few films in which he
appeared for which he did not receive top billing, in what might be
taken as an indicator of the beginning of his decline as a film star).
*Barton Fink*'s cinematic sources also extend into the period between
1941 and 1991, including perhaps most importantly Polanski's *The Tenant* (1976), a film whose plot is surprisingly similar to that of *Barton
Fink*, even though its central character is a lowly clerk who has no
involvement in the film industry. Indeed, James Mottram goes so far as
to call Polanski's film the "template" for *Barton Fink*.[7] Bergan, meanwhile, notes that additional Polanski films—such as *Repulsion* (1965),
*Rosemary's Baby* (1968), and *Chinatown* (1974)—also bear similarities
to *Barton Fink*. Bergan, meanwhile, notes the Coens' own acknowledgment that *Barton Fink* is "in the line of Polanski."[8] Along these lines, it
is worth noting that Polanski chaired the jury that awarded the Coens'
film its Palme d'Or.

In addition to its resonance with other specific films and genres,
*Barton Fink* is linked to the world of film in other ways as well. Even
the film's engagement with history is really more involved with the

history of film than with political history. By placing the film at the beginning of World War II, the Coens put their film into direct contact with a number of important historical events, to which the film refers several different times; yet it is also clearly the case that, in terms of its implications for the film, the place of 1941 in movie history is far more important than its place in world political history—a fact that speaks volumes about the kind of film that *Barton Fink* really is. As the year of Orson Welles's *Citizen Kane*, widely regarded as the greatest of American films, 1941 is an especially important year in American film history for that reason alone.[9] For the Coens, though, it is probably much more significant that 1941 was the year of Preston Sturges's *Sullivan's Travels*, one of the Golden Age films that has most influenced their work. It is also significant that the conventional timeline of film noir locates 1941—the year of such films as John Huston's *The Maltese Falcon* and Raoul Walsh's *High Sierra*—as the beginning point of the noir cycle.

Finally, as is typical of the Coens, the intertextual network that provides a cultural context within which to understand *Barton Fink* also includes the world of literature. Bergan notes, for example, that (in addition to Faulkner and Odets, who would seem to be the chief literary presences) the film contains reminders of the work of such writers as Dashiell Hammett, Raymond Chandler, Nathanael West, and F. Scott Fitzgerald, in addition to Franz Kafka.[10] Indeed, the stranger and more surreal moments of the film clearly do evoke Kafka, even if the Coens have denied any conscious debt to the Bohemian Jewish writer. Meanwhile, Hammett and Chandler function as tutelary deities almost everywhere in the Coens' work, while both were among the many established American writers who—like Odets and Faulkner (and Fink)—did stints in Hollywood writing screenplays. These writers also included Fitzgerald, whose novel *The Last Tycoon* (published, of course, in 1941) is one of the two most important Hollywood satires in all of American literature. The other was West's *The Day of the Locust* (1939), which Adams identifies (somewhat questionably) as "the primary source for the story of *Barton Fink*."[11]

*The Day of the Locust* is a rather harsh (and surreal) critique of Hollywood that, like *Barton Fink*, culminates in an apocalyptic fire, this time set off by mob violence that is triggered when a character named "Homer Simpson," of all things, becomes deranged and murders a child actor at the site of a movie premiere. For the novel's protagonist, Tod Hackett, a movie studio lot becomes a dumping ground for the detritus of the imagination, a "history of civilization . . . in the form of a dream dump. . . . And the dump grew continually, for there wasn't a dream afloat somewhere which wouldn't sooner or later turn up on it, having first been made photographic by plaster, canvas, lath, and paint."[12] Hollywood, in short, is a dream factory, but the dreams it turns out are garbage. West's novel and its interesting 1975 film adaptation lack both the occasional zaniness and the ultimate love of movies that mark *Barton Fink*, but the works have many things in common, *The Day of the Locust* being less the "primary source" for the Coens' film and something more like its evil, deranged grandparent. As I have noted elsewhere, the critique of modern consumerism that marks West's novel is both ahead of its time and bitingly effective:

> West's Hollywood is a memorable nightmare realm dominated by images of commodified sex and violence and inhabited by grotesquely dehumanized victims of the American dream factory. All of Los Angeles is, in fact, directly implicated in this characterization, which by extension becomes not a bizarre deviation from the norm of American life but the ultimate expression of it. Indeed, *The Day of the Locust* depicts Hollywood as the epitome of an American capitalist system that generates desire through the presentation of beautiful images, then drives individuals to violence and despair when they discover that these desires can never be realized.[13]

Within the world of the film itself, the most important literary referent is Faulkner, of course, and many Faulkner fans have reportedly been incensed over the rather harsh depiction of the Faulkner-based Mayhew as a broken-down, alcoholic has-been, so steeped in booze that he is no longer able to write and has to have Audrey write his scripts for him. Of course, the real Faulkner had his troubles with alcohol as well, though Meta Carpenter did not, as far as we know, write his scripts. In fact, while Faulkner himself never achieved the heights as a screenwriter that he had as a novelist, he in fact did have a reasonably productive career in Hollywood, with screenwriting credits that included such Hawks-directed classics as *To Have and Have Not* (1944) and *The Big Sleep* (1946), not to mention the extensive work he did for Hawks as an uncredited script doctor.[14] Thus, while Mayhew is transparently based on Faulkner, he is a caricature, not a serious portrayal. Mayhew is the Faulkner of a Coen Brothers alternate universe, and any resemblance to the real Faulkner should be read with a strong dose of irony. The Hollywood of *Barton Fink* seems to be a refuge not of brilliance and commitment but of decadence and greed. And yet, this Hollywood is not necessarily meant to resemble the *real* Hollywood, and none of this satire seems bitter or angry. In fact, it seems more like a performance of a critique of Hollywood than a real critique, perhaps more of a nod to all the other Hollywood satires that came before than a real satire in its own right.

One thinks again of *Sunset Boulevard* (1950), which can at times be quite strident in its depiction of the damage done to individuals by the mismatch between conditions in the real world and those in the world of Hollywood film. Yet the film, described by James Naremore as a "savage critique of modernity," seems to put at least as much blame on modern reality as on Hollywood for this mismatch.[15] Moreover, *Sunset Boulevard* also contains genuine expressions of love for film itself. In one important scene, an aspiring young screenwriter comments as she walks down a Potemkin street in the Paramount lot: "Look at this street," she says. "All cardboard, all hollow, all phony, all done with mirrors." She then follows this seeming critique with a final twist: "You know, I like it better than any street in the world."

*Barton Fink* can certainly be read as a critique of Hollywood during the studio system years, but—like *Sunset Boulevard*—it is centrally informed by a love of film itself. Fink's entire depiction would seem to make clear the Coens' low opinion of politically committed cinema, very much in line with the preference for entertainment-based cinema expressed in *Sullivan's Travels*, a film that looms time and again as one of the central influences behind the work of the Coen Brothers. Indeed, *Barton Fink* is really more of a tribute to films such as *Sullivan's Travels* than it is a critique of politically engaged cinema. Even Fink, certainly an unattractive figure in many ways, is treated with a certain amount of sympathy. For one thing, the film focuses almost entirely on his point of view, making it hard *not* to identify with him to some extent. Meanwhile, Turturro's impressive performance in the role is delivered with such clear sympathy for the character that it is almost entirely impossible for audiences not to feel some sort of sympathy for him as well. In addition, if Fink seems haughtily indifferent to Charlie's experiences as a "working stiff," it is also the case that an insurance salesman is not really a classic proletarian of the kind Fink sees as his constituency, so perhaps Fink has a reason not to want to hear Charlie's "stories." And insurance salesmen in general have often been portrayed rather negatively in movies such as *Double Indemnity* (1944), one of the noir films that has most influenced the Coens. On top of all this, Charlie himself is an annoying and obnoxious personage in his own right—who might be a serial killer. Finally, it is also possible that Charlie/Mundt doesn't even exist but is simply a figment of Fink's imagination, conjured up as the writer descends into the hellish depths of his own mind.

In the meantime, the police of the film—who appear in the persons of detectives Mastrionotti (Richard Portnow) and Deutsch (Christopher Murney)—might also be figments. Whatever their existential status, they are represented as overtly anti-Semitic in their harassment of Fink, which also wins audience sympathy for the writer. In addition, their blatantly Italian and German surnames combine with their clear disdain for Jews and the 1941 setting to make them potential emblems of fascism, further complicating the swirl of political intonations in the film. Near the end of the film, all hell breaks loose (literally) as the hotel erupts into flames. Here, Charlie/Mundt transforms into a seemingly satanic figure, at home in the fires of hell. Yet he might also be an avenging Jewish angel, emerging from the fires not of hell but of Auschwitz to destroy the two fascist cops, taunting Deutsch by snarling, "Heil Hitler" as he prepares to blow his head off.[16]

## *HAIL, CAESAR!*: MANUFACTURING STORIES

Ominous resonances constantly hover in the margins of *Barton Fink*. There are such resonances a quarter of a century later in *Hail, Caesar!* as well, mostly in the form of reminders of the Cold War era in which it is set, but now they are pushed further into the margins, while comedy is center stage. Set some time in the early 1950s, *Hail, Caesar!* begins as the central character, Eddie Mannix (Josh Brolin), sits in a confession booth, where he confesses that, though he has supposedly quit smoking at the request of his wife, Connie, he has recently snuck two or three cigarettes and then kept this transgression from Connie. It seems a pretty minor sin, and we will eventually learn that Mannix is, in fact, an extremely righteous character who commits *only* the most minor of sins, then feels obligated to confess them immediately—so much so that even his confessor ultimately suggests that perhaps he should confess a bit less often. Mannix is the head of "physical production" for Capitol Pictures, thus returning us to the world of *Barton Fink*, approximately a decade later. Moreover, we learn very early in the film that the studios of Capitol Pictures now feature a "Wallace Beery Conference Room," extending the Wallace Beery motif from *Barton Fink* and virtually ensuring that attentive viewers will link the two films.

Mannix's righteousness stands in stark contrast to the crass and ruthless behavior of his predecessor Lipnick, though we also learn in *Hail, Caesar!* that the true head of Capitol Pictures is one Mr. Schenk (pronounced "Skank"), who is headquartered back in New York. This situation closely parallels (but is not quite the same as) the real-world one in which, from 1927 to 1951, Louis B. Mayer ran the MGM studios in Hollywood but had to report to his corporate boss in New York, one Nicholas Schenck, whom Mayer was fond of calling "Skunk." Mannix's name, though, is taken from elsewhere in Hollywood history (and it always helps to know your Hollywood history when viewing the films of the Coens). The original Eddie Mannix had been Mayer's subordinate at MGM and became widely known as a "fixer" who solved (or at least hid from the public) the personal problems of MGM's stars. The Mannix of *Hail, Caesar!* performs a similar function for Capitol's stars. However, the original Mannix was reportedly a rather unsavory character with possible mob connections, again standing in stark contrast to the squeaky clean and genuinely well-meaning Mannix of the Coens' film.

The second scene of *Hail, Caesar!* shows us Mannix in his fixer role, as he rushes to a house where he finds one of the studio's starlets posing in a photograph session with clear potential to evolve into a "French postcard situation." Mannix breaks up the session, sends the photographer packing, and hustles the starlet, one Gloria DeLamour (Natasha Bassett), out of the house, pausing to bribe a couple of cops on the way. One gets the impression, though, that Mannix is not just protecting the assets of Capitol Pictures; he also genuinely wants to help Gloria. The fact that he slaps her a couple of times in the process of trying to sober her up is a bit problematic, but it also reminds us just how much of his character (like so many things in the Coens' films) has been filtered through film noir.

The film noir vibe of this scene is strengthened by the fact that it is accompanied by a highly stylized voice-over narration delivered by acclaimed Irish-born British actor Sir Michael Gambon, whose greatest role was probably as the protagonist in Dennis Potter's noir-inspired BBC miniseries *The Singing Detective* (1986). Such voice-over narrations, of course, are common in film noir. Meanwhile, this whole scene is highly reminiscent of the one in the classic film noir *The Big Sleep* (1946), in which Philip Marlowe (Humphrey Bogart) rescues young Carmen Sternwood (Martha Vickers) from a similarly scandalous photography scene. And the resemblance is probably no accident. That *The Big Sleep* is based on a novel by Raymond Chandler (who looms so large in the Coens' work) or that the screenplay was cowritten by William Faulkner (who looms so large in *Barton Fink*) is only typical of the kind of interconnections that run through the films of the Coen Brothers.

Gambon's voice-over helps to introduce Mannix and his tireless, virtually around-the-clock work for Capitol Pictures. But it also provides commentary that enhances many of the important themes of the film. For example, in his initial description of Mannix, Gambon informs us that "the studio for which he works manufactures stories, each its own day-lit drama or moon-lit dream." This characterization of the studio calls attention to its status as a capitalist dream factory but also subtly suggests that there might be something wonderful about these manufactured dreams. At a later point in the film, Gambon's voice-over makes Capitol Pictures seem even more factory-like but also casts the studio's products in an even more positive light. Gambon follows Mannix as he "hurries back to the vastness of Capitol Pictures, whose tireless machinery clanks on, producing this year's ration of dreams for all the weary peoples of the world." And, as we are about to attend the premiere of the studio's latest Western (which bears a 1951 copyright, one of the few specific dates mentioned in the film), Gambon describes the new movie as "another portion of balm for the ache of a toiling mankind."

Soothing balm or not, the production of films must go on, and Mannix is kept more than busy by trying both to ensure that things go smoothly on the sets of the various pictures currently being filmed at the studio and to deal with the considerable off-set difficulties of his stars, while keeping those difficulties out of the press, represented here primarily by the twin sisters Thora and Thessaly Thacker (both played hilariously by Tilda Swinton). The sisters are rather obvious echoes of the real-world rival Hollywood gossip columnists Hedda Hopper and Louella Parsons, though (as is always the case with the Coens) they differ from their sources in ways that go beyond the fact of being twins.[17]

The first film to which we are introduced—and the most important film embedded within *Hail, Caesar!*—is the studio's biggest current "prestige" production, a biblical epic titled *Hail, Caesar!: A Tale of the Christ*. This film stars Capitol's most bankable (and most trouble-prone) star, Baird Whitlock (George Clooney), a charming (but not too bright) rogue with a weakness for the liquor and the ladies (and perhaps the gentlemen as well). In this film-within-a-film, Whitlock plays a Roman centurion who undergoes a change of heart when he encounters Jesus Christ (appearing on film for the first time) and is overcome by his majesty and goodness. It would not do, of course, to have Whitlock involved in a scandal while playing such a role but keeping Whitlock out of trouble (and his scandals out of the newspapers) has long been one of Mannix's biggest challenges. This film is no exception, though the trouble into which Whitlock is plunged is no fault of his own (though he does eventually exacerbate the situation).

Biblical epics were, of course, one of the key phenomena in Hollywood film of the 1950s (and a particular specialty of MGM), spurred partly by a desire to produce huge, elaborate, Technicolor spectacles that could not be effectively reproduced on the new medium of television, thus giving audiences a reason to leave their homes and go to the theater. Some of the most memorable films of the decade were biblical epics, of which there were so many that it is impossible to locate just one as a model for *Hail, Caesar!*[18] In reality, the first film to show Jesus Christ's face on-screen was one of the last of the biblical epics, Nicholas Ray's MGM-distributed *King of Kings* (1961), with Jeffrey Hunter as Christ. But the plot of *Hail, Caesar!* probably most resembles that of the MGM epic *Quo Vadis* (1951), while it also contains echoes of MGM's *Ben-Hur* (1959), a remake of one of MGM's first major hits, the silent film of the same title (released in 1925). In addition, it is worth noting that these latter films derived from an 1880 novel titled *Ben-Hur: A Tale of the Christ*, thus sharing a subtitle with *Hail, Caesar!*

Biblical epics were also part of an elaborate publicity program designed to assure the American public that the movies were not the havens for communism and sin that some had made them out to be and that Hollywood was, in fact, just as pious as the rest of America in that God-drenched decade. As usual, however, the Coens avoid any direct commentary on such matters and instead provide, as a commentary on the role of religion in Hollywood, a single comic set piece in which Mannix interviews a panel of religious leaders (a rabbi, a Catholic priest, an Eastern Orthodox priest, and a Protestant minister, all of whom have just read the script) to try to make sure that there is nothing in Capitol's religious epic to which they might object. The Orthodox minister is concerned that a chariot action scene is unbelievable, but all are impressed that Whitlock is in the picture. When Mannix asks the clerics to stick to religious issues, they begin to quibble among themselves and spout platitudes. Not surprisingly, the Jew gets the funniest lines. When Mannix expresses confusion over the disagreements among the three Christians, the rabbi (played by Robert Picardo) explains that "you don't follow for a very simple reason: these men are screwballs." When it becomes clear that the men can't really agree on *anything* (but that none seem seriously offended by the movie), Mannix gives up. In the 1950s, America is in the grip of a religious fervor designed to make the United States look morally superior to the Soviets, but it is an incoherent enthusiasm informed by little in the way of theological consistency.

Meanwhile, it is clear that, far from hoping to promote religious zeal, Capitol Pictures is interested in producing *Hail, Caesar!** because they think it will be a big moneymaker, just as were many of the biblical epics in our own 1950s. Scenes from the film are sprinkled throughout *Hail, Caesar!*, looking very much like (but not quite *exactly* like) scenes from a real 1950s religious epic. Indeed, one of the joys of *Hail, Caesar!* (no doubt for the Coens as well as for us) is that it gives the Coens a chance to shoot a number of reasonably authentic (but slightly askew) scenes from the films being made by Capitol Pictures. Each of these scenes is a little masterpiece, but one of the best of them is an elaborately produced synchronized swimming scene that features Scarlett Johansson playing starlet DeeAna Moran, who herself plays a mermaid in the scene. Moran is clearly based on Esther Williams, who rose to fame in the 1940s and 1950s starring in a series of "aquamusicals" and other swimming-based films for MGM, including the 1952 biopic *Million Dollar Mermaid*, which features synchronized swimming scenes of the sort seen within *Hail, Caesar!*[19] However, Moran's beauty and grace in the water contrast sharply with her vulgar mouth when off camera, while her behavior off-set causes considerable problems for Mannix, who must deal with the fact that she is pregnant out of wedlock, presenting a "public-relations problem for the studio." After all, as Mannix tells Moran, "the public loves you because they know how innocent you are," a suggestion that contrasts sharply with what we see of Moran, who (among other things) has been twice married—once to a gangster and once to a bandleader with a drug problem.

If anything, Moran's swimming scene is even more impressive than the scenes in Williams's real films, even if it is almost *too* impressive. The same might be said of the brief scene we see early on from a Western featuring singing cowboy star Hobie Doyle (Alden Ehrenreich), whose horseback acrobatics are even more preposterous than those sometimes found in real vintage Westerns. Westerns, of course, were a major force in American film of the 1950s, so it is perhaps surprising that they play such a small role in *Hail, Caesar!*, with only two Western scenes (this one and one comic scene from another film accompanied by Doyle's singing) appearing in the film.

**Scarlett Johansson as aquatic starlet DeeAna Moran in** *Hail, Caesar!* **Universal Pictures / Photofest © Universal Pictures**

The reason Doyle's Westerns are not prominent in *Hail, Caesar!* is that, early in the film, he is pulled off the Western he is currently shooting to become the leading man in *Merrily We Dance*, a posh drawing-room drama being directed by fastidious (and possibly gay) British director Laurence Laurentz (Ralph Fiennes), something of an amalgam of British maestros such as David Lean, Noel Coward, and Laurence Olivier, with perhaps a dash of the American George Cukor thrown in as well. Doyle is a mere "dust actor," who is accustomed only to action scenes and is stipulated to be barely able to talk, so he and Laurentz are about as mismatched as it is possible for an actor and a director to be. We actually see very little in the way of scenes from this film because Doyle is so bad at delivering his lines that Laurentz continually has to interrupt him to try to coach him. Indeed, the best parts of this film are not the actual scenes but the scenes between Doyle and Laurentz, as when the latter attempts to teach rough-hewn Doyle to speak in a suavely British style, a moment that clearly recalls the efforts to teach horrible-voiced silent-film star Lina Lamont (Jean Hagen) to speak in a more palatable manner so that she can transition to the talkies in the classic musical *Singin' in the Rain* (1952).

Among other things, the scenes surrounding *Merrily We Dance* comment on the dire results that were sometimes obtained in the studio era, when casting was strictly controlled by studio executives, who often assigned contracted actors to roles for which they were not well suited. Doyle is game, though (and "gamey," according to a frustrated Laurentz), and gives it his all; meanwhile, Ehrenreich's own performance as the bewildered, fish-out-of-water bumpkin is a highlight of *Hail, Caesar!* (despite the fact that the then little-known actor was surrounded by so many major stars). Indeed, Ehrenreich himself now seems headed for stardom—soon after the release of *Hail, Caesar!* he was cast to play the starring role in a *Star Wars* prequel film about a young Han Solo.

The final film-within-a-film to which we are introduced in *Hail, Caesar!* recalls Hollywood's attempts to revive the musical in the 1950s. Here, Channing Tatum stars as Burt Gurney, a gifted and athletic song and dance man clearly modeled after Gene Kelly, except that Gurney seems to have little in common with the actual Kelly other than his talent and the kinds of films in which he stars. The film from which we see a scene is a sailor musical somewhat in the mold of Kelly's *Anchors Aweigh* (1945) and *On the Town* (1949). In this scene, Gurney leads a bar full of sailors in a rousing musical number that bemoans the fact that they are about to ship out and will be without "dames" for eight months. "Can you beat it?" asks Gurney's character ruefully. "You're gonna hafta beat it," says the sarcastic, cigar-chomping proprietor of the "Swinging Dinghy," as the bar is called. Apparently, the Production Code is different in this alternate Hollywood than it was in ours.

The musical number itself, titled "No Dames," is brilliantly choreographed and impressively performed, a match for even the best musical numbers from the era of classic Hollywood. Meanwhile, Gurney's character and his fellow sailors seem blissfully ignorant of the double entendres that lace the song, as when two sailors respond to the warning that they "ain't gonna see no dames" during their time at sea by suggesting that they might see some "octopuses" or "clams," both terms suggesting female genitalia in ways that would have almost certainly not passed muster in the classic Hollywood of our world. In addition, the scene riffs on the sometimes-homoerotic implications of dance scenes from classic Hollywood films by having the sailors dance with each other in ways that are blatantly suggestive, especially when accompanied by lyrics reminding us that, while at the sea, that will have no dames but only each other. In a final reminder that the films made in this Hollywood are not quite the same as the ones made in ours, the dancing finally becomes so suggestive that the proprietor has to break it up, yelling, "This ain't that kind of a place!"

An important subplot of *Hail, Caesar!* involves the fact that Mannix is being aggressively (but surreptitiously, via secret meetings in a mysterious Chinese restaurant) recruited to leave the movie business and join the Lockheed Corporation as an executive. Not only would Mannix make more money and work saner hours, with fewer intractable problems to deal with, at Lockheed, but he would also have a chance to be a part of the "future," doing serious things in the aerospace industry, as opposed to the "frivolous" work of making movies. How serious is the work done by Lockheed? Deadly serious. Indeed, one bit of evidence of the weighty things being done by Lockheed is the revelation, in one of Mannix's meetings with their recruiter, Mr. Cuddahy (Ian Blackman), that Lockheed had been heavily involved in the recent testing of a hydrogen bomb at the Bikini Atoll. Cuddahy is distinctly proud of this participation, but Mannix is not so sure, characterizing the H-bomb as an emblem of Armageddon, clearly seeing the device, not as a harbinger of the future, but possibly as its destroyer.[20]

Ultimately, Mannix opts to stay at Capitol Pictures in what is partly a sign of his personal virtue and partly a statement by the Coens on the importance of the movies. After all, Mannix's choice of the movie business over the aerospace industry is essentially a reiteration of the choice made by John L. Sullivan in *Sullivan's Travels* to stick with light comedy rather than socially relevant seriousness in making his own films. Meanwhile, the characterization of Lockheed as the future (and a rather ominous one at that) in this 1950s setting inevitably recalls the famous warnings of President Dwight D. Eisenhower about the growing power of the "military-industrial complex" in American society as he departed office on January 17, 1961. But this characterization of Lockheed is also a key structural feature of *Hail, Caesar!* that links this subplot with the main plot of the film in important ways.

In this main plot, Whitlock is kidnapped off the set of *Hail, Caesar!*\* by a gang of communist screenwriters, who are working in league with the Soviet Union to try to sneak communist content into Hollywood films and thus further the ultimate transformation of the United States into a communist society. For example, one of their films contains a "town hall scene" in which a crooked election is overturned so that "Gus" can become the mayor. The combination of "Gus" and "town hall" is clearly meant to evoke Gus Hall, a leader of the Communist Party USA (CPUSA) in the years after World War II who spent much of the 1950s in Leavenworth Prison for his political activities and who rose to become general secretary of the CPUSA in 1959. The overthrow of the crooked election in the referenced film is clearly meant to symbolize an imagined overthrow of the U.S. government, allowing Hall to accede to the head of the new postrevolutionary government.

Meanwhile, the commie screenwriters plan to send the ransom garnered from Whitlock's kidnapping back to the Soviet Union to help the cause there. It is clear, however, that these screenwriters are just as inauthentic as Barton Fink in their devotion to the "little man," even though they are at least taking political action. After all, as they lecture Whitlock about the ways in which they, as writers, are being exploited by the Hollywood money machine, they are lounging in bourgeois decadence in a ritzy beach house belonging to Burt Gurney (who turns out also to be a communist) while munching on fancy finger sandwiches.

Meanwhile, when they try to explain their Marxist vision to Whitlock, they produce what sounds like little more than a string of communist clichés and platitudes, showing themselves to be little more than a leftist version of the panel of clerics earlier convened by Mannix. Actually, almost everything the screenwriters say (such as characterizing Capitol Pictures as an "instrument of capitalism") is arguably accurate, but the way they seem to think they can actually succeed in their battle against capitalism makes them appear ridiculous. Of course, in this alternate reality, perhaps they *can* succeed.

Importantly, in their ransom note to Capitol Pictures, the screenwriters simply identify themselves collectively as The Future, thus linking themselves to the Lockheed man and completing a perfect triangle in which capitalism, communism, and religion all turn out to be false solutions for dealing with the problems of the world—though capitalism (linked specifically with nuclear holocaust) emerges as perhaps the most sinister of the three. We should remember, however, that these are *alternate-reality* communists, capitalists, and clerics that cannot necessarily be equated with their counterparts in our reality in any simple way. The communists seem particularly unlike the leftist screenwriters who were known to have worked in Hollywood in our world, even though several of them are based on identifiable sources in our reality. Thus, Matthew Dessem, in an article that attempts to trace the real-world sources of numerous characters in *Hail, Caesar!*, concludes (correctly, I think) that the portrayal of these screenwriters represents "probably the least fair caricatures" in the film. Among other things, Dessem notes that the leader of the screenwriters is named John Howard Hermann (played by Max Baker), in an apparent reference to real-world screenwriter John Howard Lawson, the unofficial leader of the Hollywood Ten[21] and the onetime leader of the Hollywood section of the CPUSA.[22] Dessem makes this identification based mostly on the name of the character, but it is worth pointing out that many of the comments on the film industry made by Hermann in the film resemble the commentary to be found in Lawson's book *Film in the Battle of Ideas*. Dessem is also clearly correct to link the film's elderly Professor Marcuse (John Bluthal) to our world's Herbert Marcuse, who was a key member of the Marxist Frankfurt School and the author of such important texts as *Eros and Civilization* (1955) and *One-Dimensional Man* (1964), key inspirations in the rise of the American New Left, as well as favorite texts of many student radicals in the oppositional political movements of the 1960s. The real Marcuse, though, would have been roughly in his mid-fifties during the time of the events of *Hail, Caesar!*, while the Dr. Marcuse of the film (who has "come down from Stanford" to teach the screenwriters about Marxist theory and whom Whitlock at one point addresses as "Herb") appears much older. In addition, far from being a Soviet agent who worked to undermine the U.S. government, the real Marcuse was a staunch critic of the Soviet regime—as in his book *Soviet Marxism: A Critical Analysis* (1958)—who in fact worked *for* the U.S. government as an intelligence analyst from 1943 to 1950. Moreover, he never worked in the film industry or taught at Stanford and did not live in California until he assumed a position at the University of California, San Diego, in 1965.[23]

The fact that both Gus Hall and John Howard Lawson were sent to prison for their political beliefs (and that most leftist screenwriters had already been blacklisted from working in Hollywood by the time of the events of *Hail, Caesar!*) suggests just how serious the Red Scare of the 1950s and late 1940s really was. As a result, the most problematic aspect of *Hail, Caesar!* is that its alternate history turns a very dark episode in our own history into a joke. At the same time, the events of the film would appear to exaggerate the seriousness of the communist presence in Hollywood and suggest that the 1947 hearings held by HUAC (with Karl Mundt as a member) that eventually sent Lawson and other members of the Hollywood Ten to prison, far from being a misguided witch hunt, were in fact quite justified (though these hearings do not appear to have even taken place in the alternate reality of *Hail, Caesar!*).[24] These alternate-reality communists really *are* a threat to the security of the United States—even though the threat does not appear to be very serious, given that they are also depicted as bumbling incompetents. For example, having successfully collected $100,000 in ransom for Whitlock, they decide to send the money straight to the Comintern via their confederate (none other than Burt Gurney), but (despite the physical dexterity he showed in his earlier dance number) Gurney accidentally drops the money into the ocean as he boards the Soviet submarine that is to take him to Moscow.

The apparently negative depiction of leftist screenwriters in *Hail, Caesar!* resembles that in *Barton Fink*. However, as with *Barton Fink*, there is a possible alternative interpretation of this depiction in *Hail,*

*Caesar!* For one thing, we should again remember that this is an alternate-reality version of Hollywood and that depictions shown in the film are not necessarily implied to resemble anything that has ever occurred in our world. Perhaps more importantly, the depiction of these screenwriters as communist agents is so exaggerated that one is tempted to read it, not as a verification of the paranoid sensibilities of the anti-communists of the HUAC/McCarthy era (who tended to see Soviet-backed communist agents *everywhere*), but as a *parody* of those sensibilities. In this distorted, fun-house world, communist screenwriters behave exactly as they behaved in the fantasies of the HUAC investigators who imprisoned the Hollywood Ten and triggered the notorious Hollywood blacklist. They are so insidious, for example, that their captive, Baird Whitlock, is ultimately won over to their cause, joining the CPUSA—the film even gives us a glimpse of his new CPUSA membership card (#14,162), signed by none other than party president Gus Hall and dated 1951. This card, in fact, is one of the few things in the film that identifies the year of the action as 1951, while other information in the film (such as the fact that the 1954 "Castle Bravo" thermonuclear test has already occurred) clearly indicates that the 1951 of this world is somewhat out of sync with the 1951 of our world. (In addition, the real Gus Hall was never the "president" of the CPUSA and did not rise to its highest office of general secretary until 1959.)

As *Hail, Caesar!* ends, Mannix has successfully avoided all of the potential disasters that have been dogging him throughout the film, and business goes on as usual at Capitol Pictures. Whitlock has even returned from his flirtation with communism to complete the filming of *Hail, Caesar!*\*—but only after being slapped around a bit by Mannix, thus replicating Mannix's manhandling of Gloria DeLamour early in the film. The camera pans up from the studio lot toward the sky, as if to signal that the forces of heaven have, for the nonce, triumphed over the forces of evil. The communists have been thwarted in their attempt to send money to the Comintern, the capitalists of the military-industrial complex have been thwarted in their attempt to lure Mannix to their cause, and movies continue to be made. All is right with the world.

# 5

# STAR-CROSSED LOVERS

*The Hudsucker Proxy, Intolerable Cruelty,* and the
American Tradition of Screwball Comedy

In my *Historical Dictionary of American Cinema*, I define screwball comedy as "a form of romantic comedy in which a couple, seemingly ill matched due to differences in temperament, social class, or other circumstances, negotiates a series of comical obstacles on their way to establishing a romantic relationship."[1] That succinct and basic definition in itself, however, does not quite capture the wacky spirit and off-center perspective that set screwball comedy apart from ordinary romantic comedies and that made screwball comedy one of the highlights of Hollywood cinema from films such as Frank Capra's *It Happened One Night* (1934) to the beginning of the American involvement in World War II. That screwball comedy had such a short period of prominence should come as no surprise: while films with strong elements of screwball comedy have never stopped appearing, the genre is very much rooted in the 1930s, when it was, like the musical, one of the central attempts to take advantage of the new resources of sound film as a means of producing films that could provide a distraction from the hardships of the Great Depression. For example, as with film noir, screwball comedy is noted for its use of witty, rapid-fire dialogue, especially between the male and female leads, something that obviously could not have been done in the silents. In addition, screwball comedy shares with the "social problem" dramas of the 1930s a particular rootedness in the social realities of the Depression era. In particular, the obstacles in the path of the romantic protagonists of screwball comedy are quite often economic ones, typically having to do with the fact that one partner (usually the woman) has a much loftier economic status than the other. Screwball comedy is thus closely related to a growing awareness of the extremity of class inequality in America amid the hardships of the 1930s, but it also attempts to minimize the importance of this inequality by making it a subject of humor—and one that can ultimately be overcome. Finally, it is no accident that screwball comedies came into being just as the restrictive Hollywood Production Code went into full enforcement in 1934, and the sometimes extreme shenanigans that appear in screwball comedies can often be seen as a way of getting around the restrictions of the Code by using a different kind of code of their own, though in this sense screwball comedy perhaps most closely resembles film noir, which would continue this strategy for avoiding censorship in the 1940s and 1950s.

The Coens are not operating under the restrictions of the Code, but—given the obvious fascination of the Coens with 1930s and 1940s Hollywood—it should come as no surprise that screwball comedy and film noir—so rooted in those two decades, respectively—are the two film genres that the brothers draw upon most extensively in their own filmmaking. Chapter 1 of this volume discussed the Coens' creative use of elements from film noir in their own work; this chapter looks at their engagement with screwball comedy. Elements of both screwball comedy and film noir are, of course, distributed throughout the Coens' work. These two chapters, however, concentrate on the films in which these elements are strong enough to be a dominant influence on the overall style and tone of the film. In the case of screwball comedy, those films would be *The Hudsucker Proxy* and *Intolerable Cruelty*.

## THE HUDSUCKER PROXY: WORKERS OF THE WORLD, NEVER MIND

*The Hudsucker Proxy* would at first glance seem to be, above all, a somewhat lighthearted satire of the burgeoning world of corporate consumer capitalism in the 1950s. Yet, if *Intolerable Cruelty* is the closest the Coens come to pure screwball comedy, *The Hudsucker Proxy* represents their most successful and creative engagement with the genre. This film, in fact, draws extensively upon a number of Golden Age Hollywood genres, as well as specific films—especially the films of Preston Sturges, Frank Capra, and Howard Hawks. Though not one of their better-known or most widely admired films, *The Hudsucker Proxy* (written by the Coens in conjunction with their buddy Sam Raimi) indicates as well as any other film the complex multigeneric nature of the work of the Coen Brothers, as well as exemplifying their peculiar insider-outsider status with regard to Hollywood.

*The Hudsucker Proxy* begins with a shot of the Manhattan skyline, toward which the camera gradually zooms in as a voice-over narrator (Moses, an old black man who tends the clock and keeps it running, played by Bill Cobbs) explains that it is New Year's Eve, 1958. We are, the narrator explains, on the cusp of a new year and on the verge of the future. Eventually, the camera zeroes in on a clock that is approaching midnight; underneath is a sign reading "The Future is Now." We will soon learn that this clock is on the side of the towering Hudsucker Building and that this sign is the slogan of Hudsucker Industries, whose business is booming. The seeming air of optimism, however, is undercut at this point by the narrator's acknowledgment that "we got somethin' here called the rat race. Got a way of chewing folks up so that they don't want no celebratin', don't want no cheering up, don't care nothin' 'bout no New Year's. Outta hope, outta rope, outta time." Then the narrator introduces Norville Barnes (Tim Robbins), the president of Hudsucker Industries. Continuing the ominous note just sounded by the narrator, Barnes is stepping through the window of his office onto a ledge high above the street below. Whether he will jump, the narrator says, is uncertain because the future is unknowable. The past, however, is a different matter, thus setting up the rest of the film, which is the story of the events that led Barnes to his current plight.

The story begins with Barnes's initial arrival in New York, fresh off the bus from Muncie, Indiana. Already, then, the film draws upon the Coens' keen eye for geographical variations in the texture of American society, with Muncie here exemplifying the supposed innocence and naiveté of the small-town Midwest and New York exemplifying the promise (and the threat) of the bustling big city. But this motif also already indicates the Coens' keen knowledge of film history, given that this device of a small-town innocent arriving to take on the big city is such an important one in Golden Age film. Here, the most directly relevant precedent is probably Capra's *Mr. Deeds Goes to Town* (1936), in which Gary Cooper's Longfellow Deeds comes to New York from the sleepy hamlet of Mandrake Falls, Vermont. Deeds, however, arrives already rich, having just inherited $20 million, so his biggest problem is protecting his fortune from schemers, rather than trying to make a fortune, as in the case of Barnes.

Barnes (whose very name suggests rusticity) is a rube who has come to make it big in the city without any clear idea of how he plans to do so and with few resources to aid him. He has graduated from Muncie College of Business Administration, but he seems ill prepared for the business world. For example, he is surprised to learn, on arriving in New York, that virtually all available jobs require experience, which he does not have. Then fate seemingly takes a hand, as a sheet from a newspaper blows along the sidewalk and sticks to his leg. When he removes the sheet from his leg and looks at it, he finds that a ring of coffee stain has perfectly encircled an ad for employment at Hudsucker Industries, specifying that no experience is necessary. Of course, the ad also announces that employment with the firm will involve long hours and low pay, so even this seeming bit of luck has more than one side to it—as does virtually everything in this film. Barnes rushes to the Hudsucker Building, entering just as Waring Hudsucker (Charles Durning)—the company's founder, president, CEO, and chief stockholder—leaps through the window of the corporate boardroom (in the midst of a board meeting) and plummets to his death on the sidewalk below. This dark moment, however, is treated comically—and then joked about ad infinitum by the building's manic elevator operator, Buzz (Jim True), as the mixed mode of this film becomes increasingly clear.

Barnes attains a job in the company mailroom, the classic entry-level position, especially in the world of film. It is, for example, the initial position taken by Robert Morse's J. Pierrepont Finch when he goes to work for the World Wide Wicket Company in the 1967 film *How to Succeed in Business Without Really Trying*. Indeed, on closer examination, almost everything in *The Hudsucker Proxy* seems to have been taken from the world of film, not the world of reality, despite the fact that the events are so precisely located in a specific time and place. However, while Finch quickly rises to become chairman of the board at World Wide Wicket, initial signs are that, in the case of Hudsucker

Industries, advancement beyond the mailroom is unlikely for Barnes. Nevertheless, the young man has arrived in New York armed with what he sees as a big idea (which turns out to be the Hula Hoop), though others initially scoff at the invention. Barnes has also arrived at the company just as Sidney J. Mussburger (Paul Newman), Hudsucker's former second-in-command, is hatching a scheme to replace Hudsucker (who had personally owned 87 percent of the company's stock) with an incompetent so that the company's stock will tank, allowing Mussburger and his cronies to buy up the stock formerly owned by Hudsucker at a discount rate. Mussburger spots Barnes and immediately concludes that he is a bumbling idiot. He quickly moves to make Barnes the new president of the company, though Mussburger plans to retain the real power himself.

At first, the plan seems to be working, as Hudsucker stock plummets. The film then takes a sudden turn into movie history as Barnes draws the attention of the editor (played by John Mahoney) of the *Manhattan Argus*, who thinks that Barnes's story might help sell papers. He assigns Pulitzer Prize–winning journalist Amy Archer (Jennifer Ja-

**Norville Barnes (Tim Robbins) tries out his new invention in *The Hudsucker Proxy*. Warner Brothers Pictures Inc. / Photofest © Warner Brothers Pictures Inc.**

son Leigh) to find out all she can about Barnes. Archer's entrance also signals the beginning of the film's screwball comedy plot, and her whole newspaper-reporter plotline seems to be largely a pastiche of Hawks's screwball comedy *His Girl Friday* (1940), starring Rosalind Russell as fast-talking reporter Hildy Johnson. Leigh signals the artificiality of her role—and the fact that it is derived from earlier films—by hamming it up to the hilt, strutting about the screen doing a running imitation of Russell but also tossing in a strong dose of Katharine Hepburn, probably the greatest female film star of Russell's era and the star of important screwball comedies such as *Bringing Up Baby* (1938) and *The Philadelphia Story* (1940). It's an overtly cinematic performance, and Leigh clearly means to call attention to her imitation of her illustrious predecessors. To make the role effective, of course, Leigh has to exaggerate and overplay her imitations, but the purpose of this overperformance seems merely to be comic entertainment, no critique of Russell or Hepburn implied.

After her initial encounter with Barnes, Archer becomes convinced that Barnes is an "imbecile," and the *Argus* runs her story to that effect on its front page, with the banner headline "Imbecile Heads Hudsucker." Then we actually see Barnes himself reading this story—in the December 15, 1958, edition of the newspaper. Such precision in the dating of the events of the film seems to locate it at a very specific moment in history. But the date displayed on the paper means that the rest of the action leading up to Barnes's near suicide all takes place in just sixteen days. This action includes, among other things, the final design, testing, manufacture, distribution, and rise to sales success of the Hula Hoop (after a slow start), accompanied by a meteoric rise in Hudsucker stock. The company then again begins to falter as sales flatten and Barnes fails to come up with his next big idea, offering Mussburger and his minions the opportunity to oust Barnes by having him declared insane, leading to the suicide attempt that begins the film. But all of these events clearly could not take place in a mere sixteen days, and the actual Hula Hoop, while in fact introduced in 1958 as in the film, was already a huge hit in July of 1958. Time and again, this film treats viewers to realistic-seeming details, only to undermine that realism with clearly unrealistic details.

That such aberrant details involve real historical events (such as the introduction of the Hula Hoop) only adds to the sense that this film is taking place not in the real New York but in some sort of alternate-reality version of New York. The numerous shots of the city and its skyline look somewhat like New York, but it's an art deco New York with a German Expressionist tinge, filtered through the Nazi architecture of Albert Speer, with nods to Fritz Lang's *Metropolis* (1927), a film that also has many thematic points of connection with *The Hudsucker Proxy*. Indeed, like so many of the Coen Brothers' films, *The Hudsucker Proxy* clearly *does* take place in an alternate reality—the "reality" of film and especially of Golden Age Hollywood. For example, one might expect the crucial role of newspapers in the story to add an air of verisimilitude, given that newspapers supposedly contain accurate representations of real events—or were at least still seen that way in 1958. Of course, most viewers will probably know that the *Manhattan Argus* is not a real newspaper,[2] but what is more to the point is that the entire newspaper motif in *The Hudsucker Proxy* refers not to the world of real print journalism but to the worlds of the great newspaper films of the past, a phenomenon that not only spans the screwball comedy from *It Happened One Night* (1934) to *His Girl Friday* but also memorably includes *Citizen Kane* (1941). That such films were at their peak approximately two decades prior to the action of *The Hudsucker Proxy* only serves further to destabilize any sense that the film is set in the "real" 1950s. Importantly, though, the film is set, not in one alternate reality, but in several because the film draws upon a number of different cinematic worlds, producing a mishmash of elements that don't quite fit together, thus increasing the sense that the whole film is slightly (but delightfully) askew. John Harkness captures this aspect of the film nicely when he notes that "Barnes is a Preston Sturges hero trapped in a Frank Capra story, and never should that twain meet, especially not in a world that seems to have been created by Fritz Lang."[3]

Some critics have felt that *The Hudsucker Proxy* overdoes its engagement with Golden Age Hollywood, but excess and artificiality are the principal modes of *The Hudsucker Proxy*—as is perhaps appropriate for any film that is centrally about consumer capitalism, which thrives on excess and artificiality above all else. For example, all of the characters in *The Hudsucker Proxy* are, in fact, caricatures, and all of the fine actors who play them *over*play them. In his review upon the initial release of the film (written as a dialogue between an angel who loved the film and a devil who hated it), Ebert (as the devil) complains that "the performances are deliberately angled as satire." But then, as the angel, he responds, "But those performances are right on target." And indeed they are. Leigh's performance is self-consciously mannered to the point that it becomes not a parody of Russell but of itself; it is also one of the highlights of the film. Similarly, Newman's Mussburger, the ultimate corporate conniver, is excessively evil—or at least excessively open about how evil he is, which seems both appropriate and inappropriate to the backstabbing businessman that he is. And True's histrionic Buzz is perhaps the most over-the-top character of all, seemingly compounded from a combination of Jerry Lewis's antic bellboy and every elevator operator who ever appeared in the films of Hollywood's Golden Age.

Robbins also plays Barnes as an over-the-top character. In particular, he is a sort of idiot savant, unable to understand almost anything going on around him in the world of corporate intrigue but also occasionally able to come up with ideas that are brilliantly successful, even if the simplicity of such products as the Hula Hoop perhaps tells us more about the ability of the capitalist system to manipulate consumers into desiring its products than about the genius of the products themselves. The fact that, by the end of the film, he also comes up with another brilliant idea (the Frisbee) might also be read in this way, though the fact that both of his inventions are based on the idea of the circle also resonates with a circular motif (the clock, the coffee stain, and so on) that runs throughout the film—as well as other Coen Brothers films, such as *Miller's Crossing* and *The Man Who Wasn't There*—and suggests a greater significance. Circles, after all, carry with them a number of mystic resonances and have been given special significance in many systems of thought over the centuries.

Despite this seeming mysteriousness, the circle is also one of the shapes that we encounter most often in everyday life, which makes it easy for the Coens to populate their film with circles of various kinds, while also suggesting that there is something special about some of the circles. This circle motif becomes most visually effective in one particular scene in which an irate toy-store owner, frustrated at his inability to sell the new product upon its initial release, angrily tosses his stock of Hula Hoops into an alley. One of the hoops, however, escapes the alley and rolls down the sidewalk, powered by its own momentum, though in a way that perhaps violates the laws of physics. It then takes an extensive trip down the sidewalk until it encounters a young boy who picks it up and starts to use it, attracting a crowd of other kids who then rush off to buy Hula Hoops of their own. And the rest is history, or at least alternate history. Meanwhile, this motif of the hoop moving along the sidewalk on its own steam recalls nothing more than the famous blowing (circular) hat from *Miller's Crossing* (1990), a film the Coens had made just a few years before.

In the hands of the Coens, of course, such "profound" symbolism is not to be taken entirely seriously. Indeed, the devil in Ebert's review claims that *The Hudsucker Proxy* is all style and no substance and that the film never even attempts to take itself seriously. Thus, the other references to the mythological or supernatural in *The Hudsucker Proxy* cannot be taken entirely seriously, either—which is not to say that they have no significance whatsoever. *The Hudsucker Proxy* veers into the realm of the mythological/supernatural largely in a tongue-in-cheek manner intended primarily for entertainment. But such references can also be taken as part of a general quest for materials that go beyond the normal—and as part of the Coens' continual insistence that the world is richer and stranger than it might first appear to be.

For example, the clock keeper Moses turns out to be a sort of guardian angel who has the power to manipulate time itself (or at least the clock has this power), and he ultimately intercedes to save Barnes when he does, in fact, plummet from that ledge—though accidentally, and with an assist from a mysterious, malevolent-looking janitor/sign painter named Aloysius (Harry Bugin). Aloysius, meanwhile, looms in the margins throughout the film, becoming particularly visible when he changes the name painted on the door of the president's office whenever the former president dies or is deposed. This function makes it appear that Aloysius is a sort of angel of death/grim reaper figure, a suspicion that is verified late in the film when he battles with Moses in an attempt to prevent the latter from saving Barnes as he falls toward what appears to be certain death. After all, where there is a figure of supernatural good, the demands of plotting almost require that there must be a figure of supernatural evil. But both of these opposed supernatural figures seem far too pedestrian to be truly supernatural; they function more as highly cinematic plot devices than as real characters—and jokey ones at that.

Moses, meanwhile, is a clear example of the "magical Negro," a type of problematic character identified (and named) by African American filmmaker Spike Lee in 2001 to indicate black characters (typically with supernatural powers, or at least special folksy wisdom) whose only purpose in a film is to provide help and support to the (more important) white characters. Complaining specifically of then recent films such as *The Green Mile* (1999) and *The Legend of Bagger Vance* (2000), Lee argued that such roles promulgated harmful clichés by suggesting that black people have no bigger concerns than to be helpful to white people, thus reproducing longtime problematic stereotypes: "They're still doing the same old thing . . . recycling the noble savage and the happy slave."[4] Of course, the Coens, in 1994, could not have been aware of Lee's comments, but they were probably aware that Moses is a rather stereotypical character. Then again, *all* of the characters of *The Hudsucker Proxy* are movie clichés of one kind or another, self-consciously borrowed from any number of other films. That the Coens chose not to critique or even acknowledge this particular cliché is not surprising, given that the Coens here (and in most of their other films) choose not to engage in any sort of critical dialogue with their numerous cinematic sources but simply to mimic those sources without comment.

This sort of mimicry without comment is the very essence of the technique of pastiche, which is so central to the work of the Coen Brothers. Todd McCarthy, in the entertainment industry newspaper *Variety*, praised the technical accomplishments of *The Hudsucker Proxy*, calling the film "one of the most inspired and technically stunning pastiches of old Hollywood pictures ever to come out of the New Hollywood." At the same time, much in the same spirit as Ebert's "devil," McCarthy found this flashy technical accomplishment lacking in substance: "But a pastiche it remains, as nearly everything in the Coen brothers' latest and biggest film seems like a wizardly but artificial synthesis, leaving a hole in the middle where some emotion and humanity should be."

In a similar fashion, at the level of content, *The Hudsucker Proxy* is first and foremost a satire aimed at capitalist greed, but this satire is so whimsical that it almost seems to poke fun at the very idea of satirizing capitalism. Granted, at least one reviewer, James Berardinelli, found the film's satire of capitalism to be quite effective:

*The Hudsucker Proxy* skewers Big Business on the same shaft that Robert Altman ran Hollywood through with *The Player*. From the *Brazil*-like scenes in the cavernous mail room to the convoluted machinations in the board room, this film is pure satire of the nastiest and most enjoyable sort. In this surreal world of 1958 can be found many of the issues confronting large corporations in the 1990s, all twisted to match the filmmakers' vision.

"Twisted to match the filmmakers' vision" is an important caveat, however, because the vision of the Coens in *The Hudsucker Proxy* simply does not include any serious attempt to critique capitalism as a system.

Many aspects of *The Hudsucker Proxy* seem specifically designed to trigger political interpretations. After all, the basic plot is all about capitalist greed and about how the capitalist system can seduce even the most innocent into participating in this greed, though ultimately leaving them unfulfilled, no matter how much money they make. Even the Hudsucker Building itself seems designed as a sort of allegory of class inequality, with the towering structure indicating the vast gap between the grim basement (where the lowliest workers, including those in the mailroom, toil endlessly) and the posh top floor, where bloated executives loll about in luxury. The division is very reminiscent of the one in *Metropolis*, where manual laborers stoke hellish boilers far below ground, while executives lounge in comfort many floors above them in a towering structure whose architecture in fact would have been right at home in the New York of *The Hudsucker Proxy*.

Indeed, this comparison points to precisely the reason why *The Hudsucker Proxy* is not particularly effective as an anticapitalist satire (apart from the fact that it doesn't tell us anything we don't already know). And that reason is that every aspect of the film is simply too *much* like something from a movie to serve as a truly effective commentary on political reality. In the hands of a more political filmmaker, such as Orson Welles (or Capra or Altman), the principal materials of *The Hudsucker Proxy* could no doubt have been molded into an effective commentary on the corruption and inequality that drive the capitalist system, and possibly on the manipulation of gullible consumers that feeds it. But the Coens are not political filmmakers in this way. For example, when an interviewer asked Joel about the obvious commentary in *The Hudsucker Proxy* on the opposition between capitalists and workers, he simply responded, "Maybe the characters do embody those grand themes you mentioned, but that question is independent of whether or not we're interested in them—and we're not."[5]

Despite the chronological and satirical similarities between *The Hudsucker Proxy* and *The Player* (released only two years earlier), the presiding spirit of *The Hudsucker Proxy* (as in much of the Coens' work) is not Altman but Sturges, who spoke up for the little man for sure, but mostly by offering him entertainment that would help him more comfortably suffer the hardships of life in the modern world, rather than urging him to take action to bring those troubles to a just end through political means. Much of the plot of *The Hudsucker Proxy*, for example, resembles that of Sturges's *Christmas in July* (1940), in which lowly office worker Jimmy MacDonald (Dick Powell) seemingly strikes it rich via success in the capitalist system, only to discover that he has been the butt of a practical joke. MacDonald, however, ultimately succeeds anyway, just as Barnes ultimately winds up on top in *The Hudsucker Proxy*.

However, as would even more obviously be the case in the later *O Brother, Where Art Thou?* (2000), the Sturges film to which the Coens owe the most fundamental spiritual debt in *Hudsucker* is *Sullivan's Travels* (1941). In this film, movie director John L. Sullivan (Joel McCrea) decides that, in view of the suffering of the poor during the Great Depression, the light comedies he has been making are irresponsible. As a result, he vows to start making more politically engaged films, in order to help the downtrodden understand their position and perhaps change it. He himself envisions making a film that will seriously explore the plight of the Depression-era poor, a plight he then sets out to research and experience firsthand. Numerous misadventures ensue, but the gist of it all is that Sullivan concludes from his travels that the poor don't need films that remind them of their misery; instead, he decides that they need comedies that will lift them above their misery, if only for an hour or two—and resolves to continue making such films.

In *The Hudsucker Proxy*, the Coens seem to be doing very much the same thing as Sullivan, except that the political intimations of the film potentially threaten to blunt the comedy. It is perhaps no surprise, then, that Ebert's "devil" also complained about all the references to screwball comedy in *Hudsucker*, arguing that "screwball comedy needs a certain looseness, an anarchic spirit that's alien to the meticulous productions of the Coen Brothers." Of course, the very structure of his review suggests that Ebert only half agrees with this assessment, and it is certainly relevant that the relationship of Sturges to screwball comedy is also debatable: it is clear that his films push the boundaries of the screwball comedy if they are screwball comedies at all. Recognizing the fundamental spiritual compatibility of *The Hudsucker Proxy* with films such as *Sullivan's Travels* thus provides a sort of commentary on the Coens' own complex relationship with screwball comedy—and with film genre in general.

## *INTOLERABLE CRUELTY*: TILL DIVORCE DO US PART

*Intolerable Cruelty* is probably the Coen Brothers film that belongs most comfortably within the generic confines of screwball comedy, which might help to explain why it is not one of their most successful films. The best Coen Brothers films tend not to reside comfortably within any one genre but to span several. Even *Intolerable Cruelty*, though, approaches its genre in a rather oblique manner, partly because it is so thoroughly situated, not in the 1930s, where the genre is most at home, but in the early-twenty-first-century context in which the film was made and in which its action takes place. The esteemed film critic Roger Ebert captures this aspect of the film well when he declares that *Intolerable Cruelty* is definitely "in" the genre of screwball comedy "but somehow not of it. The Coens sometimes have a way of standing to one side of their work: It's the puppet and they're the ventriloquists. The puppet is sincere, but the puppetmaster is wagging his eyebrows at the audience and asking, can you believe this stuff?"[6]

One problem with *Intolerable Cruelty* is that it never quite feels like a Coen Brothers film, perhaps because it was the first film they directed that was not originally conceived by them—though it also has the distinction (thanks to changes in the rules of the Directors' Guild of America) of being the first film officially to list both Joel and Ethan as directors. After *The Man Who Wasn't There*, the Coens spent considerable time and energy trying to come up with a script and funding for an ambitious film to be titled *To the White Sea*, about an American airman who is shot down over Japan in World War II and then struggles to evade capture and make his way back home.[7] The script (based on a novel by James Dickey) materialized, but the funding didn't, and the project was shelved, leaving the Coens without a film in the immediate pipeline. So, offered the chance to make *Intolerable Cruelty*, the Coens accepted (after, of course, reworking the original script by Robert Ramsey and Matthew Stone).

*Intolerable Cruelty* satirizes contemporary California divorce culture, in which love, marriage, and divorce among the wealthier denizens of Los Angeles become part of a grasping and cynical game of cyclical cat and mouse in which couples meet, jostle for advantage, and then break up, each having extracted as much profit—sexual, financial, or otherwise—as possible before moving on to the next encounter. In the film's satirical presentation of this culture, men enter marital relationships mostly just to establish sexual control of younger, more attractive women, while protecting as many of their financial assets as possible; these women, meanwhile, enter the relationships strictly for financial gain—both during and after the marriage. This adversarial situation, of course, admits severe impediments to the marriage of true minds, especially when those minds belong to a predatory gold digger (Marylin Rexroth, played by Catherine Zeta-Jones) and a cutthroat divorce attorney (Miles Massey, played by George Clooney), both of whom have made careers out of exploiting the marriage-and-divorce game. It doesn't help that, in their first encounter, Marylin and Miles are direct adversaries in a divorce case in which Miles (as the attorney for Marylin's philandering husband) wins a smashing victory, leaving Marylin virtually penniless. The rest of the plot is driven by Marylin's elaborate plan to get revenge (and get rich) by fraudulently seducing (then divorcing) Miles, which does not make their romantic prospects seem promising.

Anything is possible in screwball comic romances, however. On the other hand, this is a film that makes us want for the two leads to wind up together but not care too much if they don't. As it happens, they do wind up together (after the requisite series of twists and turns), but then we don't care much about that either. The whole enterprise is highly entertaining and extremely funny, even if some of its funniest moments are probably in bad taste—like the hit man who confuses his pistol with his asthma inhaler and accidentally blows his brains out. Part of the problem, of course, is that neither Miles nor Marylin is very nice, even though both Clooney and Zeta-Jones exude charisma and look great—she particularly lights up the screen with her beauty and it is

The dueling lovers Miles Massey (George Clooney) and Marylin Rexroth (Catherine Zeta-Jones) in *Intolerable Cruelty*. Universal Pictures / Photofest © Universal Pictures

easy to see why Miles is so mesmerized whenever he sees her. Ebert's review, in fact, describes her beauty in this film as one of the great examples of feminine beauty in film history. Much of the chemistry between the two characters, though, comes from the admiration of each for the other's conniving ruthlessness, and one of the reasons why the film's happy ending doesn't deliver much emotional payload is that it is hard to believe that a match between two such characters will really last. In fact, the ending resolution between Miles and Marylin comes amid a swirl of final twists in which almost all of the wronged characters in the film suddenly come out on top, a swirl so sudden that it seems forced and artificial. As a result, this happy ending feels more like a parody of a happy ending than like the genuinely happy endings of the classic screwball comedies from which the film draws so much spiritual inspiration.

Don't get me wrong: *Intolerable Cruelty* is endlessly entertaining and eminently watchable—though probably not as *re*watchable as the very best Coen films. In a gushing review in *Empire* magazine, Damon Wise might have inadvertently touched on the reason why this is *not* one of the very best Coen films when he declared that the newly released film was sure to be a box-office smash:

> Unabashedly commercial, crowd-tickling stuff, this dazzling screwball comedy—following proudly in the footsteps of Preston Sturges, Howard Hawks and Billy Wilder—stars George Clooney at his most charming and Catherine Zeta-Jones doing what she does best (however little that is) in an immediately accessible story about avarice, divorce and love, in that order. Tight as a drum, glamorous and exquisitely funny, this one should earn them enough cash to make five more offbeat minor masterpieces like *The Man Who Wasn't There*—and the Coens deserve that as much as we do.[8]

This description of the film is fairly accurate (though it might undersell the multiple talents of Zeta-Jones, a gifted musical stage performer, among other things). The film does *look* relatively mainstream, lacking the usual offbeat visual flair of the Coens' films. And the subject matter is relatively commercial as well—much more so than, say, a film noir set in Texas or a film about a leftist screenwriter on the eve of World War II. Wise was wrong about one thing, though: the film did not do especially well at the U.S. box office, taking in a mere $35 million in domestic receipts. The reason for this surprisingly modest return is probably that *Intolerable Cruelty* is still too much like a Coen film to be a box-office smash, though it is also too mainstream commercial to be among the best efforts of the Coens, who thrive on eccentric effects outside the Hollywood mainstream (while nevertheless keeping a toe dipped in the waters of that stream).

Interestingly enough, though, *Intolerable Cruelty* did ultimately manage to be a commercial success (though still not an absolute blockbuster) thanks to an international box-office take of nearly $85 million. That a film so rooted in the contemporary culture of Los Angeles and so closely attached to the American screwball comedy tradition should take in well over twice as much in box-office receipts abroad as at home is probably telling. The Coens are filmmakers whose films are, in general, more thoroughly rooted in various American cultural traditions than are those of almost any other filmmaker. Yet there is something vaguely European about the Coens' sensibilities as well—a fact that perhaps accounts for *Barton Fink*'s Palme d'Or or for the fact that the Coens were selected to make one of the eighteen short films that are included in the anthology *Paris je t'aime* (2006)—which is, as the name implies, a sort of love letter to the city of Paris.[9] Still, despite the skewing of its box-office numbers, *Intolerable Cruelty* is one of the most American of the Coens' films. One might say the same for *The Hudsucker Proxy*, which perhaps says something about the Americanness of the screwball comedy as a genre.

# 6

# LAUGHING TO KEEP FROM DYING IN THE SUBURBS

Black Comedy in *Fargo* and *A Serious Man*

Given the tendency of the Coen Brothers to place their films in very specific geographic locations (or at least in alternate-reality versions of those locations), it was perhaps inevitable that they would eventually set one of their films in the suburban Minnesota where they grew up. In fact, they returned to film in Minnesota relatively early in their careers with the production of their sixth film, *Fargo* (1996). They returned to Minnesota once again to make *A Serious Man* (2009), which is set in a world much more like the one in which the brothers actually spent their childhoods—and is even set in the time period during which they were living in Minnesota. In both films, though, it is clear that the Minnesota portrayed differs in important ways from the Minnesota of our reality. *Fargo* is set amid a criminal conspiracy that descends into deadly violence of a kind never encountered by the Coens in Minnesota. And *A Serious Man*, while involving events that would mostly, on the surface, be possible in the real world of suburban Minnesota, veers in the aggregate toward dark absurdist comedy.

## *FARGO*: TAKE MY WIFE, PLEASE

There is a moment in *Fargo* in which murderous thug Carl Showalter (Steve Buscemi) goes on a date (with a hired escort) to the Carlton Celebrity Room, where the couple dine and observe a live performance by well-known Puerto Rican singer José Feliciano. The film is set in 1987, but Feliciano had reached the height of his fame as a performer many years earlier with the release of such hits as "Light My Fire" (1968) and "Feliz Navidad" (1970). For many viewers of the film, Feliciano's appearance (in which we hear him sing much of the song "Let's Find Each Other Tonight," which he had in fact recorded in 1983) is thus something of a nostalgia trip. In fact, it might be such a trip for the Coens themselves, given that they were young teens or preteens in Minnesota when he was at the height of his fame. Meanwhile, the appearance essentially as a lounge singer by a former A-list star might seem like something of a comedown. However, the real Carlton (located in Bloomington, Minnesota) was in fact a large (seating capacity roughly 2,200) and prestigious venue, which in its time hosted such acts as Johnny Cash, Ray Charles, and Prince. Then again, the Carlton of the film is clearly not the real one, given that the real one was bulldozed in 1986 (to make way for the building of the Mall of America). Its appearance in a film set in 1987 is thus a classic Coen Brothers move and one that identifies the Minnesota of *Fargo* as an alternate-reality location that resembles, but is not identical to, the Minnesota of the real world.

This sense of an uneasy boundary between reality and unreality is also furthered by the on-screen claim at the beginning of *Fargo* that it is based on real events that occurred in Minnesota in 1987; this claim might seem to suggest that this particular film might exist in a world more representative of the real one than the alternate-reality constructions of the Coens' earlier films. Nothing, however, could be further from the truth. Indeed, the fact that the film is not actually based on real events, despite this opening claim, only distances it further from reality. The Coens have acknowledged that they were attempting, in *Fargo*, to create a crime-infused world that is more interesting than our own world. In particular, while evading the question in numerous interviews, the Coens eventually admitted that the story is a complete fiction, manufactured because all of the true crime stories they researched seemed insufficiently compelling.[1] In short, *Fargo* may exist even *more* straightforwardly in an alternate reality than had the Coens' earlier films, even as it takes us to the region where the Coens grew up and therefore to one they presumably know well enough to represent accurately.

That *Fargo* does not reside in a world that is simply a re-creation of reality can also be seen in the gestures toward the mythical version of the Minnesota Northlands that is represented by the numerous shots we see of a statue of Paul Bunyan that complements the sign welcoming visitors to the town of Brainerd (a key location in the film), identifying the town as Bunyan's "home." This statue is itself a bit of movie magic: there are, in fact, numerous Paul Bunyan statues scattered across Minnesota, but this particular one is a fake, constructed specifically for use in the film (and located in northeastern North Dakota, nowhere near the real town of Brainerd, which sits in almost the exact center of Minnesota).[2]

Bunyan, incidentally, is not particularly associated with the town of Brainerd. He is, however, one of the most prominent figures in the entire phenomenon of American tall tales, a giant lumberjack generally accompanied by the equally gargantuan Babe the Blue Ox as he performs various astounding feats. There are many versions of Bunyan's story, almost all of which involve superhuman exploits, and some of which employ Bunyan as a warning against the dehumanizing potential of capitalist modernization, as Bunyan's vast strength and manual skill as a lumberjack are eventually outstripped by more efficient (but inhuman) machines, somewhat in the mold of the equally mythical John Henry. Ironically, though, Bunyan has also been widely employed as a marketing tool by the very capitalist system that his stories sometimes critique—as when a motel featured in the film takes its name from Bunyan's sidekick or when the city of Brainerd attempts to use his image to attract cash-paying visitors. Indeed, Bunyan first became widely known through his use in a series of advertising pamphlets for the Red River Lumber Company, beginning in 1916. Meanwhile, Bunyan's stories were themselves largely manufactured for commercial publication, rather than evolving organically like genuine folklore. Thus, folklorist Richard M. Dorson regards Bunyan as a chief example of the phenomenon he refers to as "fakelore," his stories having been hijacked by advertisers and fiction writers until they bore little relation to their original roots. For Dorson, Bunyan is the "archetype" of the "mass-culture hero," his image manufactured partly for profit and partly to promote a nationalistic vision of America's greatness.[3] Bunyan, then, is the perfect figure to represent a film such as *Fargo*, with its patently false claims to authenticity. He also helps to reinforce the sense that this film takes place in a setting that both is and is not the Minnesota we all know.

*Fargo* calls attention to its far north setting immediately, beginning with an all-white screen that we quickly discover is a view of the northern winterscape, the snow-covered earth almost indistinguishable from the white sky. As slow, melancholy music (a bit reminiscent of the music of *Miller's Crossing*) plays, a car appears, towing another car down a highway so covered with snow that it is virtually indistinguishable from the empty fields around it. The cars then arrive in Fargo, North Dakota, where Jerry Lundegaard (William H. Macy) is delivering the towed car to two thugs with whom he has agreed to meet in order to arrange the kidnapping of his wife, Jean (Kristin Rudrüd); he hopes thereby to collect ransom money from her wealthy father, Wade Gustafson (Harve Presnell). The thugs, Showalter and Gaear Grimsrud (Peter Stormare), are puzzled by the deal, but all Jerry will reveal is that he needs the money because he is in a bit of "trouble." The arrangement made between Jerry and the thugs sets in motion a series of misadventures that plays out across North Dakota and (especially) Minnesota, as the Coens continue their mapping of an alternative America.

At this point, at least in terms of plot, *Fargo* seems to be shaping up like a mildly interesting but ultimately run-of-the-mill thriller, though the artistically presented opening snowscape and the introduction of these three terrific character actors so early on hold considerable promise that the film might contain at least a few special touches. And, of course, the film automatically holds promise for anyone who has been following the Coens' earlier films, though most critics felt that the brothers reached a new level of achievement in this particular film. *Fargo* premiered at the 1996 Cannes Film Festival, where it won the Best Director award for Joel Coen, though of course *Barton Fink* had won even more accolades at the French festival. Perhaps more telling was the review of the film by Roger Ebert, who had been singularly unimpressed by the Coens' first five films but who waxed poetic in his praise of *Fargo*. "To watch it," he says, "is to experience steadily mounting delight, as you realize the filmmakers have taken enormous risks, gotten away with them and made a movie that is completely original, and as familiar as an old shoe."[4] This same description, of course, applies perfectly well to the Coens' earlier films as well, but the fact that it took *Fargo* to make such an astute observer as Ebert finally begin to realize what the Coens were up to tells us what an important film this truly is in the Coens' career, which gained significant new momentum as a result of the film.

*Fargo* was nominated for seven Academy Awards (including Best Picture) and ultimately won two, including a joint Best Original Screenplay Oscar for the brothers. These Oscar nominations represented the first to have been gained by a Coen Brothers film, and the screenwriting win is still (as of this writing in 2018) the only Oscar won by the brothers outside of the three they took home for *No Country for Old Men* (2007). *Fargo* also won a well-deserved Best Actress Oscar for Frances McDormand as Marge Gunderson, the seven-months-pregnant police chief of Brainerd. It is Marge who is primarily tasked with investigating the constellation of crimes associated with Jean Lundegaard's kidnapping and its aftermath, and it is a task that she performs well, though nearly a million dollars in ransom money does go missing and many of the principals (including Jean) are killed in the process. But, of course, neither the crimes nor their investigation is the real point of *Fargo*, which is part ironic homage to the Minnesota milieu the Coens know so well and part character study—featuring the Coens' usual array of amusing eccentrics, some of whom spill over into the grotesque, but at least one of whom (Marge) is portrayed with a degree of warmth and humanity not previously achieved in the Coens' films.

As the film proceeds, the scene quickly shifts from Fargo to Minneapolis, as we see Jerry back there in his home, where the true patriarch is clearly not Jerry but his father-in-law, a domineering figure with whom the unimposing Jerry cannot compete in masculine power. Soon afterward, we see Jerry at work as the "executive sales manager" at a car dealership, which is (of course) owned by Gustafson, ensuring that Jerry remains in the shadow of his father-in-law there as well. Jerry is also up to no good here, having fraudulently extracted some $320,000 in loan money from GMAC (at that time the financing arm of General Motors) for cars that do not, in fact, exist. He also cheats his customers, maneuvering them into paying extra for accessories they neither need nor want. It is clear that Jerry, driven by the desire to compete with his far more successful father-in-law, has completely abandoned all sense of ethics—though his unscrupulous dealings are so incompetently executed that they tend simply to get him deeper and deeper into debt (and other forms of trouble). For her part, Jean seems a virtual nonentity, spending her time engaged in domestic tasks such as knitting and cooking, having little true communication with her husband or son, and remaining dominated by her powerful father—as she doubtless has been her entire life.

The dysfunction of the Lundegaard household should come as no surprise to viewers of the Coens' earlier films. Scenes of domestic harmony and genuine love seem almost entirely absent from the brothers' earlier work. (The occasional moments of connection between Hi and Ed in *Raising Arizona* merit the "almost," but those moments are seriously flawed.) In *Fargo*, however, we actually see one family that is almost too ideal to be believable. The marriage between Marge and her husband, Norm (John Carroll Lynch), presents us with a genuine utopian enclave in which mutual love and understanding reign supreme, even as that enclave is surrounded by a world of violence and corruption. Indeed, it is the fallen world at large that makes the domestic space ruled by Marge and Norm (as they await the birth of their first child) all the more special. And it is indeed ruled by both, the two seeming very much to be equal partners. Meanwhile, one of the things that makes *Fargo* so special is that the idyllic marriage of the Gundersons is centrally informed by a gender reversal in which Norm occupies an essentially domestic space, while it is Marge who goes out into the cold (in this case, *really* cold), cruel world and deals with its nasty realities so that Norm won't have to.

One of the charms of *Fargo* is that the folksy, gravid Marge seems so unsuited to take on ruthless (if inept) thugs like Showalter and Grimsrud but ultimately proves more than up to the task. Easy to underestimate (which is one of her key strengths), Marge turns out to be shrewd, courageous, and wise in the ways of the world. She is no supersleuth, but she is a competent cop. We see her perhaps at her best when she interviews Shep Proudfoot (Steve Reevis), the hulking Native American parolee who works as an auto mechanic at Gustafson Motors. It was Proudfoot, with his own connections in the criminal world (Gaear is his "buddy"), who originally got Jerry in touch with the kidnappers, who had in turn called Proudfoot from the Blue Ox Motel, leaving a phone record that led Marge to the mechanic. The large, menacing, taciturn Proudfoot is this film's central ethnic stereotype,[5] and he clearly hopes to intimidate the small, pregnant, unassuming white woman who comes to interview him. The chipper Marge holds her ground quite nicely, though, and it is Proudfoot who ends up being unsettled by the interview, though he also manages to avoid giving up any information about the kidnappers. One feels that Norm, on the other hand, would be completely lost in the criminal world into which Marge must venture in the course of her professional duties. Like Jerry, Norm lacks stereotypically macho attributes. Unlike Jerry, this does not mean that Norm is not a good husband who loves his wife; one suspects that he will be a good father as well. He need not be able to take on and defeat murderous thugs in order to play those roles. Someone, however, has to deal with the evils of the world, and there is no reason why that someone has to be male, just as there is no reason why someone who holds down the home front has to be female.

Norm, though, is never presented as effeminate. He's just ordinary. He does, however, have his own talents as a maker of various forms of arts and crafts. For example, one part of the domestic subplot of the film involves his work on a painting of a mallard that he is preparing to enter into a competition to appear on a postage stamp. (He wins but only for the 3-cent stamp, losing out to a local rival for the more prestigious 29-cent first-class stamp.) For her part, Marge is a loving and supportive wife who never shows any sign of loving or respecting Norm less because of his lack of traditional machismo. He functions very well in the domestic space of the home, and that's fine with Marge. Jerry, meanwhile, is no better equipped than Norm to deal with the criminal underworld of the thugs with whom he attempts to do business; Jerry, though, is equally incompetent even in his own "natural" environments: the conventional world of business at the car dealership and the domestic space of marriage (as his willingness to use his own wife as a pawn in his kidnapping scheme amply illustrates).

If Norm is seen as embodying a "good" form of alternative masculinity and Jerry and Carl as occupying "bad" forms, all of the characters of *Fargo* who represent conventional forms of masculinity are represented negatively. The patriarchal Wade is hardly a likable character, and his insensitive treatment of Jerry is merely one aspect of a pattern of behavior in which he is clearly more devoted to making money and exerting control than to any form of human relationship. It should thus come as no surprise that his first reaction to the news of the ransom demand is that they should negotiate with the kidnappers for a lower ransom. Meanwhile, the film's two paragons of masculine "strength"—Gaear and Shep—are both depicted as violent, abusive, and virtually incapable of verbal communication or of controlling their tempers. Perhaps the most enigmatic masculine character in the film is Mike Yanagita, Marge's former high-school classmate, who arranges a meeting with Marge in order to hit on her and is then undeterred by the discovery of her pregnancy. For her part, Marge is sympathetic and kind when Mike tearfully explains his extreme loneliness in the wake of his wife's death from leukemia, though of course she is uninterested in his overtures. Mike then comes off as significantly less sympathetic (to both Marge and the viewing audience) when we later learn that he was lying about his wife's death and has never been married. But this news is also mitigated by the revelation that he has "psychiatric problems" and is now living at home with his parents, rather than living the successful life as an engineer for Honeywell that he had described to Marge.

Mike's narrative thus comes off as rather touching, instead of as the farcical tale it might have been in many of the Coens' films. It is thus very much in keeping with the kinder and gentler feel of *Fargo* in general. Many aspects of the film, though, are vintage Coens, as when Jerry contrives to cheat both sides in the transaction surrounding Jean's kidnapping: he tells Wade that the kidnappers have demanded a ransom of $1 million, while he tells the kidnappers that the ransom is only $80,000, which he plans to split with them 50-50, throwing in a brand-new Oldsmobile Cutlass Ciera to sweeten the deal (and to help the criminals with their transportation during the crime). Then again, Jerry's plan to outsmart everyone is seriously hampered by the fact that he isn't very smart. Moreover, the plan is also hobbled by the fact that Wade, clearly a control freak (especially where his money and his daughter are concerned), immediately insists on interfering, despite Jerry's pleas that he not get involved in the transaction other than putting up the cash. But Wade demands that he be allowed to deliver the ransom money to Carl himself; he then comes armed to the transaction, which he refuses to carry out on Carl's terms. For once, though, Wade is not in charge, and he ends up being shot dead by Carl—but not before he shoots Carl (who is fresh from a beating at the hands of Shep

Proudfoot and who serves as this film's punching-bag character) in the face, though the wound is relatively superficial.

Jerry's problems are exacerbated by the fact that the criminals he hires to do his bidding aren't any smarter than he is—on top of which they refuse to actually do his bidding. Instead, they insist on being paid the entire $80,000; when Carl discovers that Wade has brought $1 million instead, he buries $920,000 of it in the snow by the side of a road to avoid sharing it with Gaear. As is quite typical for a Coen Brothers film, numerous characters in this film are bent on double-crossing numerous other characters, but they then carry out these betrayals rather incompetently, contributing to the series of errors that ultimately leaves seven people dead, including Jean, Wade, and Carl—not to mention a state trooper, a parking lot attendant, and two witnesses, all four of whom accidentally run afoul of the two thugs.

All of this, of course, is quintessential Coens. One might also see *Fargo* as the film in which the Coens perfected the technique of mixing genres, moods, and tones that is perhaps the most distinctive feature of their work, in which odd mixtures of disparate materials tend to mesh brilliantly. But *Fargo* effects its mixtures of materials more quietly and subtly than is usually the case in a film by the Coens, who often effect such mixtures with gleeful violence and intrusiveness. Perhaps the most obvious mixture in *Fargo* is its unhesitating combination of crime and comedy, a feature that is typical of the Coens' work as a whole—and one of the things that most clearly contributes to its air of taking place in alternate, off-kilter realities.

In one of the comic highlights of *Fargo*, a staple scene of the police procedural turns into an all-out comedy routine as Marge interviews the two hookers who had serviced Carl and Gaear at the Blue Ox. For one thing, the Minnesota accents of the two innocent-looking young women are among the funniest in the film. For another, their descriptions of the two criminals are classic. Carl's hooker informs Marge that "he was funny lookin'—more'n most people, even." Gaear's, meanwhile, suggests that he looked like the Marlboro man, though she admits that she might have gotten that impression from the fact that he smoked so many Marlboros, "you know, like a subconscious type of thing." They are, though, able to provide Marge with the information that the two men were headed for the Twin Cities, which at least provides her with a direction for her investigation.

The hooker's identification of Gaear with the Marlboro man—an icon of conventional testosterone-soaked manliness somewhat in the mode of the Stranger in *The Big Lebowski*—points to the way in which this film (so ultimately dominated by its female lead) is centrally concerned with the topic of masculinity. With the exception of Norm (who is not conventionally masculine), men do not come off well in this film. Gaear—big, strong, and tight-lipped—does indeed show many of the traits that are conventionally coded as masculine, but he is also a psychopathic killer. Wade is successful in ways that have traditionally been endorsed by American society, but it is also clear that he can be ruthless, self-serving, and oblivious to the feelings of others, traits that have no doubt contributed to making Jerry feel less than a man and thus turn to crime as a form of compensation. Meanwhile, Jerry and Carl both try desperately to achieve conventional masculinity but fail miserably in doing so, partly because they are in the respective shadows of Wade and Gaear, suggesting both that society's stereotypical expectations of men might put unreasonable pressures on them and that those who do behave in these stereotypically masculine ways place toxic limitations on the development of others, including other men.

Jerry is a little man in every sense of the word, but he dreams of being a big man like his father-in-law. In this, Jerry is the successor to a long line of literary characters (Gogol's mild-mannered copyist Akaky Akakievich Bashmachkin, from "The Overcoat," might be the prototype) who are so extraordinary in their ordinariness as to be virtually unnoticeable by others. In *Fargo*, Jerry's ill-fated kidnapping scheme is a bid not just to solve his (apparently considerable) money problems but also an attempt for once to be somebody special and to escape from the confinement of his day-to-day life.[6] That this plan collapses so miserably, leaving him in the very unmasculine position of screaming and squirming in his underwear as police arrest him in a seedy motel, is a testament to just how ill suited he is for the role of criminal mastermind. Jerry is depicted as having suffered so much humiliation over the years that it is hard not to have a little sympathy for him; however, he is so pathetic in his lack of prowess and in his lack of concern about how his actions will affect others that it is impossible to have more than a little.

Perhaps the only character in *Fargo* more hapless than Jerry is the diminutive Carl. After all, one of the comic highlights of this very funny, very bloody film occurs when Marge discovers Gaear feeding Carl's body into that wood chipper, just one sneaker-clad foot still sticking out. This scene, meanwhile, is the culmination of the ongoing squabble between the two criminals that runs—along with their bumbling incompetence as they go about their work—as a comic thread throughout the film. Much of the brilliance of *Fargo*, however, comes in its ability to make these criminals funny without ever really asking us to sympathize with them and without any attempt to suggest that they are anything but bloodthirsty killers. *Fargo* is a sort of buddy film in which the relationship between Carl and Gaear is a crucial element of the plot. One might compare here the relationship between Vincent Vega (John Travolta) and Jules Winnfield (Samuel L. Jackson) in Quentin Tarantino's *Pulp Fiction* (1994), which is also something of a cross between a violent crime film and a humorous buddy film. But the criminal pair in *Pulp Fiction* are both clearly coded as conventionally masculine, while in *Fargo* the relationship between Gaear and Carl takes on an extra dimension because the first is coded as masculine, while the second has numerous feminine characteristics. As Adams astutely observes, Carl and Gaear function in the film as a sort of dysfunctional couple—which places them essentially as the negative counterpart of the positive couple constituted by Norm and Marge, both in terms of their moral positions and in terms of the largely hostile attitudes they hold toward each other. The two of them constantly bicker and argue over minutiae; at one point they even have sex together—though with the mediation of the two young (and enthusiastic) hookers they hire to join them in their room at the Blue Ox truck stop and motel in Brainerd (midway between Fargo and Minneapolis), on their way to kidnap Jean in Minneapolis. Then the two thugs relax together to watch some postcoital late-night TV, very much like so many other American couples, but with an added layer of irony.

Especially given the way their association ends up, Gaear and Carl represent a seriously bad alternative version of the typical couple, just as Norm and Marge constitute an ideal alternative form of the typical couple. Both relationships, though, are very much in keeping with the alternate-reality feel of this film as a whole. When the Coens returned to Minnesota with *A Serious Man*, they would create a world that is both more ordinary and more strange than the one in *Fargo*, a seemingly paradoxical feat that is quintessentially Coenesque.

Marge Gunderson (Frances McDormand) takes aim in *Fargo*. Gramercy Pictures /
Photofest © Gramercy Pictures

## *A SERIOUS MAN*: "ACCEPT THE MYSTERY"

*A Serious Man* is the Coen Brothers' "Jewish" film. Something like a
comic riff on the book of Job, it includes scenes in Hebrew school, in a
synagogue, and at a bar mitzvah. Almost all of the characters are Jewish,
and several are rabbis. The opening scene is entirely in Yiddish, set in
an Eastern European *shtetl*. The central (Jewish) character—physics
professor Larry Gopnik (Michael Stuhlbarg)—is not only something of
a figure of Job, but his unending troubles make him something of a
figure of the historical Jewish experience. Several major reviewers,
however, questioned whether the film—in its gleeful torture of this
character and in its presentation of so many Jewish characters as caricatures—might be a work of "Jewish self-loathing": one online reviewer
went so far as the call it "certainly the most anti-Jewish film Hollywood
has ever produced."[7] Bergan, on the other hand, praises the film as a
landmark in Jewish American culture, as the moment "when Judaism
came of age in American cinema."[8] It is certainly the case that *A Serious Man* is anything but mean spirited in its treatment of Jews. It is also

(despite the title) anything but entirely serious. A jokey notation that is displayed at the end of the credits captures the self-consciously light-hearted spirit of the film perfectly: "No Jews were harmed in the making of this motion picture."

Perhaps no *real* Jews were harmed, but many of the Jewish characters take quite a buffeting, either in terms of the events that occur in the film or the way in which they are portrayed in the film. One of the many ironies of *Fargo* is that the dark, violent world of the film is so very unlike the uneventful suburban Minnesota world in which the Coens grew up—though suggestions that decadence and violence lie beneath the placid surface of suburbia long have been a staple of American film, from *Peyton Place* (1957) to recent horror films such as *Get Out* (2017). However, as opposed to the events of these films (or of *Fargo*), the troubles encountered in *A Serious Man* are generally more mundane, though some of them border on the metaphysical. Indeed, the suburban world of *A Serious Man* has an air of mystery added to its ordinariness, helping to make it once again a sort of alternate-reality version of the world in which it is ostensibly set.

*A Serious Man* begins on a seemingly philosophical note, with an on-screen quote attributed to the medieval French rabbi and Talmudic scholar Rashi: "Receive with simplicity everything that happens to you." This seems, at this point, to be a movie with a message, but we will eventually find that the film is filled with such tidbits, all of which have seemingly profound implications, but none of which ultimately seems to provide much in terms of practical advice on how to live our lives. The film then shifts directly into a cold (in more ways than one) open that is set, like the opening of *Fargo*, in a scene of snow. This snow, however, appears to be falling in a *shtetl* in Eastern Europe, perhaps in the nineteenth century. While we see glimpses of the snow, the scene is set mostly in a dark, claustrophobic interior, in muted tones, with a compressed 4:3 aspect ratio that contributes to the antique feel and to the claustrophobia. In the scene, a sort of folktale that draws on Jewish mythology, a Jewish couple are visited by a supposedly deceased rabbi who might or might not be a *dybbuk*, a malevolent spirit risen from the dead. As a result, the couple might or might not be cursed. Nothing is ever quite certain in this film.

This scene, in any case, is not directly related to the rest of the film that occurs (in a more modern setting) after the opening credits—as the aspect ratio expands and the lighting level increases significantly. There is no indication of how the two parts of the film are related, though it certainly seems reasonable to assume that the couple in the prologue *is* cursed and that they are the ancestors of Gopnik, who has in turn somehow inherited the curse. In any case, Gopnik does certainly seem cursed in this film, but the uncertainties about the meaning of the prologue are never resolved. This film is one that produces lots of questions but very few answers, just as Gopnik—a smart, rational, educated man—is a seeker of certainty whose life gradually unravels into more and more uncertainty as the film proceeds. As Gopnik puts it, consulting a rabbi a bit more than halfway through the film, "Why does He [God] make us feel the questions if He's not gonna give us any answers?"

One might ask the same about the Coens. In any case, not much goes right for Gopnik, though he (and we) never find the reason for his suffering. His constant mantra throughout the film—"I didn't do anything"—is generally true, but that buys him no dispensation from life's woes. Gopnik is clearly the central character of the film, but he seems responsible for almost none of the film's major events, instead simply being knocked about by blind fate or by the actions of others. Seemingly powerless, he is apparently not even the "serious man" of the title, an appellation that is applied multiple times in the film to his condescending, touchy-feely rival Sy Ableman (Fred Melamed), would-be second husband of Gopnik's shrewish wife, Judith (Sari Lennick). Indeed, when Gopnik at one point attempts to declare himself a serious man, he cannot even manage to speak the words without a disclaimer. Not only is Judith unfaithful (though in a chaste way), but his kids are unruly and disobedient, his daughter saving up for the nose job that she has been forbidden to have and his son more interested in watching *F Troop* than sitting shiva after Ableman is killed in an auto accident. The only thing over which one might expect Gopnik to be able to exert a modicum of control—his professional life as a college physics professor—is in danger of spiraling out of control as well.

All of this, we will eventually learn, takes place in 1967 in a Minnesota suburb, which places it both geographically and temporally in the childhood of the Coens.[9] This temporal setting is indicated early on, as the opening credits appear (after the East European prologue) with rock music in the background, then morph into the opening scene of the main part of the film, which reveals that the music we have been hearing—Jefferson Airplane's rock classic "Somebody to Love" (released April 1, 1967, on the album *Surrealistic Pillow*)—is actually playing on a transistor radio that is being secretly listened to via an earbud worn by Gopnik's son, Danny (Aaron Wolff), to entertain him while he ignores what is going on in his Hebrew school. Danny, we will later learn, is a fan, not just of rock music, but of marijuana. He is thus very much a child of his times in 1967, year of the "Summer of Love" and the year that "Somebody to Love" was ubiquitous among young Americans, as it is in the world of the film, popping up at key moments throughout. The prominence of this song helps to establish the setting of the film in 1967 and to remind us of how crucial that year was to the 1960s counterculture. But the well-known opening words to the song—heard several times in the film—are perfectly in keeping with the overall theme of the film: "When the truth is found to be lies / And all the joy within you dies, / Don't you want somebody to love?"

At the same time as the opening scene in the Hebrew school, Gopnik is undergoing a thorough physical exam, the results of which he gets from his cigarette-smoking doctor, who offers Gopnik a smoke as well. Surprisingly, given the way the rest of the film goes, Gopnik is given (at this point) a clean bill of health. It's all downhill from there, though. We next see him on the job in the classroom, teaching the paradox of Schrödinger's cat. He seems competent, if uninspiring, as a teacher, though his students seem about as engaged as the bored students at Danny's Hebrew school. After class, Gopnik is visited in his office by the kind of student all professors dread—a student who wants to complain that the grade he was given on the recent midterm exam was "unjust." In this case, the student is Korean immigrant Clive Park (David Kang), whose argument is that the test was unfair to him because it depended too much on mathematics, at which he (going against Asian American stereotypes) is very poor. As a result, he failed the test and experienced dreadful "shame" (this time verifying a stereotypical Asian characteristic), though he understands the physics. Gopnik tries to explain that one can't do the physics without the mathematics, but Clive is unmoved by the argument, opting instead to leave an envelope full of cash, clearly meant as a bribe.

Gopnik later attempts to give the money back to Clive, who refuses to take it or to acknowledge that it is his. Soon afterward, Clive's father (played by Steve Park—who had been Mike Yanagita in *Fargo*) comes to Gopnik's home to deliver a paradoxical threat to sue the professor both for accepting a bribe and for defaming his son by falsely accusing him of offering a bribe—unless he gives Clive a passing grade. Befuddled, Gopnik grapples with the logic of the threat. "It doesn't make sense," he tells Park. "Either he left the money, or he didn't." "Please," responds Park, offering still another gloss on the events of the film as a whole, "accept the mystery."

The ability simultaneously to accept seemingly contradictory propositions is often associated with Eastern philosophy, so Park here would seem to be as much of an ethnic stereotype as the various stage Jews who populate the rest of the film. On the other hand, this sort of paradoxical thinking should not be foreign to Gopnik at all because it is also central to the quantum physics in which he appears to specialize in his work. "Schrödinger's cat," for example, is a well-known thought experiment from 1935, in which Austrian physicist Erwin Schrödinger conceived of a situation in which, due to the phenomenon known as "quantum superposition," a cat must be considered simultaneously dead and alive under the conditions of the experiment. Schrödinger developed this experiment as a critique of the absurdity of certain interpretations of quantum mechanics, but it has become widely known as a serious illustration of some of the implications of quantum mechanics, and Gopnik himself appears to be teaching it in this way.

Clearly, Gopnik is unaccustomed to applying the principles of quantum physics to macro-scale events in his daily life—and rightfully so. He thus appears to make no connection whatsoever between the principles he teaches in class and the attitude being espoused by Mr. Park. However, within a few years of the 1967 setting of the movie, it would become quite commonplace to note parallels between the kind of thinking involved in quantum physics and that which informs Eastern mysticism. In 1975, for example, Fritjof Capra's *The Tao of Physics*, which touts such parallels, became a popular best-seller; that book has gone through several successful editions since then. Similar parallels were also important (though less central) to Gary Zukav's *The Dancing Wu Li Masters*, which won a National Book Award in the category of science for 1979.

One could, in fact, read *A Serious Man* as an exploration of various sources of wisdom, from the glib soundbites of popular music, to traditional Jewish culture, to science, to Eastern mysticism, all of which seem to have certain things in common, including an acknowledgment that life always includes a certain amount of uncertainty—a key theme in the film. At one point in the film, Gopnik appropriately lectures on the Heisenberg uncertainty principle, ending his presentation with the announcement that "it proves we can't ever really know what's going on," perhaps spinning his interpretation to reflect the circumstances of his private life. As his students hastily depart the lecture hall when the bell rings, he adds, "But even though you can't figure anything out, you will be responsible for it on the midterm." When a physics professor lectures on this topic, it certainly has a different feel than when it is propounded by Freddie Riedenschneider in *The Man Who Wasn't There*. One feels, for example, that Gopnik actually knows what he is talking about. On the other hand, it is also clear that Gopnik's interpretation of the uncertainty principle is as much a gloss on his own life as on subatomic physics. Time and again in this film, he finds himself being held responsible for dealing with circumstances that are beyond his understanding or control. But his gloss on the uncertainty principle (and warning about the exam) can also be taken as the central message of the film: like it or not, we have to deal with what life throws at us, even if it isn't fair and even if we don't understand it. The film, however, has little or no advice on *how* to deal with life's problems.

One of Gopnik's biggest problems is that he is currently being considered for tenure at the suburban university where he teaches, so Clive's disruption comes at an inopportune moment. This is especially the case because Gopnik seems to have few publications or other achievements to submit in support of his tenure case—but also because the tenure committee has been receiving anonymous (there are unverified hints that they might have come from Ableman) denigrating letters accusing Gopnik of being morally unfit. Every possible problem seems to be hitting Gopnik at once.

After the Heisenberg lecture, Gopnik appears to be visited (in what turns out to be a dream) in the lecture hall by Ableman's ghost, who advises him not to rely so much on mathematics, which is, after all, merely "the art of the possible." "I don't think so," replies Gopnik, haltingly, thinking hard. "The art of the possible, that's . . . I can't remember. Something else." That even an educated man like Gopnik cannot identify Otto von Bismarck's famous definition of politics might be taken as a subtle suggestion on the part of the Coens that politics is not the answer to Gopnik's (or anyone's) problems, a suggestion that would certainly be in keeping with the attitude toward politics that the Coens display throughout their career. Alternatively, this moment could be taken as an indication that scientists are not necessarily well educated in the general sense but (like rabbis) are learned only in a narrow, specialized field.

In any case, "Ableman" advises Gopnik that there is a simple solution to his problems: "See Marshak," he says, referring to a local elderly rabbi of near-legendary wisdom. But, of course, Gopnik has been trying to see the elusive Rabbi Marshak (or to find some other source of rabbinical wisdom) throughout most of the film. When Gopnik first learns of Judith's demand for a divorce, he questions the fundamental meaning of the universe. "Everything," he declares, "that I thought was one way turns out to be another." The truth, in other words, has been found to be lies—but now he has no one to love. So he is advised to seek solace in the wisdom of the Jewish tradition; he thus goes to see Rabbi Nachtner (George Wyner), the senior rabbi at his local synagogue (the film employs the same B'nai Emet Synagogue that the Coens attended as boys). Nachtner, however, is unavailable, so Gopnik speaks instead to the young Rabbi Scott, who offers him nothing but platitudes on "perspective." Later, when Gopnik is finally able to see Nachtner, he gets nothing but a long and inconclusive story about a Jewish dentist who finds an ominous message engraved (in Hebrew) on the backs of the lower front teeth of a gentile. When Gopnik demands an explanation of what this story is supposed to mean in terms of his own predicament, Nachtner merely shrugs. In another of the film's bits of capsulized wisdom, he simply states (in his own version of the uncertainty principle), "We can't know everything."

Nachtner's story is accompanied throughout by Jimi Hendrix's antiwar song "Machine Gun" playing on the soundtrack, which furthers the film's project of interweaving contemporary rock culture with traditional Jewish wisdom. The inclusion of Hendrix (like Jefferson Airplane a key icon of the 1960s counterculture) also helps to establish the late-1960s setting of the film. The only problem is that "Machine Gun" was not recorded until 1970, making its inclusion anachronistic and providing a subtle reminder that, as one would expect by now of the Coens, *A Serious Man* is not set in a representation of the real Minnesota suburbs in which the brothers grew up but is instead set in an alternate-reality Minnesota composed of a loose collection of cultural memories, not all of them accurate.

One could, of course, argue that "Machine Gun" is not playing diegetically in the film, so that it need not have been recorded by 1967. Later, however, Gopnik is informed by the Columbia House Record Club, which hounds him for payment throughout the film, that his next regular selection will be *Cosmo's Factory*, which was an album by Creedence Clearwater Revival, the band so beloved by Jeff Lebowski. This album, however, was also released in 1970 and so could not have been a record club selection in the real world of 1967. Such "errors" occur far too often (and too strategically) in the work of the Coens to be unintentional but instead seem intended to remind us of the fictionality of the film we are watching.

Gopnik never does manage to get an audience with Marshak, who is too generally busy contemplating the universe to offer practical advice to individuals. As the capstone to his bar mitzvah ceremony, however, Danny is brought in for an audience with the distinguished wise man. At this meeting, Marshak returns Danny's transistor radio, which had been confiscated earlier in Hebrew school. Meanwhile, the doddering Marshak himself has apparently been listening to the radio because the only wisdom he has to impart involves quoting (or rather misquoting) the opening lines from "Somebody to Love": "When the truth is found to be lies / And all the hope within you dies . . . then what?" Perhaps the substitution of "hope" for "joy" shows the difference between Marshak's Jewish tradition and the Airplane's own worldview, or maybe the rabbi is trying to remember the song but fails. In any case, a bewildered and speechless Danny sits silently as the rabbi then attempts (not quite successfully) to name the members of Jefferson Airplane, something Danny himself could no doubt easily do. Marshak then tops off the meeting with the profound admonition that Danny should "be a good boy."

This interview represents a convergence of ancient Jewish wisdom with modern popular culture that is gestured toward in *The Big Lebowski* when Walter identifies Moses and Sandy Koufax as the two greatest figures in the Jewish tradition. But this convergence emerges fully formed only in *A Serious Man*, though even here it is not clear what we should make of this motif. One could take a positive tack and suggest that this convergence suggests both the ongoing relevance of ancient Jewish wisdom in our modern secular world and the presence of genuine insights into the meaning of life even in the most seemingly trendy works of popular culture. After all, when Grace Slick suggests that, amid the uncertainties of life, love might be our only true refuge, she offers wisdom that might have come from the Judeo-Christian tradition, even if she has replaced a love of God and of fellow humans with a suggestion that drug-fueled free sex might just be the cure for what ails us in the modern world.

More cynically, one could just as well see the convergence of ancient religious thought and modern secular thought in *A Serious Man* as suggesting that both are equally unable to provide us with genuinely useful guidance about how to live our daily lives.[10] Thus, while the events depicted in the film seem to bear out Job's famous Old Testament declaration that "man that is born of a woman is of few days, and full of trouble," it is not clear what we are supposed to do with this information. In any case, the indication that life is full of woe does little in either the film or the Bible to help us deal with those woes, other than providing company to misery by providing a "shit happens" reminder that trouble is universal.

Granted, such reminders are not totally without value, especially in helping us to deal with the small everyday problems that everyone encounters from time to time, though it is certainly the case that it is unusual to encounter as many of these problems as does Gopnik, whom many reviewers have seen as a modern figure of Job, while just as many have seen him as a modern figure of the *schlemiel* from Yiddish lore. The *schlemiel*, though, is usually the bungling source of his own troubles, while Job generally has trouble thrust upon him, making the identification of Gopnik with Job more accurate than identifying him as a *schlemiel*. Indeed, as Bergan notes, if one wishes to classify Gopnik according to Yiddish folk traditions, he is more of a *schlimazel*—one who encounters misfortunes through no fault of his own.[11]

Much of the film consists largely of a nonstop sequence of ordinary problems of the sort we all encounter, making him a sort of Everyman figure as well—though popular stereotypes about intellectuals would suggest that Gopnik would be unable to handle these ordinary problems well, being too immersed in the intellectual problems of his abstract work to engage effectively with the real world. One of the more amusing threads that runs through the film concerns the way Gopnik is being hounded by Columbia House, a club he has never joined. Gopnik suspects the music fan Danny of being the culprit, which seems logical, though we never learn the true source of this particular problem. Danny, meanwhile, is constantly hounding Gopnik to go up on the roof to adjust the family antenna to alleviate another common household problem of the 1960s: poor television reception.

In one of those trips to the roof, Gopnik spies the neighbor, Mrs. Samsky (Amy Landecker), sunbathing nude inside her privacy fence next door. His obvious interest seems to foreshadow suburban hanky-panky, no doubt leading to even more trouble. When Gopnik visits her later, offering to help out with any chores she might have around the house as part of his new project to "help others," the film seems on the verge of descending into a satire of suburban infidelity, especially as Mrs. Samsky, a walking stereotype of the jaded and lonely housewife (her husband "travels"), seems quite receptive. We also know that sexual adventures, in the films of the Coens, often lead to dire results, but, in this case, Gopnik manages to avoid an entanglement (beyond smoking pot together on the couch) with Mrs. Samsky. On the other hand, his failure to respond to her obvious attempt at seduction (she hints that she likes to take advantage of the "new freedoms") seems to owe less to the fact that he exercises good judgment (for once) and more to his own clumsiness and infelicity with such matters.

Music (with Carter Burwell as the film's music director) is probably less important in *A Serious Man* than in most Coen Brothers films, but the near-seduction scene between Gopnik and Mrs. Samsky involves some very dexterous (and funny) use of background music, in this case music from *Surrealistic Pillow*, which is playing in the Samsky household when Gopnik pays his visit. As Gopnik arrives, we hear "Today," the fourth track on *Surrealistic Pillow*, which means that Mrs. Samsky would have almost certainly been listening to "Somebody to Love" (the second track) just a few moments earlier. "Today" continues to play as Mrs. Samsky, taking the lead, positions Gopnik on the couch and makes her reference to the new freedoms. As she turns to take out a reefer, we hear the lyrics of the song announce, "Today, everything you want / I swear it will all come true," leading us to believe that a seduction scene is under way. The song then turns into a fervent declaration of love, but the scene descends into the mere friendly smoking of marijuana, which

The seductive neighbor Mrs. Samsky (Amy Landecker) hosts physics professor
Larry Gopnik (Michael Stuhlbarg) in *A Serious Man*. Focus Features / Photofest ©
Focus Features

clearly makes Gopnik a bit nervous at first, though he soon seems quite
mellow. As the album comes to an end, a clearly stoned Gopnik won-
ders whether all his problems might just be matters of perception after
all, just as Rabbi Scott suggested.

The film's musical thread continues soon afterward when Gopnik
has a (rather unerotic) erotic dream about having sex with a bored Mrs.
Samsky (who smokes a cigarette even during the sex act). "Somebody to
Love" predictably plays during the erotic portion of the dream sequence (and is presumably part of the dream itself), though Gopnik's
tryst with Mrs. Samsky is quickly interrupted by the appearance of the
now-deceased Ableman in the dream. "Nailing it down," says Ableman,
in a bit of double entendre, "so important." Then we see a coffin closing
and Gopnik jolts into consciousness.

Ultimately, Gopnik's encounter with Mrs. Samsky only serves to
further diminish his flagging sense of masculinity. His masculinity is
also threatened in a different way by his encounters with his next-door
neighbor on the other side, the gentile, gun-toting, deer-slaying neigh-

bor Mr. Brandt (Peter Breitmayer), who seems very much the type who might these days be a member of a right-wing militia. The hypermasculine über-goy Brandt clearly intimidates (and appalls) Gopnik in a general way, though Gopnik does not back down when Brandt initiates a dispute over their property line. Instead, he refers the matter to the law firm that is already handling his divorce case. And it appears that he might, for once, win a battle. Gopnik seems on the verge of getting good news when he is told that Sol Schlutz (Michael Lerner), a senior partner in his divorce attorney's firm, has discovered a nifty solution to Gopnik's property-line dispute with his neighbor. Sol is about the announce the solution when he drops dead of a heart attack on the spot. Neither we nor Gopnik ever learn what the solution had been.

However cursed Gopnik seems in the film, there is at least one character who has it even worse—his brother, Arthur. Arthur, much more of a *schlemiel* than his brother, has no family, no job, and no home—leading him to camp during the film on his brother's couch. To make matters worse, he is plagued with a sebaceous cyst that he spends much of his time draining. Much of the rest of his time is spent constructing an elaborate "Mentaculus," which he describes as a "probability map of the universe." A combination of mathematics and mystical doodling, this Mentaculus is meant to unlock the secrets of the universe and thus joins all of the other potential sources of wisdom in the film. However, while Arthur's project might seem the least legitimate of such sources, it seems to work to some extent, apparently providing Arthur with the insights he needs to win big in a local card game (ominously run by "Italians"). The game, however, is illegal, getting Arthur into some minor trouble with the police. This trouble then becomes more serious when he is eventually arrested on charges of solicitation and sodomy, leading him to feel that his life is collapsing around him and that Larry is the *fortunate* brother. As his troubles mount, Arthur, in his underwear, sits weeping by the side of the pool at the local motel (the "Jolly Roger," in another case of double entendre) where Larry took up residence after being booted out of the family home by Judith. Arthur then makes his own pronouncement on the meaning of life: "It's all shit!" he proclaims to his brother, who stands by at a loss for anything helpful to say.

But the troubles of others tend to become troubles for Larry Gopnik as well. Just as he had been expected to pay for Sy Ableman's funeral, so too is he nominated to pay Arthur's legal bills, which might be considerable. Then, in a flurry of events that ends the film, Gopnik is first given a hint by his department chair that his candidacy for tenure is likely to be successful. Then we get a quick cut back to Hebrew school, where Danny (having retrieved his transistor radio) is listening to another cut from *Surrealistic Pillow*—this time "3/5 of a Mile in 10 Seconds." Apparently some things never change (or perhaps he took his meeting with Marshak as an official endorsement of Jefferson Airplane). Then we are back to Gopnik's office, where Gopnik receives a bill for $3,000 for a retainer for top-notch criminal defense attorney Ronald Meshbesher[12] to defend Arthur. Realizing he's going to need the money, Gopnik decides to compromise his principles in favor of his dysfunctional brother's needs and reluctantly changes Clive's "F" to a "C-" so he can keep the bribe. Then, as if in retribution for this decision, Gopnik immediately gets a call from his doctor from the beginning of the film telling him that he needs to speak with him in person immediately because he has now spotted something on Gopnik's X-rays that he prefers not to discuss over the phone. Ominously, he has cleared his schedule to be able to speak with Gopnik. Outside, an apocalyptic-looking tornado approaches at this very moment; "Somebody to Love" again begins to play on the soundtrack; and the screen cuts to black, followed by the end credits, perhaps (in this case) end-of-the-world credits.

Midway through the credits, however, the music switches to a song we also heard earlier on the soundtrack, "Dem Milners Trern" ("The Miller's Tears"), a deeply sorrowful Yiddish lament about the sufferings of Jews driven into exile by the czarist pogroms conducted in early twentieth-century Russia. The end credits, then, perform one last juxtaposition of modern American pop culture with more traditional Jewish culture, though in this case the effect is to emphasize the contrast between the two as methods for dealing with the troubles of the world. American pop culture of the kind represented by "Somebody to Love" is designed to provide entertainment and enjoyment and to encourage its audience to seek pleasure wherever they can as a respite from life's troubles. Superficial and escapist, this sort of culture might provide some momentary relief but does little to deal with the underlying conditions that caused the troubles to begin with. The Jewish culture represented by "Dem Milners Trern," on the other hand, deals with misery head-on, as it were, somewhat along the lines of American blues music but with a more somber tone.

*A Serious Man*, incidentally, does not seem to favor one of these strategies over the other. Neither sex nor religion tends to bring much solace in the cinematic world of the Coens, and this film is no exception. Instead of real advice, all the film has to offer is platitudes such as "accept the mystery," "we can't know everything," and allied examples such as the Heisenberg uncertainty principle. The film itself, though, is oddly comforting, partly because Gopnik is likely to be worse off than any of us and partly because some of us might just take a bit of pleasure in the fact that an unusual little jewel of a film such as *A Serious Man* even exists in the first place.

# 7

# FROM SOGGY BOTTOM TO GREENWICH VILLAGE

American Music in *O Brother, Where Art Thou?* and *Inside Llewyn Davis*

**M**usic is a key ingredient in American film in general—though it is used more centrally and more effectively by the Coen Brothers than by most other filmmakers. Music is important in all of their films, though certainly more important in some than others. In *No Country for Old Men*, for example, the music is barely noticeable. In two of the brothers' films, though, music is particularly central, though for different reasons. In *O Brother, Where Art Thou?* (2000), music is the central tool used by the brothers to evoke the cultural context of the American South in the 1930s. *Inside Llewyn Davis* (2013), on the other hand, is literally about music, featuring an eponymous protagonist who is struggling to make a name for himself amid the burgeoning folk revival of the early 1960s.

## *O BROTHER, WHERE ART THOU?*: GOING HOME TO THE ROOTS OF AMERICAN MUSIC

By the time of *O Brother, Where Art Thou?*, the Coen Brothers' particular bag of tricks was well known to American film audiences and critics. After all, each of the previous seven films that had been written, directed, and produced by the brothers involved many of the same elements, even if each of the films was a unique piece of cinematic art with a character very much of its own. *O Brother*, in that sense, was simply a continuation of what the Coens had been doing all along. It had some of the zany comedy of *Raising Arizona*, a period setting like *Miller's Crossing*, and faux social commentary like *The Hudsucker Proxy*. It even featured several actors—such as John Turturro, John Goodman, Holly Hunter, and Charles Durning—who had already successfully collaborated with the Coens. In addition, one of the things audiences had come to expect from the Coens was a particularly effective and original use of music, with Carter Burwell producing impressive soundtracks for all of the first seven films, and *O Brother* doesn't disappoint. With this film, however, the brothers went in a different musical direction, employing T Bone Burnett to write the score and (perhaps more importantly) to compile a collection of traditional American music to serve as the soundtrack. The result was some of the most striking and memorable music in movie history. Burnett himself has described the music of the film thusly:

> We were tapping into a beautiful and powerful musical stream. What is often called Bluegrass may have been in the middle of this stream, but it's all part of a long history that includes everyone from Duke Ellington to Lefty Frizzell, from Billie Holiday to Elvis Presley, and maybe most of all, to Louis Armstrong. This stream we explored is the extraordinary music of the last century—an incredible treasure that comes to us directly from an age when music was made by everyone. It was analogue. It was made before the rise of the machines. [1]

Shockingly, *O Brother* received no Oscar nominations for its music, but the film's soundtrack has been widely credited with spurring renewed interest in vintage country, bluegrass, and roots music nationwide. For its own part, the soundtrack album became a runaway hit in 2001 and—with approximately eight million sales—has now likely grossed more than the film itself originally grossed at the box office. Among numerous other awards, the album ultimately won the Grammy Award for Album of the Year, as well as both the Country Music Association and the Academy of Country Music awards for Album of the Year, so the film's music certainly did not go unnoticed on the awards circuit, despite the Oscar snub.

One way in which *O Brother* resembles earlier Coen Brothers films is that it gets off to such a rich start, evoking a wide range of cultural contexts and predecessors within its first few minutes. *O Brother* begins with an on-screen epigraph taken from the beginning of Homer's *Odyssey*, in which the poet asks the Muse to help him tell the story of his protagonist, Odysseus:

> O Muse!
> Sing in me, and through me tell the story
> Of that man skilled in all ways of contending,
> A wanderer, harried for years on end . . .

We then shift from the world of classical Greek epic poetry to a scene from the Depression-era South, as we see a chain gang breaking rocks with picks and sledgehammers, recalling films such as Mervyn LeRoy's 1932 film *I Am a Fugitive from a Chain Gang*, which helped to call attention to the brutal conditions that often held sway in the Southern penal system of that era. The prisoners swing their heavy tools in unison, with the help of the rhythm supplied as they apparently sing a surprisingly well-done version of the traditional work song "Po Lazarus" to help them get through the day. The opening credits are then presented via a series of retro-looking title cards, reminiscent of the silent-film era, intercut with scenes of three prisoners escaping from the chain gang, running across a field accompanied by the music of Harry McClintock's original 1928 recording of "Big Rock Candy Mountain," which recounts a hobo's vision of a perfect, utopian world, a "land that's fair and bright," "where the box cars all are empty, and the sun shines every day." Perhaps more importantly, in this mythical land of plenty, "all the cops have wooden legs, and the bulldogs all have rubber teeth," thus relieving hoboes of some of the dangers they face daily in the real world. The change in the music thus perfectly reflects the sudden change in status of the three running men, as they go from prisoner to escapee. Meanwhile, the evocation of an alternate reality in "Big Rock Candy Mountain" provides a clue that, as always with the Coens, this film will take place in a reality that is different from our own. Or, as Nathan puts it, the film is set in "an imaginary South."[2]

Even those opening title cards contain layers of richness. For one thing, the clear reference to the silent-film era is overtly anachronistic, as the film is clearly set in the 1930s, perhaps providing a subtle hint that the 1930s of the film are not quite the same as the 1930s of our own history. Moreover, each of the title cards contains an icon in each of its four corners, inviting viewers to try to understand their meaning. In the first card (which contains the title of the film itself), the four icons include a human ear and a musical note, both of which perhaps suggest the unusual importance of music in the film we are about to see. The other two icons are a crossed hammer and wrench and a storm cloud with a lightning bolt coming out the bottom. These two images perhaps suggest the world of work and the turbulence of storms, two phenomena that would be absent in the world of "Big Rock Candy Mountain." The next card, which announces George Clooney, John Turturro, and Tim Blake Nelson as the film's top-billed stars, also perhaps references the song, with a key (perhaps to a jail cell) and a piece of cake in opposite corners, suggesting freedom and plenty. The other two diagonally opposed images on this card—a Christian cross and a

**The three protagonists of *O Brother, Where Art Thou?* bolt from the chain gang.**
**Buena Vista Pictures / Photofest © Buena Vista Pictures**

Star of David—are a bit more enigmatic, though they could be taken to link the paradise of the song with the heaven envisioned in Judeo-Christian theology. The rest of the main cast is then identified on a card that features a stack of books, a pair of sunglasses, a slice of pie, and an old-style gramophone as its corner icons. The books might (or might not) suggest the richly intertextual nature of *O Brother*, the pie again suggests the pleasures of the song's utopia, and the gramophone again suggests the importance of music in the film. The sunglasses are more problematic: perhaps they refer to the sunny weather on the Big Rock Candy Mountain, but perhaps they more ominously foreshadow the sinister (and satanic) sunglass-wearing prison guard who tracks the protagonists through the film. And so on, with some images requiring more unpacking than others and some even hard to identify. The next-to-last card informs us that the film is "based on 'The Odyssey' by Homer," linking back to the epigraph. After the last card, identifying Joel Coen as the film's director, we see one last sequence in which the three escapees, still chained together, attempt to board a moving train by climbing into a boxcar but fail miserably in a moment that recalls the cartoonish comedy of *Raising Arizona*. (Luckily, their violent fall from the train does them no damage, as in the tradition of Looney Tunes cartoons.) Had there ever been any doubt, considering that this is a Coen Brothers film, this scene announces the fact that *O Brother* is going to be a far different film than grim social-problem dramas of the 1930s such as *I Am a Fugitive from a Chain Gang*.

Of course, anyone who knows film history—and knows the typical fixations of the Coens—will have already discerned this last fact from title of *O Brother, Where Art Thou?*, which just happens to be the title of the Depression-era social-problem drama that director John L. Sullivan hopes to make in *Sullivan's Travels*, from which the brothers had already drawn considerable inspiration in their earlier films. Sullivan (after various travels, including by jumping boxcars and including imprisonment and work on a chain gang) ultimately decides the poor and downtrodden will be better served by films that make them laugh than by films that make them angry. The Coens, we have every right to expect at this point, will be making their film in the same comic spirit—and we won't be disappointed.

By now, we have been introduced to the three main characters of *O Brother*: Ulysses Everett McGill (Clooney), Pete Hogwallop (Turturro), and Delmar O'Donnell (Tim Blake Nelson). We have also learned that the film will have a rich variety of intertextual referents, ranging from ancient Greek poetry to modern American film; that it is a period comedy set in the Depression-era South; and that music will be crucial to the workings of the film, including the establishment of its period atmosphere. We have been presented with a series of symbols to decode in relation to the film. We have been teased with the possibility that this film might be a serious examination of important social problems from the historical past, then informed that it is instead going to be more of a slapstick comedy. All of this and we are five and a half minutes into the film.

If one begins to track down the allusions that have already been included in this brief sequence, one finds that they are surprisingly rich in significance. For example, one might expect (knowing the Coens) that the identification of *The Odyssey* as the basis of the film is spurious—and it surely is, in a literal sense, especially as the Coens claim never to have read Homer's masterpiece. On the other hand, numerous episodes in the film (and it is a *highly* episodic film, just as *The Odyssey* is highly episodic) can be linked directly to corresponding episodes of Homer's epic. For example, soon after the opening sequence described above, the three escapees hitch a ride on the railroad track on a handcar being pumped by an old, blind black man. The man, who says he has "no name," can nevertheless be linked directly to the blind seer Tiresias, who figures prominently in ancient Greek myth and literature, including the *Odyssey*. That the old man has Tiresias's powers of clairvoyance can be seen in the way he prophesies a future for his three passengers that is eventually realized in the course of the film.[3] In another episode, the three fugitives come upon a one-eyed Bible salesman, Big Dan Teague (John Goodman), who attacks them with extreme violence, thus playing the role of Polyphemus, the Cyclops who sets upon Odysseus and his men. Perhaps the most memorable Homeric moment in *O Brother* occurs when the three travelers are overcome by the haunting singing of three seductive young women who are washing clothes in a pond, thus recalling the Sirens episode of *The Odyssey*. Finally, the very plot of the film is highly reminiscent of *The Odyssey*, as McGill employs every trick at his command to try to get home to Ithaka, Mississippi, and his wife, Penny (Holly Hunter), before she marries someone else, though it is certainly the case that Penny seems considerably less devoted to her spouse than does Homer's Penelope.

Many aspects of McGill's character correspond to those of Odysseus, including the fact that Odysseus is a rather vain figure, just as McGill shows an almost epic concern with keeping his hair perfectly pomaded in place. Moreover, both Odysseus and McGill are fast-talkers who are not necessarily always honest. As Janice Siegel puts it, McGill "fancies himself a trickster and a wordsmith in the style of Odysseus." She does, however, question the validity of this comparison when she goes on to note that "far from having achieved the success of an Odysseus, Everett is just a run-of-the-mill con man, and not a very good one at that."[4] Indeed, the connection with *The Odyssey* in *O Brother* is extensive but ironic throughout.[5] Then again, McGill's first name is not Odysseus but Ulysses, the Romanized version of the name of Homer's hero, thus perhaps reminding us that the most famous work of modern culture to draw extensively upon Homer, James Joyce's *Ulysses* (1922), also employs the Roman version of the name. And Irish Everyman Leopold Bloom, the protagonist of Joyce's novel, is similarly an ironic reinscription of his epic predecessor. I myself have argued elsewhere that Joyce's use of Homer is primarily parodic and subversive, meant to undermine the authority of the epic past rather than as an appeal to it.[6] That McGill has an Irish name might suggest an additional connection to *Ulysses*. Of course, it is worth remembering that parodic renditions of the *Odyssey* are almost as old as the *Odyssey* itself. Thus, the Russian literary theorist Mikhail Bakhtin has noted that the figure of the "comic Odysseus" is a classic one in the parodic tradition.[7]

In some ways, then, *O Brother* has more in common with Joyce's masterpiece than with Homer's, the point being not that *O Brother* is actually based on *Ulysses*, rather than the *Odyssey*, but that—as is typically the case with the Coens—it is based on a wide variety of sources and participates in a number of genres and traditions from both literature and film. Again, however, music—particularly traditional Southern folk and bluegrass music—is what stands out as the cultural background most crucial to the texture of *O Brother*, something that can already be seen in the first few minutes of the film. The rendition of "Po Lazarus" used to open the film, for example, was initially recorded by ethnomusicologist Alan Lomax in 1959 at the Mississippi state prison, as part of a trip he made through the South making recordings of authentic Southern folk and blues music soon after he had returned from spending most of the 1950s in Europe to escape the anti-communist witch hunts that ravaged America during that time. This particular recording features inmate James Carter as the lead singer, backed by a group of his fellow prisoners. It therefore certainly seems to fulfill Lomax's quest for authenticity, as well as providing perfect musical accompaniment for the chain-gang sequence in *O Brother*.

"Po Lazarus" exists in various versions (and probably dates back to slave days), but it is roughly about a big black man who is unjustly hunted down and killed by a white sheriff. It is, in a sense, a tragic tale, which would seem to place it in stark contrast with the utopian "Big Rock Candy Mountain" that follows immediately after it. However, as a prison work song, "Po Lazarus" contains certain subversive energies. Not only does the song subtly portray Lazarus as a sort of folk hero (and the sheriff as a villain), but it also (in the tradition of the spirituals adopted by American slaves) becomes a source of strength to the prisoners who sing it, helping them to survive any and all hardships that are thrust upon them. Moreover, the very name of Lazarus suggests a potential resurrection, and some versions of the song make him an obvious figure of Christ, thus suggesting resurrection even more strongly.

"Big Rock Candy Mountain" also carries strong political intonations, both in its lyrics and in its background. McClintock claimed to have written the song in 1895, though it has roots that go back even further. It first became a hit when it topped *Billboard* magazine's country chart in 1939 but reached its maximum popularity in a bowdlerized version recorded by Burl Ives and marketed as a children's song in 1949. It has since come to be regarded as a classic of American children's music, despite its rough origins. Identified (as was Lomax) as a communist sympathizer in the 1950 pamphlet *Red Channels*, Ives cooperated with HUAC in 1952 and was thus able to continue his career as an entertainer, ultimately achieving mainstream success as both a singer and an actor. His cooperation with HUAC, however, led to a bitter feud with other leftist folk singers who had been blacklisted, including Pete Seeger, a performer who had also been listed in *Red Channels* and who himself recorded a version of "Big Rock Candy Mountain" in 1957. Both Ives and Seeger, meanwhile, were among the performers whose work was collected by Lomax over the course of his long career of collecting American folk music, dating back to the 1930s context of *O*

*Brother.* "Big Rock Candy Mountain" was among the songs included by Lomax in his collection *The Penguin Book of American Folk Songs* (1964); it also supplied the title for Lomax's 1955 ballad opera.

Thus, these first two songs not only already suggest to us the kind of music that will be so crucial to the overall impact of *O Brother* but also suggest the richness of the web of intertextual connections evoked by the film's music. Because of the Lomax involvement, the two songs have an extensive connection with each other, while both are also connected to the McCarthyite anti-communist crusades of the 1950s, linking them to important parts of the backgrounds of both *Barton Fink* and *Hail, Caesar!*, as well as American cultural history in general. By placing the action of *O Brother* in the 1930s, *before* the anti-communist witch hunts, and by never explicitly linking anything in the film to anti-communist repression, the Coens, as usual, avoid any overt engagement with serious political issues—recall that even *Barton Fink* and *Hail, Caesar!* omit any reference to the anti-communist campaigns that rocked Hollywood in the 1950s. Nevertheless, the ways in which the legacy of anti-communist repression in American history keeps cropping up in the margins of their films suggests that the Coens are very well aware of this legacy and that they regard it as an important element of the cultural background of their careers as filmmakers.

This initial chain-gang escape sets in motion the plot of the film, which is basically a trying-to-get-home story—the kind of story for which *The Odyssey* is the most important prototype in Western culture, but of which there are many other important examples as well, including many from American film. *It Happened One Night* (1934) is one such story, for example, and it is worth noting that Clooney as McGill comes off essentially as a cartoonish version of Clark Gable, the male lead of *It Happened One Night*. *Sullivan's Travels* itself is such a film, though perhaps the central example of a trying-to-get-home film from roughly the same time period as the action of *O Brother* would have to be *The Wizard of Oz* (1939), a film that Joel Coen has suggested was more fundamental as a model for the basic plot structure of the film than was *The Odyssey*.[8]

Then again, *O Brother* is a film in which the plot is largely beside the point. Instead, it is a film in which a collection of colorful characters and a series of striking scenes (almost all of which are built around music) provide a framework through which to present the cultural milieu of (an alternate-reality) 1930s Mississippi. Many of these scenes, in fact, have little or nothing to do with the actual plot of the film. For example, having barely escaped capture when ratted out to the authorities after they take refuge on the farm of one of Pete's relatives, Everett, Pete, and Delmar find themselves on the fringe of a strange scene in which a white-clad congregation of seemingly mesmerized devotees marches in formation to a nearby river, where a preacher waits to baptize them in the muddy water. As they walk, they appear to be singing the traditional gospel hymn "Down to the River to Pray," a song that was first published in 1867 but that was recorded especially for *O Brother* by contemporary bluegrass star Alison Krauss. The scene is one of several haunting, surreal moments that punctuate the film, as realism is thrown to the wind in the interest of creating a perfect fusion of music and theater. Both Pete and Delmar are caught up in the moment, rushing into the river to be "saved." For his part, the nonbelieving Everett merely scoffs at their foolishness. They then continue on their travels, which seem little affected by the supposed conversion of two of the three members of the group.

Nathan suggests that the entranced congregation can be related to the lotus eaters from *The Odyssey*, a race of people who live their lives in a drugged-out state thanks to a diet that consists mainly of narcotics. They threaten to seduce Odysseus's men into joining them, until the hero manages to usher his men back aboard their ship to get on with their journey.[9] Odysseus's men soon recover from the narcotics, just as Pete and Delmar ultimately seem little affected by their baptisms. In fact, about all these baptisms do in the film is set up the punch line for what is probably Everett's funniest line in the film. Soon after the baptism scene, the three stop to pick up a young, guitar-toting black man who is standing at a crossroads. The black man, Tommy Johnson (blues singer Chris Thomas King), quickly announces that he has just sold his soul to the devil in return for being given the ability to play the guitar "real good," thus recalling the famous legend that Mississippi blues legend Robert Johnson might have gained his talents in a similar fashion. Everett informs the new arrival that Pete and Delmar have just been baptized and saved, then delivers the punch line: "I guess I'm the only one that remains unaffiliated." It's a funny moment, but Everett's irreverence, combined with the later moment in the film in which Everett and Delmar are viciously set upon and robbed by a supposed Bible salesman, casts doubt on the efficacy of Christianity as a frame within which to deal with reality—or at least this *particular* reality. As Nathan puts it, Christianity is not treated particularly seriously in the film but is just part of the "mythical brew" involving the Homeric references.[10]

Everett, in fact, is a consistent skeptic who fancies himself a voice of reason and rationality and a strong proponent of scientific modernization who stands in stark opposition to the reactionary intransigence with which the South has so often been associated. In one late speech (he loves to speechify), he welcomes the coming of electrification and envisions it as the beginning of a new day:

> The South is gonna change. Everything's gonna be put on electricity and run on a payin' basis. Out with old spiritual mumbo-jumbo, the superstitious and the backward ways. We're gonna see a brave new world where they run everyone a wire and hook us all up to the grid. Yessir, a veritable age of reason like the one they had in France—and not a moment too soon.

Everett delivers the speech with his customary enthusiasm, but the particular wording tends to nullify his position, given that phrases such as "hook us all up to the grid" have clearly dystopian intonations, made more emphatic by the embedded reference to Aldous Huxley's dystopian classic *Brave New World*, which takes its title from a phrase uttered by a naif in Shakespeare's *The Tempest*, who believes wonderful things are afoot when in fact they are not.

Soon after picking up Johnson, the group gets an opportunity to snag some quick cash by recording a song for one Mr. Lund (Stephen Root), a blind radio-station owner who is looking for material to broadcast over his station. What follows is not particularly impressive in a visual sense, but it does involve some Hollywood magic, as the new quartet (calling themselves the "Soggy Bottom Boys") delivers an amazingly effective performance of "Man of Constant Sorrow" that is one of the musical highlights of the film—so much so that it is repeated in a slightly different form later. Everett turns out to be a brilliant vocalist, and the group—despite never having performed before and having had no rehearsal whatsoever—is perfectly in sync. It's a moment reminiscent of the Big Rock Candy Mountain, where everything always works out in an ideal manner. Of course, Everett's rousing lead vocals on the song were actually performed by Dan Tyminski, a member of Krauss's bluegrass band Union Station, backed by Nashville songwriter Harley Allen and Pat Enright of the Nashville Bluegrass Band. This trio of real singers won a Country Music Association Award for Single of the Year for their soundtrack recording of the song, as well as a Grammy Award for Best Country Collaboration with Vocals. For its own part, "Man of Constant Sorrow" is a version of a traditional folk song originally published in 1913 (under the title "Farewell Song") by Dick Burnett,[11] a partly blind fiddler from Kentucky, though its roots go back much earlier. Various versions of the song have been recorded by such luminaries as Bob Dylan and the Stanley Brothers, the latter's version (from the 1950s) being the most direct basis for the one in the film.

In any case, the initial performance of this song plunges us into a world of pure music, the plot of the film having been suspended for the performance of the song. Soon afterward, we experience another moment in which time is simply suspended in *O Brother* as the three main characters encounter the sirens. Enthralled by the voices and bodies of these seemingly supernatural women, Everett, Pete, and Delmar forget about their quest for material wealth and are seemingly transported into another world of pure sensuality and pure bliss. Or pure cinema, as I have suggested elsewhere, given that the scene involves such a perfect combination of the visual and auditory resources of film.[12] What is important for my argument here, though, is how central music is to this scene. Of course, the sirens were always about music, but the rendition in this scene of the song "Didn't Leave Nobody but the Baby" by a country/bluegrass supertrio composed of Krauss, Emmylou Harris, and Gillian Welch is almost as entrancing as Homer reported his original sirens to be. Meanwhile, that this song—updated with additional lyrics by Burnett and Welch—is based on the traditional Mississippi lullaby "Go to Sleep, You Little Baby," discovered and documented by (of course) Alan Lomax, only adds to the complex intertextual richness of *O Brother*.

The sirens scene serves as a sort of counterpoint to the earlier baptism scene, both involving musical moments of transcendence (and water). At first glance, the two scenes stand as diametrically opposed moments of sacred versus profane bliss, but a closer look shows that the relationship between the two scenes is far more complex. In point of fact, what the two scenes really reveal is the similarity between the

spiritual pleasures of religion (which can have a strong sensual component) and the sensual pleasures of sex (which can have a strong spiritual
component). The Coens, of course, are not attempting here to make
any profound statement about such matters, preferring simply to put
their emphasis on the music and on the fact that music itself can have
both spiritual and sensual impacts and that it is, in fact, the combination
of the two that gives music its special power.

This power is also central to the final mesmerizing moment of pure
cinema in *O Brother*, which occurs at the unlikely scene of a Ku Klux
Klan rally, which the three protagonists happen upon just as the Klansmen are preparing to lynch Tommy Johnson. First, however, the Con-
federate-flag-toting Klansmen execute an elaborately choreographed
musical production number that, among other things, makes them look
comically ridiculous—which is, of course, a delicate matter, given that
there is nothing funny about the real-world Klan, whose members
might also be ridiculous but which has a sinister and deadly past. However, the musical production number actually captures this doubleness
quite nicely as the silliness of the chanting and dancing Klansmen is
punctuated by a genuinely haunting rendition of the traditional Appala-
chian dirge "O Death," sung by their leader—an Imperial Wizard who
turns out to be none other than politician Homer Stokes (Wayne Duvall), a "reform" candidate for governor. This stunning vocal performance (actually delivered by bluegrass legend Ralph Stanley, who won
a Grammy Award for Best Male Country Vocal Performance for his
recording of the song for the film) adds an extra layer of richness to this
key moment in the film, which comes as close as anything in the Coens'
film to overt political commentary. For example, when Stokes exhorts
his charges to protect their white women "from Darkies, from Jews,
from Papists, and from all those smart-ass folks say we come descended
from monkeys," the implication—that racism, fundamentalist Christianity, and hostility to the theory of evolution go hand in hand as
manifestations of hatred and ignorance—is pretty clear.

This scene is rife with cultural resonances as well. For one thing, the
Klansmen feature Big Dan Teague among their number, and his status
as a figure of Homer's Cyclops is reinforced by the fact that his Klan
hood has only one eyehole. Meanwhile, the Klan itself has played an
important role in American film history via the central role played by
the Klan in D. W. Griffith's groundbreaking *The Birth of a Nation*

(1915), a film whose racial politics very much match those of Homer Stokes, making its status as a founding text of American cinema highly problematic. The central cinematic referent of this scene, however, is clearly *The Wizard of Oz*, which is echoed more clearly here than in any other scene of *O Brother*. In particular, the entire scene is an almost direct replication (at times almost shot for shot) of the scene in *The Wizard of Oz* in which the Winkie minions of the Wicked Witch of the West perform a synchronized musical routine very similar to that performed here by the Klansmen, while the Scarecrow, Tin Man, and Cowardly Lion approach, ultimately rescuing Dorothy (and killing the Witch), just as Everett, Pete, and Delmar here manage successfully to rescue Johnson (killing Teague in the process).

With the protagonists reunited with Johnson, the reconstituted Soggy Bottom Boys ultimately play a key role in taking down Homer Stokes as well. Within the world of *O Brother*, "Man of Constant Sorrow" becomes a runaway hit all over Mississippi. A live performance of the song sends Stokes into a racist tirade, but in this alternate-reality Mississippi town of Ithaka, such tirades are not favorably looked upon, leading the white townspeople to ride Stokes out of town on a rail. Meanwhile, Stokes's opponent in the upcoming gubernatorial election, incumbent Governor Menelaus "Pappy" O'Daniel (Charles Durning) makes the Soggy Bottom Boys a key part of his successful reelection campaign, promising to make them his "brain trust" in his next administration.[13] O'Daniel (who is also the magnate of a local flour empire) takes his given name from the Greek king who led the assault on Troy from which Odysseus is trying to get home in *The Odyssey*. But the governor also has a real-world source in the person of one W. Lee "Pappy" O'Daniel, a onetime singer, radio personality, and flour entrepreneur (as founder of the Hillbilly Flour Company) who was the governor of Texas from 1939 to 1941 and then served in the U.S. Senate until 1949.[14] The rotund, white-suited O'Daniel of *O Brother* comes off as a version of the stereotypical Southern demagogue (Huey P. Long comes to mind as a predecessor, as does the Longesque Willie Stark, from Robert Penn Warren's 1946 novel *All the King's Men*), except that, in this alternate reality, O'Daniel is ultimately a benevolent figure.

One last brush with death is averted by a deus ex machina flood (with the emphasis on the *machina*, given that the flood is caused not by nature but by a dam project of the kind that the federal-sponsored

Tennessee Valley Authority built in much of the South during the Depression, bringing about the electrification that McGill is so enthused
by). After that, it is clear that O'Daniel is headed for another term,
McGill is headed for a reunion with Penelope, and all is right with the
world—as should be the case in a comedy. "All's well that ends well,"
says McGill, as the film approaches its end. *O Brother*, though, is an
unconventional comedy in which happy endings can come in various
forms. For example, gangster George "Baby Face" Nelson (Michael
Badalucco), who makes a brief appearance in the film, seems quite
gleeful at his fate, which is to be hauled off for execution in the electric
chair (even though all executions in the real Mississippi were carried
out by hanging until 1940 and even though the real Nelson was killed in
a gun battle with FBI agents just outside Chicago in 1934). As with
everything else in the film, though, the ending is summed up in the
final music—the end credits roll to the sound of the Stanley Brothers'
version of the popular nineteenth-century gospel song "Angel Band."
The hymn suggests the approach of heaven, which seems apt for a
happy ending, but it also announces the coming of death (rather than
the expected marriage), which makes the ending a bit macabre. It's an
appropriately odd ending for the film we have just seen—though it is
also immediately corrected by a shift midway through the credits to the
upbeat "Keep on the Sunny Side" (a different version of which had also
appeared within the film itself), which perhaps provides a less troubling
ending.

## *INSIDE LLEWYN DAVIS:* INSIDE THE FOLK REVIVAL

Among other things, the various kinds of American roots music featured
in *O Brother* formed an important part of the background of the early-
1960s folk revival that would come to play such a crucial role in
American popular music in the coming decades. Perhaps it is appropriate, then, that the next Coen Brothers film to place music at its center
instead of in the background—*Inside Llewyn Davis*—would focus on
the folk revival. On the other hand, despite this direct musical link
between the two films, *O Brother, Where Art Thou?* and *Inside Llewyn
Davis* could not, in many ways, be more different. The first is flamboyant, over the top, rural, and avowedly comic; the second is muted,

understated, urban, and existentially serious—almost to the point of gloominess, though it does have its occasional moments of low-key comedy. Gone in the later film is the typical ensemble cast of Coen regulars (though John Goodman does make a notable appearance), replaced instead by rising star Oscar Isaac and top-line box-office stars such as Justin Timberlake and Carey Mulligan. Most of the music in *O Brother* is performed by stars, or even legends, in the field, drifting into the film almost as if from another reality; most of the songs in *Llewyn Davis* are performed by the actors themselves, live in front of the camera, though none of them (including Timberlake) has credentials as a folk singer. But the music is still the heart and soul of the film, and (if nothing else) the fact that the music of such different films could be so directly linked provides a reminder of just how varied such music can be.

Ian Nathan has made an interesting argument about why it was entirely appropriate for the Coens to make a film about folk music. Folk songs, he notes, tend to be reworked in each generation to meet the requirements of changing times. Meanwhile, the Coens do very much the same thing in their films, reworking "old films, books and whole genres."[15] Isaac plays the eponymous Davis, the son of a merchant seaman who has himself spent time at sea but is now trying to carve out a niche in the Greenwich Village folk scene in 1961. Davis (Isaac does his own singing in the role) is a sort of generic figure, though he is based most directly on Brooklyn-born folk singer Dave Van Ronk. However, the gregarious and expansive Van Ronk differs from Davis in that he was certainly more politically engaged and more centrally located as a leader among the many folk artists who congregated in and around Greenwich Village at the time. Indeed, the film is anything but a biopic, and the Coens (not surprisingly) do not strive in the film for documentary realism of this important time and place in American cultural history. Instead, they seek to capture the essence of the music and to explore some of the cultural energies that informed it, including the Bohemian lifestyles of the participants. Timberlake and Mulligan play Jim and Jean Berkey, a husband-and-wife folk singing duo who are among those on whose couches Davis crashes, having no abode of his own. Jean has also had a dalliance with Davis that she bitterly regrets, now finding herself pregnant with a child that might have been fathered by Davis— much to her displeasure, to say the least.

One of the most direct nods to *O Brother* in *Llewyn Davis* resides in the fact that the latter film features a ginger cat named "Ulysses" that becomes lost and has to make its way back home, in the mode of Homer's epic hero (or of the not-so-epic Ulysses Everett McGill). The role of the cat as a Ulysses figure is further emphasized when we see, within the film, a poster for the early-1960s film *The Incredible Journey*, about two dogs and a cat who must make their way through 250 miles of Canadian wilderness in order to get back to their home. The film poster not only reinforces the thematic role of the film's cat as a Ulysses/Odysseus figure but also adds to the period feel of the film, even though it is slightly anachronistic, given that the film was released in 1963, two years after the action of the film. The cat also plays an important role in the film, as Davis is humanized via his attempts (inept and unsuccessful though they may be) to get it back home safely, mitigating to some extent his portrayal in much of the film as a self-centered asshole. Finally, the cat even cleverly links *Llewyn Davis* to its sources in the Greenwich Village folk scene. After all, the cover of Van Ronk's 1964 album *Inside Dave Van Ronk* (the album that presumably gave *Inside Llewyn Davis* its title) shows the folk singer being shadowed by a cat. And, more famously, the cover of the 1965 album *Bringing It All Back Home* shows Bob Dylan holding a somewhat alarmed-looking cat as well.[16]

That the music of *Llewyn Davis* is directly connected with the music of *O Brother* is indicated in the former film in a number of ways—including the fact that T Bone Burnett helmed the music for both films. Perhaps the most direct indication of the complex connection between the music featured in the two films appears in a sequence that occurs in the beginning of the film but is not entirely elucidated until it is repeated in expanded form at the end. Here, an Arkansas folk singer by the name of Elizabeth Hobby (played by real-world Ozark folk singer Nancy Blake) makes an appearance in the Gaslight Club, the real-life Greenwich Village club that is featured prominently in the film and where Davis frequently performs as well. Hobby, playing an autoharp, performs a down-home version of the old-time country classic "The Storms Are on the Ocean." Hobby might have stepped straight out of *O Brother*, and she can be taken as a figure of authenticity in the film, as a performer who is still connected to the roots from which the folk revival has grown but away from which it has already begun to move. Davis is

**Llewyn Davis (Oscar Isaac) holds the cat Ulysses on the subway in *Inside Llewyn Davis*. CBS Films / Photofest © CBS Films**

in a foul mood from the never-ending stream of setbacks he has suffered throughout the rest of the film, and he is an angry man to begin with, though the anger is often repressed. In any case, something about Hobby's performance triggers a bout of viciousness; he heckles the woman mercilessly, though some of the bile is obvious self-directed. "I hate fuckin' folk music!" he yells. Davis then pays for his outburst the next night when Hobby's husband (played by Stephen Payne) calls him into the back alley behind the club and kicks the shit out of him, expressing his disgust at the New York city slickers and their corruption of his culture in their own cultural "cesspool."

This scene thus dramatizes both the connection and the conflict between the authentic blues-country-folk traditions (especially in the South) and the new, much more commercialized folk music that was beginning to emanate from New York, reaching a zenith of inauthenticity in the heavily produced pop-folk hits of the manufactured trio Peter, Paul, and Mary—who are obliquely referred to in *Llewyn Davis* when music producer Bud Grossman (F. Murray Abraham) suggests that Davis might join a trio he is putting together.[17] One of the models for Bud

Grossman is real-world manager/producer Albert Grossman, who put together the real-world version of Peter, Paul, and Mary in 1961 but who is best known as the manager who helped Bob Dylan rise to fame.[18] Dylan, of course, is a key figure here; as the greatest mainstream success to arise from the Greenwich Village folk scene, he is also the key figure in the commercialization of folk music that *Llewyn Davis* implicitly (though half-heartedly) critiques.

That Dylan plays such a role can be seen in the closing of the film. After Davis finishes his set at the Gaslight Club (after which he will go out behind the club to be beaten up by Mr. Hobby), we see, from a distance, the scrawny, scruffy figure who follows him on the stage. We can't see the figure well, but the voice we hear is unmistakably Dylan's, in an originally unreleased studio recording of the song "Farewell," which continues to play as the ending credits begin to roll.[19] The song is very much what its title implies, as the singer bids farewell to his lover as he prepares to set out on a journey for parts unknown. It's a perfect accompaniment to the end of the film, which leaves Davis's future very much in doubt. It's also the perfect follow-up to the two songs Davis has just played (both of which, incidentally, had been recorded back in the 1960s by Van Ronk). One of these is the traditional "Hang Me, Oh Hang Me," about a man about to be hanged who doesn't mind the hanging itself but just the idea of lying dead in his grave for so long afterward. In "Farewell," Dylan similarly declares that he doesn't mind the leaving itself, just the leaving behind of his loved one. Davis's other song, "Fare Thee Well" (aka "Dink's Song"), is even more directly linked with Dylan's, as the title perhaps indicates. Indeed, "Dink's Song" (first published in 1934 in a volume coedited by Alan Lomax) was itself recorded by Dylan shortly before he wrote and recorded "Farewell," suggesting a potential direct influence.

This sudden appearance by Dylan (the only "real" singer to figure in the film) further complicates the particularly complex relationship with reality that informs *Llewyn Davis* throughout. It complicates, in fact, the entire texture and meaning of the film. The simple interpretation would be that Dylan, about to become a big commercial star (and then soon to go electric, a move that some saw as a betrayal of his folk roots), represents the beginning of the end of the authentic folk revival that Davis and others have been pursuing in the film. Read this way, this last scene would seem to be a criticism of Dylan. But it is equally possible to see Dylan as a sort of alter ego of Davis throughout the film, making him a figure of the kind of success Davis might have had if he had only made a few better decisions and perhaps had a bit more integrity—and luck. One could even argue, in fact, that Davis is in many ways based more on Dylan than on Van Ronk and that the apparent link to Van Ronk is just another bit of Coen chicanery.[20]

In between the opening scene and the final scene (which are essentially the same scene), Davis stumbles through a gloomy winter landscape without an overcoat, a condition that pretty much sums up his existence. His former singing partner has committed suicide, and Davis's first solo album isn't selling. Davis's one shot at commercial success comes when he joins Jim Berkey and a singer who calls himself Al Cody (Adam Driver) to record a novelty song ("Please Mr. Kennedy") that promises to become a big hit—but Davis has to sign away his right to royalties in return for a quick payment of $200 to pay for Jean's abortion. This missed opportunity seems typical of his entire existence, in keeping with the mood of loss that permeates the film, whose colors are mostly blues and grays, so muted that the film often feels like it is in black and white. Almost everyone is in a bad mood, and no one has the energy and exuberance of a Ulysses Everett McGill.

In most ways, *Llewyn Davis* comes very close to a realistic depiction of the Greenwich Village folk scene of the early 1960s and, as such, seems less like it is set in an alternate reality than probably any other Coen Brothers film. Eileen Jones, however, has argued that the focus on characters (especially the title character) who are losers makes the film a sort of "alternate vision of America," given that it focuses on failure in an era when prosperity and success reigned supreme. For Jones, "The Coens have made a movie about failure in an era when, the standard pop-histories tell us, nobody really failed. They continue to look at the struggle of those on the margins, at failure among bungling strivers with grandiose dreams."[21]

Moreover, even this film has its peculiar moments when it seems to veer off into another reality. For example, "Please Mr. Kennedy" is so ridiculous that one is tempted to see it as an intrusion of Coenesque whimsy into the generally realistic texture of the film. Indeed, the song received a Golden Globe nomination for Best Original Song, with the Coens and Burnett listed as composers, along with Timberlake, Ed Rush, and George Cromarty. The problem is that Rush and Cromarty originally wrote and recorded (as "The Goldcoast Singers") a version of the song back in 1961, making it appropriate to the period setting of *Llewyn Davis*, though making it questionable for categorization as a song original to the movie. What is perhaps even more interesting, though, is that the original song was an appeal to the new President Kennedy not to draft the singers into the military, with the ramp-up of U.S. forces in Vietnam just beginning. In *Llewyn Davis*, however, the song has been completely retooled as a plea not to conscript the singers into the space program and launch them into outer space. The change makes the song considerably stranger (and funnier), considering that this sort of conscription would clearly never happen in the first place. The result is one of the few points at which *Llewyn Davis* genuinely feels that it is taking place in an alternate reality. For one thing, the original "Please Mr. Kennedy" was not a huge hit: it is only within the alternate reality of the film that the song's commercial success seems assured. More importantly, in this reality, Vietnam and other political issues do not even seem to exist, and the whole (extremely important) political dimension of the folk revival has been elided completely. The folk singers of the film do not seem all that devoted even to folk sing- ing—at one point Llewyn tries (but fails, of course) to return to the sea, and all Jean really seems to want is to settle down in suburbia and raise kids with Jim. But they are *definitely* not devoted to employing their music in the interest of causes like peace and social justice, just as the Coens similarly do not see the furthering of such causes as the purpose of their art, wherever their personal sympathies might lie.

Another moment when the realism of *Llewyn Davis* seems to flicker involves the two-day road trip to Chicago that Davis takes in the middle of the film, hitching a ride there in return for sharing the driving and the cost of gas. Though this trip is based partly on a real trip once undertaken by Van Ronk, Llewyn's companions on the trip—the strange and surly jazz man Roland Turner (Goodman) and Turner's "valet," one "Johnny Five" (Garrett Hedlund)—give the trip a sort of surreal quality. Turner and Johnny Five are like mythological figures who have stepped into the film from another reality—and from differ- ent cultural universes. The massive Turner is a literally larger-than-life figure who makes quite clear his contempt for folk music as an art form, clearly feeling that jazz is far superior. However, that he also apparently dabbles in the "black arts" and seems blanked out on heroin much of the time calls the reliability of his critical judgments into question. For his part, Johnny Five looks and talks like a refugee from the Beat poetry scene. He even reads aloud from the work of Beat poet Peter Orlovsky, a longtime lover and associate of Allen Ginsberg, the most famous of all the Beats.[22] Meanwhile, in a bit of clever casting, the Coens found an actor who could give Johnny Five the Beat look by casting Hedlund, who just the year before had starred as Dean Moriarty (a fictionalized version of Beat writer Neal Cassady) in the film adaptation of Jack Kerouac's classic 1957 Beat novel *On the Road*.

The mythological resonance of this trip is enhanced by the fact that Davis travels to Chicago in order to try to convince Grossman to represent him, his current management not exactly breaking down doors to further Davis's career. Grossman manages a club called the "Gate of Horn," which did, in fact, exist in Chicago between 1956 and 1971—and which had been managed by Albert Grossman in its earliest years. Davis gets nowhere when he meets with Grossman inside the club, but the club itself adds a mythological touch because its name comes from Greek mythology, in which the gates of horn and ivory are associated with true and false dreams, respectively. The name of the club thus suggests that performing there might help aspiring acts to fulfill their dreams as entertainers. Importantly, though, the best-known reference to these gates occurs in *The Odyssey*, linking *Llewyn Davis* to Homer (and to *O Brother*).

When we last see Johnny Five, he is being carted roughly away by the police,[23] while Turner is abandoned by Davis, unconscious in the back of the car, along with a stray cat that Davis had earlier picked up, mistakenly thinking it was Ulysses. Thus, while Davis does not exactly come off well for abandoning a stray animal and an unconscious man (it is possible that he later runs over and kills the cat, though that scene is left ambiguous), neither Beat poetry nor jazz comes off particularly well as a rival to folk music as a contender for the title of most authentic American cultural form. To make Turner and Johnny Five even less authentic, the former is actually based on bluesman "Doc" Pomus rather than any jazzman, while Johnny Five is not really a poet but just an unsuccessful actor who reads other people's poetry rather than writing his own. The poetry, incidentally, sounds silly, as if the author thought he could reach some deep and shocking truths simply by using words like "fuck" and "asshole" in his poems.

Davis also meets denizens of other cultural worlds, including the academics who hang out in the apartment of the Gorfeins, Davis's couch-holders of last resort and the owners of the cat Ulysses. Almost stereotypically, these academics seem effete, pretentious, and disengaged from reality, including one who is a musician and scholar of "early" music.[24] They certainly seem no more authentic than Davis and his folkie colleagues or than Turner and Johnny Five. *Llewyn Davis* is, in fact, gently critical of the whole notion of authenticity, suspicious that the quest for authenticity that has driven so much American cultural production is simply a pretense, simply a *style*.

One useful explanatory referent here is again *Sullivan's Travels*, in which (among other things) filmmaker John L. Sullivan feels that the serious social-problem drama he hopes to make will be more authentic than the formulaic comedies on which he has hitherto built his career. In the end, however, Sullivan concludes that his comedies provide precisely the sort of artificial release from reality that his audiences need and desire. *Llewyn Davis* differs from all previous Coen Brothers films (with the possible exception of *A Serious Man*) in the extent to which it seems ambivalent about endorsing Sullivan's conclusion.[25] Despite its grimly humorous moments, *Llewyn Davis* is a serious film, indeed, one that has been compared, for example, to the work of Kafka in its exploration of the absurdities of the human condition.[26] Jonathan Romney captures the film's seriousness when he calls *Llewyn Davis* "a bleak but tender story with the direct, timeless honesty of a folk ballad," ultimately "the most moving film the Coens have ever made, the compassion leavened by calm detachment and by the cruel irony directed at its hero."[27]

*Llewyn Davis* is not, however, *too* serious, and it makes no claims with regard to its own authenticity as a document of an important moment in American cultural history. The oddly dispassionate tone of the film (and its protagonist) is one sign of this lack of any such claim. Some of the film's potentially most emotionally intense scenes come off, in fact, as darkly comic. Jean's confrontation with Davis about her pregnancy might, for example, have been an emotionally powerful moment, but the strange mismatch in the scene between Jean's overwrought emotion and Davis's almost complete *lack* of emotion defuses the intensity and makes one simply start to wonder how many times she can call him an "asshole" in one scene. Similarly, potentially poignant scenes such as Davis's visit with his father in a rest home are muted by the fact that they seem to have little emotional impact on Davis himself. We've seen Davis's odd emotional emptiness before in the Coens' work—in characters such as Ed Crane. A more telling referent, however, is probably Barton Fink because Fink's emptiness is both personal and political. Leftist screenwriters and socially committed folk singers are among the central figures of the political artist in American cultural history. Through their portrayal of the falsely political Fink and the apolitical Davis, the Coens make clear their belief, however problematic, that the true role of art is not to help us take arms against a sea of troubles, but simply to help us bear the slings and arrows of outrageous fortune.

# 8

# INTO THE SUNSET

Variations on the Western in *No Country for Old Men*
and *True Grit*

**G**iven their fascination with other key genres of Hollywood's "Golden Age"—including film noir and screwball comedy—it should come as no surprise that the Coens would eventually take on the genre of the Western. After all, if the Coens' project can be described as the creation in film of a sort of alternate-reality version of America, one might also describe the Western in the same way. No other film genre is so centrally concerned with constructing (or later deconstructing) a mythic version of America as is the Western. And the Coens had already indicated their interest in this genre several times in their early films. Elements of *Blood Simple* and *Raising Arizona* evoke the Western, for example, if only because of their Southwestern settings. And this interest in the Western is suggested quite strikingly when the Stranger of *The Big Lebowski* wanders into that film looking (and sounding) as if he might have just stepped off the set of a Western. In *No Country for Old Men* (2007) and *True Grit* (2010), however, the Western genre moves to center stage, though it is typical of the Coens that both films address the general mythic framework of the Western genre rather than the specific *movie* genre of the Western. Indeed, even though *True Grit* is, in a sense, a remake of a classic Western film, both it and *No Country for Old Men* are really direct adaptations of Western *novels* rather than re-creations of Western movies.

## NO COUNTRY FOR OLD MEN:
## APOCALYPSE IN SOUTH TEXAS

Between 2001 and 2007, Joel and Ethan Coen made only two feature-length films, *Intolerable Cruelty* (2003) and *The Ladykillers* (2004). Moreover, these two films have both been rated by many critics as among the worst and least inventive films of the Coens' entire career. In 2007, meanwhile, the brothers released *No Country for Old Men*, which some might also have expected to continue their streak of diminished creativity. After all, though many of their earlier films had been influenced in important ways by novels, *No Country for Old Men* was the first film made by the Coens that was literally an adaptation of a novel, in this case the 2005 novel of the same title by Cormac McCarthy. And the adaptation is rather faithful—certainly more faithful than one might expect of artists with the creative chops of the Coens. But the adaptation is also highly creative, and the film is the only one by the Coens to date that has won the Oscar for the year's Best Picture. It also won Oscars for the brothers for Best Director and Best Adapted Screenplay (as well as a Best Supporting Actor Oscar for Javier Bardem) and was nominated for four other Oscars, making it arguably the high point in the Coens' career, at least in terms of mainstream success. In terms of its overall tone, it is also perhaps the single Coen Brothers film that seems most unlike all the others, though the Coens were certainly never known for producing cookie-cutter films from a set formula. A careful dusting, however, shows that *No Country for Old Men* displays far more of the brothers' fingerprints than might be immediately obvious.

The film, like the novel, is set in 1980, which adds a certain irony to the fact that both versions of the story (though perhaps more the novel) are informed by an apocalyptic, end-of-the-world feel. After all, the novel and the film appeared essentially a generation after the time in which the story is set, yet the world goes on. The film follows the plot of the novel quite closely, even incorporating much of its dialogue directly. And both works are generically similar, in that both are clearly updates of the Western (and somewhat cynical updates that call into question many of the mythic implications of the genre in its classical form).[1] In particular, if the classical Western captures a sense of the United States as a young nation, expanding westward with great days ahead, both versions of *No Country for Old Men* depict a United States and a West that are old and tired, with little hope for the future.

The overall plots of the novel and the film are quite similar, beginning with a drug deal that goes wrong in the Southwest Texas desert, leading local welder (and Vietnam veteran) Llewelyn Moss (played by Josh Brolin in the film) to discover a large stash (over $2 million) of abandoned cash. Most of the plot of the film involves the attempts of various parties involved in the original transaction to recover the cash from Moss—and Moss's attempts both to keep the cash and to stay alive. It is never made completely clear exactly who these parties might be, though one group seems to be associated with a Mexican drug cartel,[2] while another seems associated with forces within the corporate world of the United States, identified in the novel (but not in the film) as the "Matacumbe Petroleum Group," suggesting a level of corruption and ruthlessness with which the oil industry has often been associated (and making an anti-capitalist point in the novel that is far more specific than anything in the film). The principal danger to Moss through most of the story, however, is menacing hit man Anton Chigurh (played by Bardem in the film), who seems aligned with some sort of shadowy third force that is never identified.

Most of the action involves Moss's attempts to evade the forces that pursue him, while local sheriff Ed Tom Bell (played by Tommy Lee Jones in the film) does everything he can (which is basically nothing) to protect Moss and his young wife, Carla Jean (played by Kelly Macdonald in the film). Along the way, the forces of corporate America employ an ex–Special Forces colonel, Carson Wells (Woody Harrelson), to kill Chigurh, but the almost unstoppable Chigurh kills Wells instead. Numerous other bodies litter the landscape of the book and the film as well, ultimately including that of Moss, as well as a number of Mexican hit men. In the novel, Chigurh kills Carla Jean as well, while the film leaves her fate unclear, thus providing one of the moments in which the Coens tweaked the novel to make it a bit less bleak—or at least a bit more ambiguously bleak. After Chigurh confronts Carla Jean in her mother's home (just after her mother's funeral), the film suddenly cuts to him leaving the home. He does check his boots, possibly for signs of blood (he has avoided the blood of his victims throughout the film), but there is no other evidence of what might have happened. However, two boys riding by on bikes do not appear to have heard a gunshot, whereas Chigurh shoots Carla Jean in the novel.

Both the novel and the film of *No Country for Old Man* contain all the trappings of a classic Western, including the South Texas setting and a story that is replete with desert landscapes, firearms, cowboy hats, cowboy boots, lawmen, and outlaws. There are even a few horses, though the modes of transportation are generally more modern and mechanized, while the weaponry used is also considerably more advanced than that seen in typical Westerns. The film makes particularly good use of Texas accents as well—especially in the case of Texas native Jones's portrayal of Bell. The regional accents here, however, seem authentic and mostly lack the comic intonations of those in a film such as *Fargo*.

Of course, it was no surprise by 2005 for McCarthy's writing to participate in the Western genre, as he had written several Westerns by this point. His Westerns, however, might really be seen as anti-Westerns that call attention to shortcomings in the genre, as when the shocking violence of his masterpiece, *Blood Meridian* (1985), reveals the violent tendencies that underlie both the genre and American history itself. One thinks here of Richard Slotkin's *Gunfighter Nation*, a scholarly study of the Western film that treats the genre as a cultural representation of the violent tendencies in American society as a whole. Slotkin argues that the Western is indicative of the way in which the American national identity is built on the notion of expansion into the frontier through violent (but triumphant) conflict with "savage" foes. In the world of McCarthy's Western fiction, however, the expansion and the triumphs are all behind us, and we are left to contemplate the notion that we Americans are ourselves the only savages left.

The modes of violence pursued in the classical Western are clearly coded as masculine, and one key aspect of the Western as a genre is its exploration of masculinity and masculine modes (and codes) of conduct. Stacey Peebles thus argues that the conventional Western is the perfect genre for displays of masculine power; however, she also argues that *No Country for Old Men* undercuts the traditionally masculine solutions that are typical of the Western. "When we talk about Westerns," she says, "we talk about the representation of masculinity and the assignation of power."[3] But *No Country*, for Peebles, defies the conventions of the Western, revealing "a particularly masculine dread—that you can't always keep things in front of you and under your control. Things won't hold still, waiting for the assertion of mastery."[4] It is certainly the case that numerous characters are virtual paragons of masculinity, from the traditional cowboy sheriff Bell, to the swaggering ex-Special Forces operative Wells, to the working-class ex-soldier Moss. Yet Chigurh, who seems a virtually sexless (and even inhuman) figure, trumps them all and is able to deploy violence more effectively than any of them. Bell is never able to catch up with Chigurh; the ultra-cocky Wells is dispensed with by Chigurh with laughable ease; and the manly Moss is reduced to running for his life, at one point wandering the streets of Mexico and then South Texas in a comically un-masculine hospital gown—made all the more ridiculous and unmanly by the fact that he is also wearing Larry Mahan cowboy boots in the film, a touch that is absent from the same scenario in the novel. In the worlds of both the novel and the film, the kinds of masculine conduct that tamed the West no longer serve as viable solutions to the problems of a society that is winding down rather than just coming into its own.

This concern with interrogating conventional codes of masculinity makes the story a perfect one for the Coens, who so often perform similar interrogations in their films. The apocalyptic tone is also suited to the Coens, despite the typical comic intonation of their films. Apocalyptic notes have arisen in their films from time to time at least since *Barton Fink*—and it is notable that *A Serious Man*, released only two years after *No Country for Old Men*, also ends on a strongly apocalyptic note, even if it is one with a dash of humor added in. An apocalyptic tone is also typical of the fiction of McCarthy, whose work in general resembles that of the Coens far more than a superficial examination would suggest. Nor should it be surprising that, for his next novel after *No Country*, *The Road* (2006), McCarthy would depart from the Western genre and shift to an all-out postapocalyptic narrative in which the American civilization that seems in such a crisis in much of McCarthy's earlier fiction has finally been destroyed altogether. Of course, the conventional Western and postapocalyptic fiction have much in common, in that both typically feature individuals who are trying to make their way in a world without the conventional protections (but also without the conventional restraints) offered by modern civilization. In the Western, though, that civilization lies in the future, supplying a potentially utopian dimension of hope, while the postapocalyptic narrative is much darker, with civilization lying in the past and frequently seeming unlikely to resurrect itself.

Both the novel and the film of No Country for Old Men partake of a number of genres, in addition to the Western and apocalyptic fiction. Importantly, Slotkin notes that the Western film declined in importance as a mythic exploration of the American national identity in the 1970s, to be largely supplanted by other genres, including the crime film and horror films, especially slasher films.[5] From this point of view, it is worth noting that the 1980 setting of No Country for Old Men places it at a time in which the decline of the Western was quite advanced. But it might be even more significant, in terms of Slotkin's argument, that both the novel and the film versions of No Country for Old Men strongly supplement their basic Western matrix with elements from both the crime drama and the slasher narrative.

Chigurh is in many ways the story's most striking figure, especially in the film. The film's key "criminal" figure, he reverses the usual terms of both the Western and crime fiction by being the hunter rather than the hunted. At times, he seems like judge, jury, and executioner, and at other times he seems almost like an agent of the Old Testament God, wreaking vengeance on those whom he feels have violated a code of conduct. Yet he is also a ruthless killer who seems to enjoy killing just for the sake of it. He also apparently enjoys toying with his victims, though his habit of having them call a coin toss to determine whether they live or die also has philosophical implications: he seems to like the idea that whether innocent people live or die can be determined by a coin toss—as if it verifies his vision of the capriciousness of the world. He does seem to behave according to a certain code and a certain logic, but it is almost impossible for ordinary humans to decipher just what they might be. He is the kind of man that one might associate with apocalyptic times. Large and menacing, Chigurh moves beyond the bounds of normal hit man territory in almost every way. For example, his favorite weapon of death is a compressed-gas-driven bolt pistol of a kind used to slaughter livestock. The weapon is not really a practical one—it requires that Chigurh get close enough to his victims to place the barrel of the pistol against their foreheads, and it also requires him to carry around a heavy cylinder of compressed gas wherever he wants to use it. But it is certainly a colorful and gruesome weapon, if only because of the association with slaughterhouses. He literally slaughters his victims, helping to give his character an almost comic-book quality, though what the large, frightening, shambling, and virtually indestructible Chigurh resembles most is probably Michael Myers, Jason Voorhees, and other slasher-film villains.

In the film, Bardem's Oscar-winning performance imparts a sense of almost supernatural menace to the character of Chigurh, which makes him seem even more like a slasher-film serial killer while also enhancing the apocalyptic tone of the film. The book, on the other hand, relies more on Sheriff Bell's clear sense that things are coming to an unpleasant end to achieve its apocalyptic tone. Seemingly a character from an earlier age (and an earlier genre), Bell is the virtual embodiment of the sense in both novel and film that the world itself has become old and tired. Bell (in both versions of the story) feels that the world has developed in strange new directions that have largely passed him by. He feels, he says, "overmatched" by the world of 1980, which includes people such as Chigurh who are beyond Bell's understanding. The events of the story then confirm this feeling, to the point that Bell retires from law enforcement by the end of both the novel and film, preferring to spend his time sitting idly out of the path of the inexorable march of time toward a seemingly apocalyptic future. Bell, though, is a slightly darker figure in the novel, in which he has spent most of his life trying to make amends for an incident during World War II when he abandoned his unit and then accepted an inappropriate Bronze Star for his actions. He is thus dogged by shadows of guilt that are not mentioned in the film, pointing toward the fact that, whenever the film differs from the novel, it is generally to remove some of the darkness and to take a somewhat lighter tone.[6] Bell also dominates the novel to a far greater extent than he does the film, giving the novel a sort of moral center and leaving the less-centered film an occasional chance for Coenesque unruliness.

Peter Bradshaw, writing for the *Guardian*, saw *No Country for Old Men* as a sort of corrective to the "quirky excesses" that, for him, sometimes undermine the Coens' work. Nevertheless, he felt that he could detect a typical Coenesque style in the film, noting that "the savoury, serio-comic tang of the Coens' film-making style is recognisably present, as is their predilection for the weirdness of hotels and motels." But, he added, in the case of this film, such Coenesque touches have been supplemented by "a real sense of seriousness, a sense that their offbeat Americana and gruesome and surreal comic contortions can really be more than the sum of their parts."[7] Other critics were equally enthusiastic. The Coens' old naysayer Roger Ebert, by this time fully won over by the brothers, proclaimed the film a "miracle" on the order of *Fargo*.[8]

In fact, *No Country for Old Men* has much in common with *Fargo*, even if it is presented with an altogether darker tone. Even the film of *No Country*, though, has its moments of dark comedy—a type of moment that is missing in the novel altogether. Perhaps the film's funniest line is delivered by Carla Jean, whose exaggerated Texas accent (as delivered by the marvelous Scottish actress Macdonald) comes as close as any in the film to sounding inherently comic. As Llewelyn puts Carla Jean on a bus for Odessa and her mother's home, where she will presumably be safely out of the line of fire, the seemingly naïve young woman (she is only nineteen in the novel, though her age is not specified in the film) complains to her husband that her mother will "cuss you up and down." "You should be used to that," he replies, suggesting a problematic relationship with his mother-in-law. "I'm used to lots of things," she says sardonically. "I work at Walmart." This line and the comic attitude it implies are not found in the book, though the novel does specify that she works at "Wal-Mart," using the designation for the retail chain that was current in 1980.

Walmart, often criticized for ill treatment of its workers, is perhaps an easy target here, and it is typical of the work of the Coens that this potentially anti-capitalist jab is delivered as a joke rather than as a serious expression of outrage at corporate malfeasance. One might compare here a line in the director's cut of the Joss Whedon–scripted *Alien: Resurrection* (1997), in which we are informed that the predatory Weyland-Yutani Corporation, a principal villain of the earlier *Alien* films, has now succumbed to a hostile takeover by the presumably even more predatory Walmart.[9] In neither of the films do we learn anything new about Walmart, while in both films the satirical treatment of the retail giant is performed with a light enough touch that one could even imagine Walmart executives being amused.

Later, we are treated to another comic scene as Carla Jean and her mother (played by Beth Grant) ride in a cab as they head for the bus station so they can travel to El Paso to join up with Moss and the money. The mother makes it clear, in a Texas accent even more outrageous than her daughter's, that she *really* hates Moss. "No" and "good," she tells her unreceptive daughter, have, when used in combination, always been the only words she could think of to describe Moss and Carla Jean's future with him. And now here she is, suffering from cancer in 90-degree heat and heading for El Paso, where she knows no one—all because of her feckless son-in-law, whose troubles, she seems to feel, were gotten into just to cause more miseries for her. And she isn't even aware of the fact that their cab is being closely tailed by a carload of Mexican gangsters. She then tops off her contribution to the film when she encounters one of the gangsters, well dressed, at the bus station, finding herself unable to resist commenting, "It's not often you see a Mexican in a suit."

There are also other self-conscious hints that we are, in fact, in another of the Coens' alternate realities (and not in the real Southwest Texas or even in the fictional Southwest Texas of McCarthy's novel). As Joel Coen put it in an interview, the brothers were trying to produce a version of Texas that was like "something preserved in legend, a collection of histories and myths."[10] For Coen fans, the casting of Coens regular Stephen Root as the unnamed corrupt businessman who hires Wells cannot help but raise a flag. Root is perfectly fine in the role and only seems slightly off-key, but the fact that we have seen him in so many odd roles in Coen films before increases the sense that he somehow does not belong in the dark and dangerous world depicted in McCarthy's novel—and in the bulk of the Coens' film. Granted, he ends the film gurgling to death on the floor after Chigurh shotguns him in the throat, but the scene is almost darkly comic—partly because of the casting and partly because of the aftermath, in which a timid accountant claims to be "nobody" and hopes that Chigurh won't shoot him as well. (We never learn whether he does, though the film hints that he does not.)

Perhaps the most important self-referential nod in the film is one that might go entirely unnoticed. It occurs when a wounded Chigurh sets off an explosion outside a South Texas pharmacy as a distraction so that he can go inside and make off with drugs and supplies to tend his injuries. This same scene occurs in the novel, where the pharmacy is simply called "the drugstore on Main."[11] For many viewers it will mean nothing that, in the film, the drugstore is called "Mike Zoss Pharmacy." After all, it makes perfect sense in the visual medium of film that the pharmacy would have a sign on front displaying its name, something that is unnecessary in the novel. However, some viewers will no doubt be aware of the fact that the Coens' own film production company is called "Mike Zoss Productions," which in a sense means that this pharmacy is actually called "the drugstore in a Coen Brothers film." In addition, the name of the production company comes from Mike Zoss Drugs, the St. Louis Park, Minnesota, pharmacy (which was founded in 1951 and closed only in 2009) at whose soda fountain the brothers used to hang out as kids. By dropping a bit of Minnesota terrain square onto Main Street in a Texas town, the Coens are signaling that this Texas town is a movie fiction created by them partly from their own experience and not just from McCarthy's novel or the real Texas.

Perhaps the most remarkable thing about *No Country for Old Men* is that it still functions so well as a darkly apocalyptic Western/crime/horror drama despite such touches of Coenesque whimsy. No doubt this effect might be at least partly attributed to the fact that the Western is a larger-than-life genre to begin with, so that it can accommodate a considerable amount of generic play, while still remaining legitimately within the bounds of the genre. It is perhaps for this reason that the Coens' other major entry in the genre, *True Grit*, also seems like such a

The ominous Anton Chigurh (Javier Bardem) stands in front of Mike Zoss Pharmacy in *No Country for Old Men*. Miramax Films / Photofest © Miramax Films

legitimate Western, despite the fact that it breaks many rules of the genre and despite the fact that it seems so natural, knowing the Coens, to expect *True Grit* to be an *anti*-Western—and especially to be a sort of subversive rejoinder to its illustrious predecessor, the 1969 version of the same story that won John Wayne his only Academy Award.

## *TRUE GRIT*: NEW TAKES ON THE OLD WEST

The Coens' 2010 version of *True Grit* won no Academy Awards, though it was nominated for a total of ten, including Best Picture and most of the other major awards, while the 1969 film was nominated only for Best Actor and Best Original Song (the latter of which it did not win). The Coens' film, meanwhile, was avowedly based directly on Charles Portis's 1968 novel, bypassing the 1969 film altogether, though it is impossible to ignore the existence of the 1969 film when assessing the 2010 version. Indeed, comparing the Coens' adaptation of the novel with the earlier Wayne vehicle is one of the best ways to appreciate the achievement of the 2010 film. This comparison shows that the Coens' version of *True Grit* is both more faithful to the original novel and more creative in its deviations from the novel than is the 1969 film. At the same time, the Coens' film seems both more realistic and more inventively cinematic than the 1969 version. Such combinations might seem paradoxical, but they actually highlight some of the key aspects of the Coens as the creators of an alternate-reality America, both in this film and throughout their joint career.

Many critics, for example, have characterized the Coens' version of *True Grit* as their most authentic genre film and the one that involves the least in the way of postmodern play and genre subversion. In point of fact, there is a great deal of play with genre conventions in *True Grit*, but it is performed more subtly than in most Coen Brothers films. It is, in fact, a doubly coded film that works perfectly well when read as a straightforward genre exercise but becomes even more interesting when one becomes aware of the slight but important deviations from genre conventions in the film. Alternate-reality narratives often work best when their deviations from the original reality are slight, almost undetectable, and this film works very much in that mode.

All three versions of *True Grit* are built upon the same basic plot, which involves the attempts of fourteen-year-old Arkansan Mattie Ross to track down the scoundrel Tom Chaney, after he murders Mattie's father in the beginning of the story. The teenager is aided in her quest by prickly, hard-drinking U.S. Marshal Reuben J. "Rooster" Cogburn as they pursue (and eventually overtake) Chaney in the Choctaw Nation of what is now eastern Oklahoma. The differences in the ways the three versions tell this basic story are extremely telling, however, suggesting that the Coens' adaptation is more faithful to the spirit of the original novel—and perhaps superior to the novel in some aspects. These differences also make some fundamental statements about the Western as a genre.

By the late 1960s, the Western film genre was self-consciously moving in new directions, both to correct perceived flaws in the classics of the genre (such as racist depictions of Native Americans) and partly to reflect a changing understanding of America's history and national identity. To an extent, John Ford, the leading director of the classic Western, helped to initiate this trend toward revisionary Westerns with his last work in the genre, *Cheyenne Autumn* (1964), which reverses the terms of many of Ford's earlier films by sympathetically portraying Native Americans as the victims of official white American treachery (and, by extension, inaccurate Hollywood representations). Within a few years, works such as Abraham Polonsky's *Tell Them Willie Boy Is Here* (1969) and Arthur Penn's *Little Big Man* (1970) extended this trend, as films sympathetic to Native Americans became more common. During the same period, "waning of the West" films also initiated a new focus on the closing of the frontier and the fact that the onward march of civilization had made the adventurous cowboys and outlaws of earlier Westerns virtually obsolete. Richard Brooks's *The Professionals* (1966), George Roy Hill's *Butch Cassidy and the Sundance Kid* (1969), Sam Peckinpah's *The Wild Bunch* (1969), and Robert Altman's *McCabe and Mrs. Miller* (1971) made this category a major cinematic phenomenon. Finally, both *Little Big Man* and *The Wild Bunch* also took advantage of the inherently allegorical possibilities of the Western to draw parallels between the conquest of the West and the contemporary American involvement in Vietnam. Anti–Vietnam War Westerns such as Ralph Nelson's *Soldier Blue* (1970), Don Siegel's *Two Mules for*

*Sister Sara* (1970), and Robert Aldrich's *Ulzana's Raid* (1972) quickly followed.

Amid all of this revisionary activity, the original 1969 film adaptation of *True Grit* was definitely something of a throwback—as one might expect from a film starring Wayne, the biggest star of the classical Western and a man who became a sort of walking embodiment of conservative resistance to the winds of change that were sweeping America in the late 1960s. It should also be noted that the film was directed by Henry Hathaway, who had been making classic Westerns with such stars as Randolph Scott for nearly four decades and who had already developed a close working relationship with Wayne as well. The film also harkens back to earlier Westerns in that—like so many of the classic films that made Wayne a star in the first place—it features glorious Western landscapes as a crucial component of its cinematic effect. In this particular film, these landscapes are dominated by the mountains of Colorado, where the 1969 *True Grit* was filmed. However, the film nominally maintains the Arkansas/Oklahoma setting of the novel, which in reality looks nothing like Colorado. As a result, this adaptation seems a bit awkward, as if trying to force the square peg of Portis's somewhat unconventional Western into the round hole of classic Wayne vehicles like *Stagecoach* (1939) and *The Searchers* (1956).

One might argue that the 1969 film takes place in an alternate reality in which western Arkansas and eastern Oklahoma have the same terrain as the Colorado of our world. But, in the case of that film, this effect is primarily a conservative and nostalgic one intended to place this film in the world of the classic Western. As such, it misses an opportunity to critique the classic Western's heroization of the "taming" of the West; unlike both the novel and the 2010 film, it fails to remind audiences that a great deal of the effort to tame the West took place in much more mundane environments than the ones we see in classic Westerns, involving grueling labor and intense physical hardship more than glorious adventure. The Coens' version of *True Grit* was largely filmed in New Mexico, but it places much less emphasis on the landscape than does the classic Western and there is very little about the landscape of the film that stands out as something that simply couldn't be found in Arkansas or Oklahoma.

In almost every case in which the 1969 film differs from the novel, the changes are conservative ones intended to tone down and make more palatable to Wayne's fan base certain aspects of the novel. For example, a public hanging scene that occurs early in the 1969 film is enacted with the spirit of a church picnic. A man sings "Amazing Grace" as the crowd mills about in a park-like atmosphere. Kids play on swings, while vendors circulate through the crowd selling peanuts. The hanging itself occurs quickly; three young white men convicted of unspecified crimes stand on the gallows, are hooded, and are then hanged as the platform drops from beneath them. Mattie (Kim Darby) looks on with her black hired man Yarnell (Ken Renard) at her side; she seems slightly disturbed by the spectacle but is then heartened by the hope that Judge Parker, who ordered these hangings, will also be willing to hang Tom Chaney should he be captured.

This potentially chilling scene is presented in a matter-of-fact way without any discernible satirical intent. Instead, it merely helps to establish the Western ambience, identifying Fort Smith, Arkansas, as a frontier town where rough justice prevails, something one often finds in the classic Western. It also chooses not to elaborate on its basis in historical reality: the fact that, with "hanging judge" Isaac Parker leading the way as U.S. district judge from 1875 to 1896, Fort Smith developed a reputation as a sort of execution center. During his tenure as judge, Parker sentenced 160 people to death, many of them having no right of appeal, though roughly half were ultimately pardoned or otherwise escaped execution. A reconstruction of the gallows where 86 people were hanged between 1873 and 1896 (79 of them sentenced by Parker during his tenure) stands today at the historical site maintained in Fort Smith by the National Park Service, almost as if this history is something to be proud of.[12] It might be noted, though, that the town of Fort Smith opted to renounce this legacy soon after Parker left office, burning the original gallows where so many had died.

Portis, an Arkansas native who was educated at the University of Arkansas and who has spent most of his life in the state, would have been well aware of this history. For example, he identifies the executioner in the scene as George Maledon, which was in fact the name of an executioner who worked under Judge Parker from the mid-1880s until 1891 and again in 1894. Maledon, known as the "Prince of Executioners," largely because of the fame he gained after retirement by assembled a traveling road show illustrating relics from his career as a hangman, would thus not actually have been the executioner in 1878, when the novel is set. Portis clearly opted to deviate from historical fact in order to use Maledon's fame to call attention to the larger historical record of hangings in Fort Smith. Portis also presents the hanging scene in much more graphic detail, making the 1969 film's version seem sanitized in comparison. In the novel, for example, the three men being hanged are each given a chance to speak final words. One of the men is a Native American, who also turns out (somewhat to the surprise of the rather sanctimonious Mattie) to be a Christian whose last words are to express confidence that he will soon "be in heaven with Christ my savior."[13] Then, when Maledon pulls the lever, the two white men go quickly to their deaths, their necks broken in the drop. The Indian, however, jerks and spasms for more than half an hour before he dies, having lost so much weight in jail awaiting execution that he was too light for the fall to break his neck.[14]

Mattie's narration does not speculate on the reasons for the Indian's weight loss in jail, though there would seem to be a subtle implication that he might have been mistreated (because of his race) while in custody. The 1969 film omits the Indian altogether, while the Coens' film maintains the Native American but omits the gruesome details of his protracted death. They do, however, include their own reference to the unequal treatment of Native Americans in the nineteenth-century justice system. Before they are hooded, the two white prisoners give almost verbatim the same speeches that they give in the novel. When it comes the turn of the Indian, however, the hood is slapped roughly over his head just as he begins to speak, denying him the chance to have a final word that had been given to the white prisoners. Importantly, as the prisoners drop to their deaths, the crowd in the Coens' film applauds happily, emphasizing the extent to which the executions are treated callously as an entertainment and delivering a far stronger indictment of the public hangings than is to be found in either Portis's novel or Hathaway's film, both of which depict the crowd as reacting with more shock and dismay at the moment of the hanging.

The various presentations of this scene are indicative of the way in which, when Hathaway's film deviates from the novel, it does so in ways that water it down or remove material that might run counter to the mythologizing intent of the film itself. Again (especially in terms of major elements in the story), the Coens' film generally deviates far less from the novel than does Hathaway's. When the Coens do stray from the novel, however, these deviations from the original novel tend to make the narrative stronger, sharpening its treatment of potentially controversial material. Hathaway's departures from the novel, on the other hand, seem designed to make his film a more conventional genre exercise and a more effective vehicle for its star.

It should be noted, for example, that the novel is narrated by a much older version of Mattie, who is looking back on experiences from her youth. The novel also includes a final scene, set in 1903, in which Mattie, now thirty-nine, travels across Arkansas to Memphis to attend a Wild West show in which Cogburn has been performing as a sharp-shooter. To her great disappointment, the reunion never occurs be-cause Cogburn dies only a few days before she arrives. Instead, Mattie meets Cole Younger and Frank James, once-feared outlaws who are also now performers in the show and who are old compadres of Cog-burn, having served with him (and Frank's brother Jesse) in the notori-ous Confederate guerrilla unit Quantrill's Raiders. The unit was known for having committed some of the greatest atrocities of the Civil War, especially in a murderous 1863 assault on the anti-slavery town of Law-rence, Kansas, killing nearly two hundred citizens and looting and burn-ing the town.

Cogburn's participation in Quantrill's Raiders is not mentioned in the 1969 film, which allows it to avoid associating Wayne via his charac-ter with a group that was arguably engaged in mass murder. Leaving out this connection also means that the Cogburn of this film need not be associated with such outlaw figures as Younger and James. Indeed, this film omits the Memphis coda altogether, though this coda does have a basis in reality: Younger and James did, in fact, tour the South as headliners in their own Wild West show in 1903. When Mattie encoun-ters them in the novel, she remembers a story Cogburn had told her twenty-five years earlier, in which she learned that Younger had once saved Cogburn's life and that the killing of a bank clerk in Northfield, Minnesota, for which Younger had been sentenced to life in prison in 1876, might actually been carried out by Jesse James. (Both Jesse and Frank James are believed to have participated in the Northfield rob-bery, though neither was convicted of any crimes associated with that event.) When Mattie meets the two old men (who are relaxing and sipping Coca-Colas, key signs of the incipient growth of American con-sumer capitalism at that time in history), she is polite and respectful to

Younger, who is courteous in turn. Frank, whom Mattie notes is now believed to have committed the killing for which Younger served twenty-five years in prison, neither rises nor removes his hat in the presence of the lady, who gruffly tells him not to bother. "Keep your seat, trash!" she says, apparently having lost none of her sand in the quarter century since her adventures with Cogburn. The Coens' 2010 film includes an almost direct transcription of this part of the novel, including the fact that the thirty-nine-year-old Mattie is shown with her left arm missing below the elbow, having lost that part of the arm due to a snakebite received in the 1878 part of the narrative. In the sanitized 1969 film, Mattie does not lose her arm but merely must wear a sling while it heals.

The omission of the coda in the 1969 film might seem inconsequential, but the Wild West shows that are thereby removed from the narrative actually form an important part of the historical background of the Western film, beginning the mythologization of the West that those films continued.[15] It was, of course, no coincidence that the rise of Wild West shows (the one organized by Buffalo Bill Cody being the most famous) occurred at the same time as the rise of American consumer capitalism. The West and its legacy were quickly converted into consumer products to be packaged and sold to eager consumers looking for a whiff of the kinds of adventure that had once supposedly been available in the Wild West. By bringing in the Wild West show, both the novel and the 2010 film thus make important de-mythologizing points about the role of the West in modern popular (and consumer) culture, points that are absent from the 1969 film through the omission of the coda.

Perhaps the most obvious differences among the three versions of *True Grit* occur in the realm of characterization, with the characters of the Coens' film adhering much more closely to those in the novel than do those in the 1969 film, while also producing far more interesting deviations. The biggest change in characterization from the novel to the 1969 film involves the way in which Wayne's version of Cogburn dominates the film, becoming the main character, while relegating Darby's Mattie to a supporting role. Part of this effect no doubt occurs because Wayne is such a dominating screen presence and completely overshadows Darby's performance, which is perfectly creditable but not exceptionable enough to challenge the dominance of an actor with the screen presence of Wayne. But much of this effect is clearly intentional: the film (partly for marketing reasons) was intended to be a vehicle for Wayne and it is designed to put his character front and center.

Jeff Bridges does a very fine job as Cogburn in the Coens' film, though his casting adds a bit of Coenesque self-referentiality. However, it is to Bridges's credit that, once the film gets under way, we almost entirely forget that he was once the Dude, a character Wayne could have (and would have) never played and who is the virtual cinematic opposite of Cogburn. Though missing an eye and stipulated to be a bit too fond of the drink, Wayne's character quickly resolves into the type of character Wayne was known for playing. Bridges's version of Cogburn, on the other hand, seems much more like the extremely compromised figure that we meet in the novel. At the same time, Bridges plays the character with a slight twinkle in his one eye,[16] making the character far more fun than Wayne's version had been, adding a performative element not available to the medium of the novel but very much in keeping with the its often wry tone.

If Wayne had a talent for dominating films, Bridges has a talent for *not* dominating films and for generously sharing the screen with his fellow actors. And here he has some impressive fellow actors with whom to share. Darby's Mattie seems tomboyish, as Mattie does in the novel, but Hailee Steinfeld's Mattie in the Coens' film seems far more formidable—as does the Mattie of the novel. Steinfeld's Oscar-nominated no-nonsense performance holds its own with Bridges's quite nicely, and she is ultimately able to emerge as the central character of the film, partly due to the existence of the coda and to a frame provided by voice-over narration from the future Mattie, but partly due to the effectiveness of Steinfeld's strong performance. Steinfeld conveys the nineteenth-century language of the film flawlessly, while also doing a much better job than Darby had of bringing to life certain aspects of Mattie's character (such as her stern religiosity, reinforced by the use of nineteenth-century gospel music on the soundtrack) that are significantly de-emphasized in the 1969 film. That Steinfeld was nominated for an Oscar for Best Performance by an Actress in a Supporting Role (while Bridges was nominated for an Oscar for Best Performance by an Actor in a Lead Role) does not reflect the realities of the film so much as the fact that Steinfeld had been only thirteen years old at the time she filmed her role, which led to her inappropriate knee-jerk categorization as a supporting player. If one thinks back to the performance of

Scarlett Johansson in *The Man Who Wasn't There*, it would appear that discovering brilliant teenage actresses needs to be added to the list of the Coens' many talents.

Speaking of supporting players, if Steinfeld and Bridges compare quite favorably with Darby and Wayne as vehicles for conveying Portis's narrative, the supporting actors in the Coens' film are altogether more interesting as well. This is quite a feat, given that the supporting players in Hathaway's film include such important actors as Jeff Corey (who plays Chaney), Dennis Hopper (in a minor role as an outlaw named "Moon"), and Robert Duvall (who plays "Lucky" Ned Pepper, the leader of the outlaw band to which both Chaney and Moon belong). In the Coens' film, on the other hand, Pepper is played by Barry Pepper, which seems like a sort of casting in-joke, though it is made funnier by the fact that Pepper goes through the entire film doing a spot-on imitation of Duvall's distinctive voice—even if Pepper has said in interviews that he had no intention of mimicking Duvall and did not even know, initially, that Duvall had been in the first film. Pepper's performance is itself perfectly fine (every bit as good as Duvall's), but it is made more enjoyable by the obvious element of postmodern mimicry in the performance, intentional or not. The fine Irish actor Domhnall Gleason, on the other hand, is much more effectively naturalistic in the role of Moon than is Hopper, who overacts in the part for all he is worth.

The Coens' film has a particularly big edge over Hathaway's in the casting of Chaney. Corey was a fine veteran actor, and he acquits himself very well in the role, but he was also in his midfifties at the time, while Chaney is specified in the novel to be in his midtwenties. Corey's version of the character seems very unlike the one in the book in almost every way, seeming more like a broken-down loser, a pathetic minor criminal defeated by life, than like the crafty criminal created by Portis. The Coens' Chaney appears much younger than Corey's version (though the actor who played the part, in his early forties, was still somewhat older than the character in the book). For Coen fans, though, the fact that this actor is Josh Brolin surely adds some Coenesque enjoyment to the film, especially as *True Grit* comes only three years after Brolin's breakthrough performance in *No Country for Old Men*. It's a bit of intrusive casting, and (for me at least) it is as difficult to forget that the Coens' Chaney is Brolin as it is to forget that Hathaway's Cogburn is Wayne, possibly because he is not in the film long enough to overcome the original frisson of recognition when he first appears in the film.[17] Yet Brolin's performance is extremely effective, adding a great deal of energy to the latter stages of the film. It also makes Chaney's character much more like the formidable, perhaps psychopathic, criminal who is found in the novel.

Perhaps the biggest difference in characterization between the two films resides in the different performances of the character of LaBoeuf, the Texas Ranger who joins Mattie and Cogburn in their quest to track down Chaney. In the 1969 film, the role is played by then-popular singing star Glen Campbell, whose acting career never amounted to much,[18] though he did win an Oscar nomination for his performance of the film's opening title song. Campbell never seems comfortable onscreen as an actor, though his awkward performance gives LaBoeuf a certain goofiness that makes him work fairly well as a foil for Wayne's Cogburn. LaBoeuf is also redeemed to a certain extent in the 1969 film when he dies after saving Cogburn and Mattie. In the Coens' film, LaBoeuf is played by Matt Damon, an A-list star in his own right and a far more accomplished film actor than was Campbell. This LaBoeuf

**Josh Brolin as Tom Chaney in *True Grit*. Paramount Pictures / Photofest © Paramount Pictures**

also helps save Cogburn and Mattie but survives (as does the character in the novel), while the fact that Damon can hold his own with Bridges as an actor helps to decenter the Coens' film from the focus on Cogburn in the 1969 film. Damon's enactment of LaBoeuf as a pompous, preening braggard is also inherently interesting and much more in line with the portrayal of this character in the novel. The Coens' film, in fact, improves on this aspect of LaBoeuf's character, both through Damon's performance and through the addition of lines such as Mattie's initial reaction the first time she sees LaBoeuf when she awakes to find him sitting in her room. He clearly expects her to be impressed by his masculine swagger; she simply responds to his presence by expressing surprise, noting that it is rare to encounter rodeo clowns back where she is from.

As they had already done in *No Country for Old Men*, the Coens, in *True Grit*, prove themselves to be master adapters from novel to film, maintaining all of the important elements of Portis's original novel but not attempting a slavish faithfulness that would make it impossible to take advantage of the resources they have as filmmakers. These resources include both those that are inherent to film as a genre (as when they enrich the story with visuals and sound, especially music) and those that are unique to the Coens (such as the casting of actors such as Bridges and Brolin, who are already well known for their performances in other films by the Coens). The Coens also draw upon the inherent advantages of film as a medium by eliciting fine performances, not only from Bridges and Brolin but also from other actors, including Damon and Pepper and especially including newcomer Steinfeld, who has since moved into a successful career in both film and music.[19] Then again, given the track record of the brothers by this time, their ability to get the most out of their medium certainly comes as no surprise.

# NOTES

## INTRODUCTION

1. "The Coen Brothers Rule Out Sci-Fi," *Irish Examiner*, December 24, 2007, https://www.irishexaminer.com/breakingnews/entertainment/coen-brothers-rule-out-sci-fi-341859.html (accessed August 9, 2018).

2. Jeffrey Adams, *The Cinema of the Coen Brothers: Hard-Boiled Entertainments* (London: Wallflower Press, 2015), 167.

3. On the phenomenon of "quality television," see *Quality TV: Contemporary American Television and Beyond*, ed. Janet McCabe and Kim Akass (London: I. B. Tauris, 2007).

4. See T Bone Burnett, "O Brother, Where Art Thou?" *HuffPost*, August 22, 2011, https://www.huffingtonpost.com/t-bone-burnett/o-brother-where-art-thou_b_933414.html (accessed May 19, 2018).

## I. PAINT IT BLACK

1. Cathleen Falsani, *The Dude Abides: The Gospel According to the Coen Brothers* (Grand Rapids, MI: Zondervan, 2009), 31.

2. There are, however, precedents to the Southwestern setting of *Blood Simple*, as when the classic noir *Ride the Pink Horse* (1947) is set in New Mexico.

3. In an interview, Joel stated that the film is not set in the real state of Texas, but in a Texas that is like "something preserved in legend, a collection of histories and myths." William Rodney Allen, ed., *The Coen Brothers: Interviews* (Jackson: University Press of Mississippi, 2006), 26.

4. Adams, *The Cinema of the Coen Brothers*, 15.

5. In an interview with Hal Hinson in 1985, Joel Coen stated that "we didn't want to make a Venetian-blind movie" but instead wanted to "emulate the source" that film noir came from (Allen, *The Coen Brothers*, 13–14).

6. Ian Nathan, *The Coen Brothers: The Iconic Filmmakers and Their Work* (London: Aurum Press, 2017), 28.

7. Falsani, *The Dude Abides*, 31.

8. We know from earlier in the film that the gun is a six-shooter that originally contained only three bullets. One had just been fired, wounding Marty. The three clicks in this scene thus represent the three remaining empty chambers. The other two chambers are still loaded. One more click and the gun would have fired, as it eventually does in the final scene, killing Visser.

9. By the time this film was shot, it was simply not possible to acquire film literally to shoot in black and white, So the film was shot on color film but developed in black and white.

10. Nathan, *The Coen Brothers*, 104.

11. Peter Bradshaw, "The Man Who Wasn't There," in *Joel and Ethan Coen: Blood Siblings*, ed. Paul A. Woods, 2nd ed. (Medford, NJ: Plexus Publishing, 2004), 196.

12. The film is, in fact, laced with subtle allusions, as are all of the Coens' films. For example, a hotel called the Hobart Arms figures prominently in the film, in an apparent reference to the apartment building of the same name that appears in Raymond Chandler's *The Big Sleep* (1939) as the place of residence of detective Philip Marlowe.

13. *The Man Who Wasn't There* also includes a medical examiner named Diedricksen, extending the allusions to *Double Indemnity* via naming.

14. We might recall that John Wayne's J. B. Books, the protagonist of Don Siegel's *The Shootist* (1976), has his suit dry-cleaned as a sign of the incipient modernization of 1901 Carson City, Nevada.

15. It is also worth noting that Raymond Chandler's 1953 novel *The Long Goodbye* identifies Santa Rosa as the hometown of Philip Marlowe.

16. Riedenschneider's name seems to have been derived from that of Doc Reidenschneider, the criminal mastermind (played by Sam Jaffe) who plans the caper at the center of John Huston's noir heist film *The Asphalt Jungle* (1950).

17. Adams suggests that this scene resembles one in Robert Siodmak's 1944 film noir *Phantom Lady*, which he describes as an "important, if unacknowledged influence" on *The Man Who Wasn't There* (*The Cinema of the Coen Brothers*, 155). The Coens' version of the scene, however, is far more striking and exaggerated, especially with the argument concerning the Heisenberg uncertainty principle thrown into the mix.

18. Up to this point, the entire piano lesson/failed audition for master teacher motif is taken almost directly from Cain's novel *Mildred Pierce* (1941), in which Veda, the daughter of the title character, seems a promising pianist until she tries out for an important teacher and is summarily dismissed. Later, Veda admits that even her previous teacher thought she "stunk" (216). This novel was itself the basis of an important film noir of the same title in 1945, as well as an excellent television miniseries (on HBO) in 2011.

19. Caryl Flinn, *Strains of Utopia: Gender, Nostalgia, and Hollywood Film Music* (Princeton, NJ: Princeton University Press, 1992), 117.

20. Adams has suggested existentialist novelists such as Albert Camus and Jean-Paul Sartre as possible glosses on *The Man Who Wasn't There*, though he ultimately agrees with the critical consensus that Cain is the most important literary influence on the film (*The Cinema of the Coen Brothers*, 160–61). Meanwhile, Bergan adds to the suggested list of literary referents for the film by noting that Crane is "the embodiment of Ivan Turgenev's *Superfluous Man*" as well as "an illustration of Thoreau's phrase that most people lead lives of 'quiet desperation.'" Ronald Bergan, *The Coen Brothers*, 2nd ed. (New York: Arcade Publishing, 2016), 213.

## 2. WHAT'S UP, DOC?

1. In addition, "Arizona" isn't even the real name of the family in the film, it having been adopted by the family patriarch because he felt that no one would want to buy furniture from a store called "Unpainted Huffheinz."

2. Roger Ebert, "*Raising Arizona*," *Roger Ebert.com*, March 20, 1987, https://www.rogerebert.com/reviews/raising-arizona-1987 (accessed April 11, 2018).

3. Adams, *The Cinema of the Coen Brothers*, 33–34.

4. Josh Levine, *The Coen Brothers: The Story of Two American Filmmakers* (Toronto: ECW Press, 2000), 46.

5. Allen, *The Coen Brothers*, 26.

6. Bergan, *The Coen Brothers*, 96.

7. Bergan, *The Coen Brothers*, 95.

8. Ironically, Cage himself would play another sort of biker from hell exactly twenty years later in the comic-book adaptation *Ghost Rider* (2007).

9. In terms of the heist element of the film, it is worth noting that the 1969 British heist film *The Italian Job* had been successfully (but loosely) remade as an American film just a year before the release of the Coens' version of *The Ladykillers*.

10. Bergan, *The Coen Brothers*, 232. On the other hand, I would argue that the focus on black music in this film can be seen as a sort of corrective to the heavy emphasis on white music in *O Brother*.

11. Bergan, *The Coen Brothers*, 231.

12. Bergan, *The Coen Brothers*, 250.

13. Bergan, *The Coen Brothers*, 250–51.

14. Nathan, *The Coen Brothers*, 143.

15. Simmons's character is unnamed in the film and listed in the credits merely as "CIA superior." The character is named "Gardner Chubb" in the original screenplay. I used that name here merely for the convenience of having a name to refer to.

16. In terms of more specific real-world models, Bergan suggests that Linda's concern with reinventing herself might have been partly modeled on Linda Tripp, a principal in the Bill Clinton/Monica Lewinsky scandal of the 1990s.

17. Jeet Heer, "We Are Living in the Coen Brothers' Darkest Comedy," *The New Republic*, July 15, 2017, https://newrepublic.com/article/143875/living-coen-brothers-darkest-comedy (accessed June 4, 2018).

## 3. JOEL AND ETHAN DO HAMMETT AND CHANDLER

1. I have already noted the importance of James M. Cain, probably the third most important writer of hard-boiled fiction, to *The Man Who Wasn't There*, though the overall impression of that film is dominated by its visual connection to film noir.

2. Gustave Flaubert, *Madame Bovary*, 1856, trans. Eleanor Marx-Aveling, 1886 (Overland Park, KS: Digireads.com, 2015), 13. I quote here from first English translation (1886), by Eleanor Marx-Aveling, the daughter of Karl Marx, a connection that suggests the effectiveness of the novel as a critique of consumerist capitalism.

3. Arthur Asa Berger, *The Objects of Affection: Semiotics and Consumer Culture* (London: Palgrave Macmillan, 2010), 84.

4. William H. Mooney, *Dashiell Hammett and the Movies* (New Brunswick, NJ: Rutgers University Press, 2014), 159. Mooney goes on to draw upon Fredric Jameson's discussion of the particularly postmodern form of nostalgia involved in the relationship between neo-noir film and film noir, concluding that *Miller's Crossing* is not merely an adaptation of *The Glass Key* but engages in an active dialogue with it, one that requires our awareness in order to be effective.

5. Cited in Mooney, *Dashiell Hammett*, 161 and 193n7.

6. Mooney, *Dashiell Hammett*, 161.

7. Roger Ebert, *"Miller's Crossing," Robert Ebert.com*, October 5, 1990, https://www.rogerebert.com/reviews/millers-crossing-1990 (accessed June 9, 2018).

8. Bergan, *The Coen Brothers*, 113.

9. Bergan, *The Coen Brothers*, 115.

10. Adams, *The Cinema of the Coen Brothers*, 57.

11. Allen, *The Coen Brothers*, 44.

12. Adams, *The Cinema of the Coen Brothers*, 59–63.

13. Edward J. Ahearn, *Marx and Modern Fiction* (New Haven, CT: Yale University Press, 1989), 60.

14. Christopher Raczkowski, "Metonymic Hats and Metaphoric Tumble-weeds: Noir Literary Aesthetics in *Miller's Crossing* and *The Big Lebowski*," in *The Year's Work in Lebowski Studies*, ed. Edward P. Comentale and Aaron Jaffe, 98–123 (Bloomington: Indiana University Press, 2009), 99.

15. Raczkowski, "Metonymic Hats," 101.

16. The Dude claims at one point to have been one of the authors of "the original Port Huron Statement" (though he was cut from the second draft). He also claims to have been a member of the "Seattle Seven," a group of anti–Vietnam War protestors that included Jeff Dowd, whom numerous critics have identified as the model for the Dude. See Joe Blevins, "Meet the Shaggy, Shambolic Jeff Dowd, Who Inspired The Big Lebowski," *AV Club*, July 15, 2016, https://news.avclub.com/meet-the-shaggy-shambolic-jeff-dowd-who-inspired-the-1798249401 (accessed June 23, 2018). When picked up by the Malibu police, meanwhile, the Dude demands to speak to a lawyer, preferably Bill Kuntsler or Ron Kuby, both of whom became known for their defenses of countercultural figures, Kuntsler being particularly well known for his defense of the Chicago Seven.

17. Peter Körte, *"The Big Lebowski,"* in *Joel & Ethan Coen*, ed. Peter Körte and Georg Seesien, trans. Rory Mullholland, 191–208 (New York: Limelight Editions, 2001), 199–200.

18. Körte, *"The Big Lebowski,"* 200.

19. This prominence of 1970s culture in *The Big Lebowski* also places it in the company of a number of 1990s films—including Quentin Tarantino's *Reservoir Dogs* (1992) and *Pulp Fiction* (1994)—that, as I have noted elsewhere, significantly draw upon the culture of the 1970s in their music and otherwise in what amounts to "a wave of nostalgia for the 1970s—or perhaps of 1990s nostalgia for 1970s nostalgia for the 1950s." M. Keith Booker, *Postmodern Hollywood: What's New in Film and Why It Makes Us Feel So Strange* (Westport, CT: Greenwood Press, 2007), 64.

20. This song, meant to mock the drug culture of the 1960s, was quickly appropriated by that culture, a phenomenon that is echoed by its use in the film.

21. The psychedelic dreams of *The Big Lebowski* are typical Coen fare, but they also have a parallel in Chandler when Marlowe is abducted and drugged in *Farewell, My Lovely*.

22. *The Big Lebowski* shows us a mock-up of the Autobahn album *Nagelbett* ("Bed of Nails"), the cover design of which clearly resembles that of the 1978 Kraftwerk album *The Man-Machine*. The soundtrack of the film also features a selection of a song called "Technopop," presumably by Autobahn (though actually composed and performed by Carter Burwell).

23. Adams, *The Cinema of the Coen Brothers*, 128.

24. Dick Hebdige, *Subculture: The Meaning of Style*, rev. ed. (London: Routledge, 1979), 96.

25. Even Treehorn admits that "standards have fallen in adult entertainment" now that professionals like himself are forced to compete with amateurs who are ruining the art form. One might compare here Paul Thomas Anderson's near-contemporaneous *Boogie Nights* (1997), which details the decline of standards in the porn industry from its Golden Age in the 1970s to its debased condition in the 1990s.

26. Note that the only other father figure we see in the film is Arthur Digby Sellers, who is even more disabled and confined. Patriarchal power is under extreme pressure in this film.

27. In one of the strongest testaments to the strength of the cast of *The Big Lebowski*, Hoffman—one of the finest character actors of his generation— goes almost unnoticed here thanks to the outrageous performances that surround him.

28. Adams specifically suggests that Maude was inspired by Fluxus artist Carolee Schneeman (*The Cinema of the Coen Brothers*, 129).

## 4. HOW THE SAUSAGE GETS MADE

1. William Leach, *Country of Exiles: The Destruction of Place in American Life* (New York: Pantheon Books, 1999), 6.

2. Bergan, *The Coen Brothers*, 128.

3. Quoted in Levine, *The Coen Brothers*, 101.

4. James Mottram, *The Coen Brothers: The Life of the Mind* (Dulles, VA: Brassey's, 2000) 87.

5. Booker, *Postmodern Hollywood*, 145.

6. Along these lines, it is worth noting that Joel Coen has been quoted to the effect that the brothers have considered making a sequel to *Barton Fink*, set perhaps in 1967: "It's the summer of love and [Fink is] teaching at Berkeley. He ratted on a lot of his friends to the House Un-American Activities committee." Adam Rosenberg, "EXCLUSIVE: Coen Brothers Want John Turturro to Get Old for 'Barton Fink' Sequel, 'Old Fink,'" *MTV Movies Blog*, September 21, 2009, https://web.archive.org/web/20130525043057/http://moviesblog.mtv.com/2009/09/21/coen-brothers-want-john-turturro-to-get-old-for-barton-fink-sequel-old-fink/ (accessed April 29, 2018).

7. Mottram, *The Coen Brothers*, 77. Mottram also acknowledges the possible importance of other films as sources of inspiration for *Barton Fink*, including Alain Resnais's *Providence* (1977) and Stanley Kubrick's *The Shining* (1980), the latter of which seems a particularly likely connection, given that it is a horror film about a writer losing his mind while struggling to overcome writer's block in a haunted hotel, a capsule description that might apply equally well to *Barton Fink*.

8. Bergan, *The Coen Brothers*, 136.

9. Though it seems certain that Fink is based primarily on Odets (and that Fink has little in common with Welles in terms of his talents as an artist), it is worth pointing out that Welles had established quite a reputation for himself on the left-leaning New York stage before being lured to Hollywood to make films.

10. Bergan, *The Coen Brothers*, 49.

11. Adams, *The Cinema of the Coen Brothers*, 74.

12. Nathanael West, *The Day of the Locust*, 1939, in *Nathanael West: Novels and Other Writings*, ed. Sacvan Bercovitch, 239–389 (New York: Library of America, 1997), 132.

13. M. Keith Booker, *The Modern American Novel of the Left: A Research Guide* (Westport, CT: Greenwood Press, 1999), 350.

14. On Faulkner's experience with Hollywood (including the fact that he first came to Hollywood to work on a Wallace Beery picture), see John Meroney, "William Faulkner's Hollywood Odyssey," *Garden and Gun*, April/May 2014, http://gardenandgun.com/feature/william-faulkners-hollywood-odyssey/ (accessed May 10, 2018).

15. James Naremore, *More Than Night: Film Noir in Its Contexts*, updated and expanded edition (Berkeley: University of California Press, 2008), 93.

16. Charlie/Mundt's ambiguous relationship with fascism also includes the fact that his favorite actor is Jack Oakie, a burly film comedian who was something of a forerunner of John Goodman. Interestingly, in 1940 (just a year before the action of *Barton Fink*) Oakie had played Mussolini in Charlie Chaplin's anti-fascist comic masterpiece *The Great Dictator*.

17. In addition, Parsons was associated with the Hearst newspaper syndicate and other Hearst enterprises from 1923 until her retirement in the 1960s, while—in the alternate 1950s of *Hail, Caesar!*—Thora Thacker is still trying to land a deal to work for Hearst.

18. For convenience and simplicity, I will henceforth refer to the biblical epic within the Coens' *Hail, Caesar!* as *Hail, Caesar!*°

19. Johansson's water ballet scenes were actually shot on the same stage at Sony Pictures Studios (called Columbia back in Williams's day) where Williams shot most of her water scenes (Nathan, *The Coen Brothers*, 167).

20. Cuddahy characterizes the H-bomb as having been first tested a couple of weeks before his meeting with Mannix. In reality, the first full-scale hydrogen bomb test was performed on November 1, 1952, at the Enewetak Atoll in the Marshall Islands. The largest such device ever tested (and the first hydrogen bomb configuration that could be deployed as a practical weapon), in the "Castle Bravo" test, did occur at the Bikini Atoll in the Marshalls but in 1954.

21. The Hollywood Ten were a group of screenwriters, directors, and producers who were called to testify before HUAC in 1947 and who collectively decided to defy the committee and refuse to answer its questions on the grounds that such investigations into the political beliefs of American citizens were unconstitutional. The ten were convicted of contempt of Congress and sentenced to prison, while most (including Lawson) were subsequently blacklisted from working in Hollywood, though writer-director Edward Dmytryk avoided the blacklist by cooperating with HUAC in 1951, as did Clifford Odets (who was not a member of the Hollywood Ten) in 1952. On Hollywood and HUAC, see Thomas Doherty, *Show Trial: Hollywood, HUAC, and the Blacklist* (New York: Columbia University Press, 2018).

22. Interestingly, some of Lawson's important early work was as a playwright working with the Group Theater in New York, which also produced the early work of Clifford Odets.

23. The Coens appear to be conflating Marcuse with other German Marxist emigrés—such as fellow Frankfurt School thinkers Theodor Adorno and Max Horkheimer—who did, in fact, live in the posh Los Angeles coastal area of Pacific Palisades in the 1940s (though not in the 1950s). Adorno and Horkheimer did not work in the film industry and were harsh critics of the American "culture industry" in general. However, their Pacific Palisades neighbor (and fellow German exile), the Marxist playwright Bertolt Brecht, did enjoy a brief career as a screenwriter, though he had fled back to communist East Germany in 1947, after testifying before HUAC.

24. They are slyly referenced, however. A chief tactic of HUAC was to attempt to force witnesses testifying before them to "name names" of the Hollywood figures they knew to have leftist political sentiments. When Whit-

lock attempts to negotiate with his captors to get a share of his own ransom, he reminds them that he can "name names" once he is released.

## 5. STAR-CROSSED LOVERS

1. M. Keith Booker, *Historical Dictionary of American Cinema* (Lanham, MD: Scarecrow Press, 2011), 330.

2. There was, however, a newspaper called the *Daily Argus* that was published in Westchester County (just north of New York City) from 1892 to 1994.

3. John Harkness, "The Sphinx Without a Riddle," in *Joel and Ethan Coen: Blood Siblings*, ed. Paul A. Woods, 126–29, 2nd ed. (Medford, NJ: Plexus Publishing, 2004), 126–27.

4. Quoted in Susan Gonzalez, "Director Spike Lee Slams 'Same Old' Black Stereotypes in Today's Films," *Yale Bulletin & Calendar*, March 2, 2001, https://web.archive.org/web/20090121190429/http://www.yale.edu/opa/arc-ybc/v29.n21/story3.html (accessed March 18, 2018).

5. Cited in Bergan, *The Coen Brothers*, 36.

6. Roger Ebert, "*Intolerable Cruelty*," *Roger Ebert.com*, October 10, 2003, https://www.rogerebert.com/reviews/intolerable-cruelty-2003 (accessed March 21, 2018).

7. This project was part of the genesis of the script for the 2014 downed-pilot World War II film *Unbroken*, directed by Angelina Jolie and scripted by the Coens, Richard LaGravenese, and William Nicholson.

8. See Damon Wise, "*Intolerable Cruelty* Review," *Empire*, January 1, 2011, https://www.empireonline.com/movies/intolerable-cruelty/review/ (accessed August 22, 2018).

9. Ian Nathan also quotes Joel Coen to the effect that the brothers grew up watching lots of British movies, due to the tastes of their father, who had grown up in England.

## 6. LAUGHING TO KEEP FROM DYING IN THE SUBURBS

1. Adams attributes this confession to an interview between the Coens and Elvis Mitchell for the Independent Film Channel in 2000 (*The Cinema of the Coen Brothers*, 103).

2. Much of *Fargo* was shot in the northernmost reaches of Minnesota and North Dakota, well to the north of the putative settings. Unusually warm

weather meant that the snow cover farther south was insufficient to achieve the effect desired in the film.

3.  Richard M. Dorson, *American Folklore*, 1959 (Chicago: University of Chicago Press, 1977), 200.

4.  Roger Ebert, *"Fargo,"* *Roger Ebert.com*, March 8, 1996, https://www.rogerebert.com/reviews/fargo-1996 (accessed June 28, 2018).

5.  Other stereotypes in this film include Gustafson's chief financial advisor, Stan Grossman (Larry Brandenburg), who is presumably Jewish based on his name (though the film makes nothing of his Jewishness) and the Asian American Mike Yanagita (Mike Park), who claims, at least, to work as an engineer. Asians (including a character played by Park) and (especially) Jews would play a much bigger role in *A Serious Man*.

6.  See Rowell for a discussion of the ways in which the cinematography emphasizes Jerry's sense of entrapment and imprisonment by frequently showing him in scenes in which he is shot inside a frame (such as a doorway) or in his small, confining office, the window of which is covered by vertical blinds opened to look like bars. As she notes, "The screen compositions consistently show him cornered by his situations." Erica Rowell, *The Brothers Grim: The Films of Ethan and Joel Coen* (Lanham, MD: Scarecrow Press, 2007).

7.  See E. Michael Jones, "Rabbinical Despotism," *Culture Wars*, June 2010, http://www.culturewars.com/2010/Coen.htm (accessed July 19, 2018).

8.  Bergan, *The Coen Brothers*, 264.

9.  Joel Coen turned thirteen in 1967, which would make it the year of his bar mitzvah, a big moment in the life on any Jewish boy, including atheist ones like the Coens.

10.  Bergan suggests that the ineffectuality of the rabbis in this film "could be seen as the Coens' revenge after growing up 'detesting Hebrew school and their boring rabbis'" (*The Coen Brothers*, 262).

11.  Bergan, *The Coen Brothers*, 265.

12.  The joke here is that "Ronald Meshbesher" is the actual name of a prominent, longtime Minnesota criminal-defense attorney, though he would have still been relatively early in his career in 1967.

## 7. FROM SOGGY BOTTOM TO GREENWICH VILLAGE

1.  See Burnett, "O Brother, Where Are Thou?"

2.  Nathan, *The Coen Brothers*, 97.

3. That this particular version of Tiresias is black makes him another version of the "magical Negro" who figures so prominently in *The Hudsucker Proxy*.

4. Jane Siegel, "The Coens' *O Brother, Where Art Thou?* and Homer's *Odyssey*," *Mouseion: Journal of the Classical Association of Canada* 7, no. 3 (2007): 218.

5. In addition to Siegel's article, see Toscano and Flensted-Jensen for discussions of the extensive points of connection between the *Odyssey* and *O Brother*. Margaret M. Toscano, "Homer Meets the Coen Brothers: Memory as Artistic Pastiche in *O Brother, Where Art Thou?*" *Film and History: An Interdisciplinary Journal of Film and Television* 39, no. 2 (Fall 2009): 49–62; Pernille Flensted-Jensen, "Something Old, Something New, Something Borrowed: The *Odyssey* and *O Brother, Where Art Thou?*" *Classica et Mediaevalia: Revue Danoise de Philologie et d'Histoire* 53 (2002): 13–30.

6. Booker, *Joyce*, 17–43.

7. M. M. Bakhtin, *The Dialogic Imagination*, ed. Michael Holquist, trans. Caryl Emerson and Michael Holquist (Austin: University of Texas Press, 1981), 54.

8. See Zack Sharf, "The Coen Brothers and George Clooney Uncover the Magic of *O Brother, Where Art Thou?* at 15th Anniversary Reunion," *IndieWire*, September 30, 2015, http://www.indiewire.com/2015/09/the-coen-brothers-and-george-clooney-uncover-the-magic-of-o-brother-where-art-thou-at-15th-anniversary-reunion-57292/ (accessed May 18, 2018). *The Wizard of Oz*, in fact, is one of the central influences on the work of the Coens. In an interview with Frank Lidz, Joel noted this importance: "All we've been doing for the last twenty-five years is remaking *The Wizard of Oz*. It's true. Sometimes consciously, and sometimes we don't realize until after we've made the movie. Consciously in *O Brother*. *Oz* is the only film we just rip off right and left." On the other hand, both Coens characteristically followed this note of tribute by claiming that they're not really that impressed with *The Wizard of Oz* as a film but that they simply saw it on TV lots of times as kids.

9. Nathan, *The Coen Brothers*, 101.

10. Nathan, *The Coen Brothers*, 101.

11. Dick Burnett is likely no relation to T Bone Burnett, though the latter has stated that he likes to imagine that they are related. See Burnett, "O Brother, Where Art Thou?"

12. Booker, *Postmodern Hollywood*, 79.

13. Bergan identifies the mayoral campaign featured in Preston Sturges's *Hail the Conquering Hero* (1944) as an important part of the background to this gubernatorial campaign (*The Coen Brothers*, 197).

14. Flensted-Jensen evinces the Coens' use of the real-world O'Daniel as an example of the way they supplemented elements taken from the *Odyssey* with elements taken from elsewhere, including the real world.

15. Nathan, *The Coen Brothers*, 161.

16. There may be at least one other moment of potential dialogue with Dylan album covers in *Llewyn Davis*. In one scene, we see Davis trudging down a snow-covered street, drawing closed the light jacket that is clearly insufficient to protect him from the cold. The scene is highly reminiscent of the photo on the cover of *The Freewheelin' Bob Dylan* (1963), perhaps the most famous of all of Dylan's album covers. However, whereas Dylan walks arm in arm with girlfriend Suze Rotolo (in one of the central couples moments in American pop cultural history), Davis walks alone, emphasizing his existential loneliness.

17. *Llewyn Davis* also includes a scene in which another singer joins Jim and Jean on stage at the Gaslight to constitute a trio that performs the traditional folk song "500 Miles," which is best known in the version recorded by Peter, Paul, and Mary and included on their best-selling self-titled debut album in 1962.

18. Van Ronk had been briefly considered by Grossman to be a member of the trio that became Peter, Paul, and Mary, but his rough-hewn voice was judged unsuitable for such a commercial project.

19. As with *O Brother*, however, the music changes midway through the credits, continuing with Van Ronk's recording of "Green, Green Rocky Road," a song of which Davis had played a brief excerpt earlier in the film, providing the most overt link between the music of Davis and that of Van Ronk, though Davis in fact plays several songs during the film that had once been recorded by Van Ronk.

20. One blogger, "Brian," has not only overtly declared that "Llewyn Davis is Bob Dylan" but has further suggested that the Coens have been "chasing the shadow" of Dylan throughout their careers. "The Weather Is Against Me: Bob Dylan and the Coen Brothers," *Fellowship of the Screen*, January 29, 2016, http://screenfellows.com/2016/01/the-weather-is-against-me-bob-dylan-and-the-coen-brothers/ (accessed May 26, 2018).

21. See Eileen Jones, "The Great American Losers," *Jacobin*, December 6, 2013, https://www.jacobinmag.com/2013/12/the-great-american-losers/ (accessed May 29, 2018).

22. Ironically, Ginsberg went on to become a devoted fan of Bob Dylan.

23. It might be noted that "Johnny 5" is also the name of the lovable robot featured in the 1986 film *Short Circuit*; that robot is also treated roughly by the authorities, though it outsmarts them and escapes.

24. Chopin appropriately plays in the background at the Gorfeins' apartment. In fact, *Llewyn Davis* expands its coverage beyond American culture by including several snippets of classical music (by composers such as Mozart, Beethoven, and Mahler, in addition to Chopin) in its score. Perhaps the most interesting of these is the bit of Mozart's *Requiem* that plays in the beginning, which potentially carries atmospheric resonances, while also setting up the appearance later in the film of F. Murray Abraham, who had played Salieri in *Amadeus* (1984), a film that is a cousin to *Llewyn Davis* in many ways. In the world of folk music, for example, one could see Van Ronk as a sort of Salieri to Dylan's Mozart.

25. Even the ultra-serious *No Country for Old Men* is essentially an entertainment-oriented genre film.

26. For an extensive exploration of the Kafkaesque elements of both *Llewyn Davis* and *A Serious Man*, see Ido Lewit, "'This Is Not Nothing': Viewing the Coen Brothers through the Lens of Kafka," in *Mediamorphosis: Kafka and the Moving Image*, ed. Shai Biderman and Ido Lewit, 258–78 (New York: Wallflower Press, 2016).

27. Jonathan Romney, "Songs of Innocence and Experience," *Film Comment* (November–December 2013): 20.

## 8. INTO THE SUNSET

1. Such reinscriptions of the Western in modern settings are often referred to as "neo-Westerns."

2. At one point in the novel, they are referred to as "Pablo's men," suggesting that they might be working for Colombian drug lord Pablo Escobar, just entering the era of his greatest power in 1980 (p. 141). There are, however, no other details in the novel to support this possibility.

3. Stacey Peebles, "'Hold Still': Models of Masculinity in the Coens' *No Country for Old Men*," in *No Country for Old Men: From Novel to Film*, ed. Lynnea Chapman King, Rick Wallach, and Jim Welsh, 124–38 (Lanham, MD: Scarecrow Press, 2009), 125.

4. Peebles, "'Hold Still,'" 136.

5. Richard Slotkin, *Gunfighter Nation: The Myth of the Frontier in Twentieth-Century America*, 1992 (Norman: University of Oklahoma Press, 1998), 633–35.

6. Bell is in several ways made more sympathetic in the film. In the novel, as he expresses his sense that the world has passed him by, he grouses that he never thought he would see people on the streets of Texas towns with "green hair and bones in their noses," a declaration that makes him seem like some-

thing of an old fogey (McCarthy, *No Country for Old Men*, 295). The same lines recur in the film but are placed in the mouth of another character, an old lawman with whom Bell consults in El Paso.

7.  Peter Bradshaw, "*No Country for Old Men*," *The Guardian*, January 18, 2008, https://www.theguardian.com/film/2008/jan/18/drama.thriller (accessed July 24, 2018).

8.  Roger Ebert, "*No Country for Old Men*," *Roger Ebert.com*, November 8, 2007, https://www.rogerebert.com/reviews/no-country-for-old-men-2007 (accessed July 26, 2018).

9.  This line was omitted from the theatrical release of the film.

10.  Allen, *The Coen Brothers*, 26.

11.  McCarthy, *No Country for Old Men*, 162.

12.  A website maintained by the National Park Service relates the histories of all of those executed at Fort Smith during this period. See "Men Executed at Fort Smith: 1873 to 1896," *National Park Service*, https://www.nps.gov/fosm/learn/historyculture/executions-at-fort-smith-1873-to-1896.htm (accessed July 30, 2018).

13.  Charles Portis, *True Grit* 19.

14.  Portis, *True Grit*, 20.

15.  This connection is central to Robert Altman's 1976 film *Buffalo Bill and the Indians, or Sitting Bull's History Lesson*, which also portrays these shows as making a key contribution to the rise of celebrity culture in the United States.

16.  Incidentally, Portis's Cogburn has a ruined left eye but does not wear a patch over it. Wayne wears a patch over his left eye. Bridges also wears a patch but over his right eye, which he has said in interviews he simply found more comfortable, but the effect is to playfully acknowledge that the 1969 film was neither ignored altogether nor treated as authoritative.

17.  The Coens' *True Grit* also features a brief voice-over from Mattie's oft-touted lawyer, J. Noble Daggett. Though he is not listed in the credits that appear at the end of the film, many Coens fans might recognize the voice as that of Coens regular J. K. Simmons.

18.  Other than his role in *True Grit*, Campbell's most important film role was as the Vietnam-vet title character of *Norwood* (1970), also based on a novel by Portis and also featuring Darby as a key cast member. Both the 1969 *True Grit* and *Norwood* were also adapted to the screen by the same screenwriter, Marguerite Roberts, so they are sister films in multiple ways.

19.  Steinfeld's career also provides a link between *True Grit* and *No Country for Old Men* in that she appears in a small role in Jones's revisionist Western *The Homesman* (2014).

# REFERENCES

Adams, Jeffrey. *The Cinema of the Coen Brothers: Hard-Boiled Entertainments*. London: Wallflower Press, 2015.

Ahearn, Edward J. *Marx and Modern Fiction*. New Haven, CT: Yale University Press, 1989.

Allen, William Rodney, ed. *The Coen Brothers: Interviews*. Jackson: University Press of Mississippi, 2006.

Bakhtin, M. M. *The Dialogic Imagination*. Ed. Michael Holquist. Trans. Caryl Emerson and Michael Holquist. Austin: University of Texas Press, 1981.

Berardinelli, James. "The Hudsucker Proxy." http://preview.reelviews.net/movies/h/hudsucker.html. Accessed March 23, 2018.

Bergan, Ronald. *The Coen Brothers*. 2nd ed. New York: Arcade Publishing, 2016.

Berger, Arthur Asa. *The Objects of Affection: Semiotics and Consumer Culture*. London: Palgrave Macmillan, 2010.

Blevins, Joe. "Meet the Shaggy, Shambolic Jeff Dowd, Who Inspired The Big Lebowski." *AV Club*. July 15, 2016. https://news.avclub.com/meet-the-shaggy-shambolic-jeff-dowd-who-inspired-the-1798249401. Accessed June 23, 2018.

Booker, M. Keith. *Historical Dictionary of American Cinema*. Lanham, MD: Scarecrow Press, 2011.

———. *Joyce, Bakhtin, and the Literary Tradition: Toward a Comparative Cultural Poetics*. Ann Arbor: University of Michigan Press, 1996.

———. *The Modern American Novel of the Left: A Research Guide*. Westport, CT: Greenwood Press, 1999.

———. *Postmodern Hollywood: What's New in Film and Why It Makes Us Feel So Strange*. Westport, CT: Greenwood Press, 2007.

Bradshaw, Peter. "The Man Who Wasn't There." In *Joel and Ethan Coen: Blood Siblings*, ed. Paul A. Woods, 196–97. 2nd ed. Medford, NJ: Plexus Publishing, 2004.

———. "No Country for Old Men." *The Guardian*. January 18, 2008. https://www.theguardian.com/film/2008/jan/18/drama.thriller. Accessed July 24, 2018.

Brian. "The Weather Is Against Me: Bob Dylan and the Coen Brothers." *Fellowship of the Screen*. January 29, 2016. http://screenfellows.com/2016/01/the-weather-is-against-me-bob-dylan-and-the-coen-brothers/. Accessed May 26, 2018.

Burnett, T Bone. "O Brother, Where Art Thou?" *HuffPost*. August 22, 2011. https://www.huffingtonpost.com/t-bone-burnett/o-brother-where-art-thou_b_933414.html. Accessed May 19, 2018.

Cain, James M. *Double Indemnity*. 1943. New York: Vintage, 1999.

———. *Mildred Pierce*. 1941. New York: Vintage, 1989.

Capra, Fritjof. *The Tao of Physics: An Exploration of the Parallels Between Modern Physics and Eastern Mysticism*. Berkeley, CA: Shambhala, 1975.

Chandler, Raymond. *The Big Sleep*. 1939. New York: Vintage, 1988.

———. *Farewell, My Lovely*. 1940. New York: Vintage, 1988.

———. *The Long Goodbye*. 1953. New York: Vintage, 2002.

"The Coen Brothers Rule Out Sci-Fi." *Irish Examiner*. December 24, 2007. https://www.irishexaminer.com/breakingnews/entertainment/coen-brothers-rule-out-sci-fi-341859.html. Accessed August 9, 2018.

Dessem, Matthew. "The Real-Life Inspirations Behind *Hail, Caesar!*: A Star-by-Star and Movie-by-Movie Breakdown." *Slate*. February 8, 2016. http://www.slate.com/blogs/browbeat/2016/02/08/hail_caesar_s_real_life_inspirations_broken_down_star_by_star_and_movie.html. Accessed May 4, 2018.

Doherty, Thomas. *Show Trial: Hollywood, HUAC, and the Blacklist*. New York: Columbia University Press, 2018.

Dorson, Richard M. *American Folklore*. 1959. Chicago: University of Chicago Press, 1977.

Douglass, Matthew K., and Jerry L. Walls. "'Takin' 'er Easy for All Us Sinners': Laziness as a Virtue in *The Big Lebowski*." In *The Philosophy of the Coen Brothers*, ed. Mark T. Conard, 147–62. Lexington: University Press of Kentucky, 2009.

Ebert, Roger. "*Fargo*." *Roger Ebert.com*. March 8, 1996. https://www.rogerebert.com/reviews/fargo-1996. Accessed June 28, 2018.

———. "*Hudsucker Proxy*." *Chicago Sun-Times*. March 25, 1994. https://www.rogerebert.com/reviews/hudsucker-proxy-1994. Accessed March 17, 2018.

———. "*Intolerable Cruelty*." *Roger Ebert.com*. October 10, 2003. https://www.rogerebert.com/reviews/intolerable-cruelty-2003. Accessed March 21, 2018.

———. "*Miller's Crossing*." *Roger Ebert.com*. October 5, 1990. https://www.rogerebert.com/reviews/millers-crossing-1990. Accessed June 9, 2018.

———. "*No Country for Old Men*." *Roger Ebert.com*. November 8, 2007. https://www.rogerebert.com/reviews/no-country-for-old-men-2007. Accessed July 26, 2018.

———. "*Raising Arizona*." *Roger Ebert.com*. March 20, 1987. https://www.rogerebert.com/reviews/raising-arizona-1987. Accessed April 11, 2018.

Falsani, Cathleen. *The Dude Abides: The Gospel According to the Coen Brothers*. Grand Rapids, MI: Zondervan, 2009.

Flaubert, Gustave. *Madame Bovary*. 1856. Trans. Eleanor Marx-Aveling, 1886. Overland Park, KS: Digireads.com, 2015.

Flensted-Jensen, Pernille. "Something Old, Something New, Something Borrowed: The *Odyssey* and *O Brother, Where Art Thou?*" *Classica et Mediaevalia: Revue Danoise de Philologie et d'Histoire* 53 (2002): 13–30.

Flinn, Caryl. *Strains of Utopia: Gender, Nostalgia, and Hollywood Film Music*. Princeton, NJ: Princeton University Press, 1992.

Frank, Thomas. *The Conquest of Cool: Business Culture, Counterculture, and the Rise of Hip Consumerism*. Chicago: University of Chicago Press, 1997.

Gonzalez, Susan. "Director Spike Lee Slams 'Same Old' Black Stereotypes in Today's Films." *Yale Bulletin & Calendar*. March 2, 2001. https://web.archive.org/web/20090121190429/http://www.yale.edu/opa/arc-ybc/v29.n21/story3.html. Accessed March 18, 2018.

Hammett, Dashiell. *The Glass Key*. 1931. New York: Vintage, 1989.

———. *Red Harvest*. 1929. New York: Vintage, 2010.

Harkness, John. "The Sphinx Without a Riddle." In *Joel and Ethan Coen: Blood Siblings*, ed. Paul A. Woods, 126–29. 2nd ed. Medford, NJ: Plexus Publishing, 2004.

Hebdige, Dick. *Subculture: The Meaning of Style*. Rev. ed. London: Routledge, 1979.

Heer, Jeet. "We Are Living in the Coen Brothers' Darkest Comedy." *The New Republic*. July 15, 2017. https://newrepublic.com/article/143875/living-coen-brothers-darkest-comedy. Accessed June 4, 2018.

Horkheimer, Max, and Theodor W. Adorno. *Dialectic of Enlightenment*. Trans. John Cumming. New York: Seabury Press, 1972.

Huxley, Aldous. *Brave New World*. 1932. New York: Harper, 2010.

Jones, Eileen. "The Great American Losers." *Jacobin*. December 6, 2013. https://www.jacobinmag.com/2013/12/the-great-american-losers/. Accessed May 29, 2018.

Jones, E. Michael. "Rabbinical Despotism." *Culture Wars*. June 2010. http://www.culturewars.com/2010/Coen.htm. Accessed July 19, 2018.

Körte, Peter. "*The Big Lebowski*." In *Joel & Ethan Coen*, ed. Peter Körte and Georg Seesien, trans. Rory Mullholland, 191–208. New York: Limelight Editions, 2001.

Lawson, John Howard. *Film in the Battle of Ideas*. 1953. Whitefish, MT: Literary Licensing, 2012.

Leach, William. *Country of Exiles: The Destruction of Place in American Life*. New York: Pantheon Books, 1999.

Levine, Josh. *The Coen Brothers: The Story of Two American Filmmakers*. Toronto: ECW Press, 2000.

Lewit, Ido. "'This Is Not Nothing': Viewing the Coen Brothers through the Lens of Kafka." In *Mediamorphosis: Kafka and the Moving Image*, ed. Shai Biderman and Ido Lewit, 258–78. New York: Wallflower Press, 2016.

Lidz, Frank. "Raising Minnesota." *GQ*. September 14, 2009. https://www.gq.com/story/coen-brothers-joel-ethan-serious-man-lebowski. Accessed May 22, 2018.

Marcuse, Herbert. *Eros and Civilization*. 1955. Boston: Beacon Press, 1974.

———. *One-Dimensional Man: Studies in the Ideology of Advanced Industrial Society*. 1964. 2nd ed. Boston: Beacon Press, 1991.

———. *Soviet Marxism: A Critical Analysis*. 1958. New York: Vintage, 1961.

McCabe, Janet, and Kim Akass, eds. *Quality TV: Contemporary American Television and Beyond*. London: I. B. Tauris, 2007.

McCarthy, Cormac. *No Country for Old Men*. New York: Knopf, 2005.

McCarthy, Todd. "The Hudsucker Proxy." *Variety*. January 30, 1994. http://variety.com/1994/film/reviews/the-hudsucker-proxy-1200435097/. Accessed March 18, 2018.

McHale, Brian. *Postmodernist Fiction*. London: Routledge, 1987.

"Men Executed at Fort Smith: 1873 to 1896." *National Park Service*. https://www.nps.gov/fosm/learn/historyculture/executions-at-fort-smith-1873-to-1896.htm. Accessed July 30, 2018.

Meroney, John. "William Faulkner's Hollywood Odyssey." *Garden and Gun*. April/May 2014. http://gardenandgun.com/feature/william-faulkners-hollywood-odyssey/. Accessed May 10, 2018.

Mooney, William H. *Dashiell Hammett and the Movies*. New Brunswick, NJ: Rutgers University Press, 2014.

Mottram, James. *The Coen Brothers: The Life of the Mind*. Dulles, VA: Brassey's, 2000.

Naremore, James. *More Than Night: Film Noir in Its Contexts*. Updated and expanded edition. Berkeley: University of California Press, 2008.

Nathan, Ian. *The Coen Brothers: The Iconic Filmmakers and Their Work*. London: Aurum Press, 2017.

Peebles, Stacey. "'Hold Still': Models of Masculinity in the Coens' *No Country for Old Men*." In *No Country for Old Men: From Novel to Film*, ed. Lynnea Chapman King, Rick Wallach, and Jim Welsh, 124–38. Lanham, MD: Scarecrow Press, 2009.

Portis, Charles. *True Grit*. 1968. New York: Overlook Press, 2012.

Postman, Neil. *Amusing Ourselves to Death: Public Discourse in the Age of Show Business*. 1985. New York: Penguin, 2005.

Raczkowski, Christopher. "Metonymic Hats and Metaphoric Tumbleweeds: Noir Literary Aesthetics in *Miller's Crossing* and *The Big Lebowski*." In *The Year's Work in Lebowski Studies*, ed. Edward P. Comentale and Aaron Jaffe, 98–123. Bloomington: Indiana University Press, 2009.

Romney, Jonathan. "Songs of Innocence and Experience." *Film Comment* (November–December 2013): 18–22.

Rosenberg, Adam. "EXCLUSIVE: Coen Brothers Want John Turturro to Get Old for 'Barton Fink' Sequel, 'Old Fink.'" *MTV Movies Blog*. September 21, 2009. https://web.archive.org/web/20130525043057/http://moviesblog.mtv.com/2009/09/21/coen-brothers-want-john-turturro-to-get-old-for-barton-fink-sequel-old-fink/. Accessed April 29, 2018.

Rowell, Erica. *The Brothers Grim: The Films of Ethan and Joel Coen*. Lanham, MD: Scarecrow Press, 2007.

Sharf, Zack. "The Coen Brothers and George Clooney Uncover the Magic of *O Brother, Where Art Thou?* at 15th Anniversary Reunion." *IndieWire*. September 30, 2015. http://www.indiewire.com/2015/09/the-coen-brothers-and-george-clooney-uncover-the-magic-of-o-brother-where-art-thou-at-15th-anniversary-reunion-57292/. Accessed May 18, 2018.

Siegel, Janice. "The Coens' *O Brother, Where Art Thou?* and Homer's *Odyssey*." *Mouseion: Journal of the Classical Association of Canada* 7, no. 3 (2007): 213–45.

Slotkin, Richard. *Gunfighter Nation: The Myth of the Frontier in Twentieth-Century America*. 1992. Norman: University of Oklahoma Press, 1998.

Toscano, Margaret M. "Homer Meets the Coen Brothers: Memory as Artistic Pastiche in *O Brother, Where Art Thou?*" *Film and History: An Interdisciplinary Journal of Film and Television* 39, no. 2 (Fall 2009): 49–62.

West, Nathanael. *The Day of the Locust*. 1939. In *Nathanael West: Novels and Other Writings*, ed. Sacvan Bercovitch, 239–389. New York: Library of America, 1997.

Wise, Damon. "*Intolerable Cruelty* Review." *Empire*. January 1, 2011. https://www.empireonline.com/movies/intolerable-cruelty/review/. Accessed August 22, 2018.

Zukav, Gary. *The Dancing Wu Li Masters: An Overview of the New Physics*. New York: William Morrow, 1979.

# FILMS CITED

Adler, Lou, and Tommy Chong, dirs. *Up in Smoke*, 1978.

Aldrich, Robert, dir. *The Big Knife*, 1955.

———, dir. *Kiss Me Deadly*, 1955.

———, dir. *Ulzana's Raid*, 1972.

Altman, Robert, dir. *McCabe and Mrs. Miller*, 1971.

———, dir. *The Player*, 1992.

Anderson, Paul Thomas, dir. *Boogie Nights*, 1997.

Aronofsky, Darren, dir. *The Wrestler*, 2008.

Badham, John, dir. *Short Circuit*, 1986.

Brooks, Richard, dir. *The Professionals*, 1966.

Burton, Tim, dir. *Ed Wood*, 1994.

Cameron, James, dir. *The Terminator*, 1984.

Capra, Frank, dir. *It Happened One Night*, 1934.

———, dir. *Mr. Deeds Goes to Town*, 1936.

Collinson, Peter, dir. *The Italian Job*, 1969.

Cukor, George, dir. *The Philadelphia Story*, 1940.

Darabont, Frank, dir. *The Green Mile*, 1999.

Dassin, Jules, dir. *The Naked City*, 1948.

———, dir. *Rififi*, 1955.

Dmytryk, Edward, dir. *Crossfire*, 1947.

———, dir. *Murder, My Sweet*, 1944.

Donaldson, Roger, dir. *The Bank Job*, 2008.

Donen, Stanley, and Gene Kelly, dirs. *On the Town*, 1949.

———, dirs. *Singin' in the Rain*, 1952.

Eastwood, Clint, dir. *Million Dollar Baby*, 2004.

Evans, David Mickey, dir. *The Sandlot*, 1993.

Ford, John, dir. (uncredited). *Flesh*, 1932.

Forman, Milos, dir. *Amadeus*, 1984.

Garnett, Tay, dir. *The Postman Always Rings Twice*, 1946.

———, dir. *Slave Ship*, 1937.

Gilliam, Terry, dir. *Brazil*, 1985.

Goulding, Edmund, dir. *Nightmare Alley*, 1947.

Gray, F. Gary, dir. *The Italian Job*, 2003.

Griffith, D. W., dir. *The Birth of a Nation*, 1915.

Haley, Jack, Jr., dir. *Norwood*, 1970.

Hathaway, Henry, dir. *Kiss of Death*, 1947.

——, dir. *True Grit*, 1969.

Hawks, Howard, dir. *The Big Sleep*, 1946.

——, dir. *Bringing Up Baby*, 1938.

——, dir. *His Girl Friday*, 1940.

——, dir. *To Have and Have Not*, 1944.

Heckerling, Amy, dir. *Look Who's Talking*, 1989.

Hill, George Roy, dir. *Butch Cassidy and the Sundance Kid*, 1969.

Hitchcock, Alfred, dir. *Shadow of a Doubt*, 1943.

Huang, George, dir. *Swimming with Sharks*, 1994.

Huston, John, dir. *The Asphalt Jungle*, 1950.

——, dir. *Key Largo*, 1948.

——, dir. *The Maltese Falcon*, 1941.

Jeunet, Jean-Pierre, dir. *Alien: Resurrection*, 1997.

Jones, Tommy Lee, dir. *The Homesman*, 2014.

Kasdan, Lawrence, dir. *Body Heat*, 1981.

Kubrick, Stanley, dir. *Killer's Kiss*, 1955.

——, dir. *The Killing*, 1956.

——, dir. *Quo Vadis*, 1951.

Landis, John, dir. *Spies Like Us*, 1985.

Lang, Fritz, dir. *Metropolis*, 1927.

LeRoy, Mervyn, dir. *I Am a Fugitive from a Chain Gang*, 1932.

——, dir. *Million Dollar Mermaid*, 1952.

Linklater, Richard, dir. *Dazed and Confused*, 1993.

——, dir. *Slacker,* 1990.

Mamoulian, Rouben, dir. *The Golden Boy*, 1939.

McDonagh, Martin, dir. *Three Billboards Outside Ebbing, Missouri*, 2017.

McKendrick, Alexander, dir. *The Ladykillers*, 1955.

Montgomery, Robert, dir. *Ride the Pink Horse*, 1947.

Nelson, Ralph, dir. *Soldier Blue*, 1970.

Niblo, Fred, dir. *Ben-Hur: A Tale of the Christ*, 1925.

Nimoy, Leonard, dir. *Three Men and a Baby*, 1987.

Pakula, Alan J., dir. *The Parallax View*, 1974.

Peckinpah, Sam, dir. *The Wild Bunch*, 1969.

Peele, Jordan, dir. *Get Out*, 2017.

Penn, Arthur, dir. *Little Big Man*, 1970.

——, dir. *Night Moves*, 1975.

Polanski, Roman, dir. *Chinatown*, 1974.

——, dir. *Repulsion*, 1965.

——, dir. *Rosemary's Baby*, 1968.

——, dir. *The Tenant*, 1976.

Pollack, Sydney, dir. *Three Days of the Condor*, 1975.

Polonsky, Abraham, dir. *Tell Them Willie Boy Is Here*, 1969.

Rafelson, Bob, dir. *The Postman Always Rings Twice*, 1981.

Raimi, Sam, dir. *Spider-Man*, 2002.

Ray, Nicholas, dir. *In a Lonely Place,* 1950.

——, dir. *King of Kings*, 1961.

Redford, Robert, dir. *The Legend of Bagger Vance*, 2000.

Robson, Mark, dir. *Champion*, 1949.

——, dir. *The Harder They Fall*, 1956.

——, dir. *Peyton Place*, 1957.

Rossen, Robert, dir. *Body and Soul*, 1947.

Scorsese, Martin, dir. *Raging Bull*, 1980.
Scott, Ridley, dir. *Blade Runner*, 1984.
Shyer, Charles, dir. *Baby Boom*, 1987.
Sidney, George, dir. *Anchors Aweigh*, 1945.
Siegel, Don, dir. *The Shootist*, 1976.
———, dir. *Two Mules for Sister Sara*, 1970.
Siodmak, Robert, dir. *Criss Cross*, 1949.
———, dir. *The Killers*, 1946.
———, dir. *Phantom Lady*, 1944.
Stone, Oliver, dir. *Wall Street*, 1987.
Sturges, Preston, dir. *Christmas in July*, 1940.
———, dir. *The Great McGinty*, 1940.
———, dir. *Hail the Conquering Hero*, 1944.
———, dir. *Sullivan's Travels*, 1941.
Swift, David, dir. *How to Succeed in Business Without Really Trying*, 1967.
Tarantino, Quentin, dir. *Pulp Fiction*, 1994.
———, dir. *Reservoir Dogs*, 1992.
Tourneur, Jacques, dir. *Out of the Past*, 1947.
Ulmer, Edgar G., dir. *Detour*, 1945.
Various directors. *Paris je t'aime*, 2006.
Vidor, King, dir. (uncredited). *The Champ*, 1931.
Walsh, Raoul, dir. *High Sierra*, 1941.
———, dir. *White Heat*, 1949.
Welles, Orson, dir. *Citizen Kane*, 1941.
———, dir. *The Lady From Shanghai*, 1947.
———, dir. *Touch of Evil*, 1958.
Wilder, Billy, dir. *Double Indemnity*, 1944.
———, dir. *One, Two, Three*, 1961.
———, dir. *Sunset Boulevard*, 1950.
Wise, Robert, dir. *The Set-Up*, 1949.
Wyler, William, dir. *Ben-Hur*, 1959.
Zhang Yimou, dir. *A Woman, a Gun, and a Noodle Shop*, 2009.

# INDEX

# ABOUT THE AUTHOR

**M. Keith Booker** is professor of English at the University of Arkansas. He is the author or editor of more than fifty books, including *The Encyclopedia of Comic Books and Graphic Novels* (2010), *Historical Dictionary of Science Fiction Literature* (Rowman & Littlefield, 2014), *"Mad Men": A Cultural History* (Rowman & Littlefield, 2016), *Tony Soprano's America: Gangsters, Guns, and Money* (Rowman & Littlefield, 2017), and *"Star Trek": A Cultural History* (Rowman & Littlefield, 2018).